I0828397

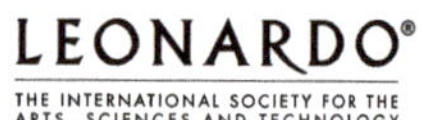
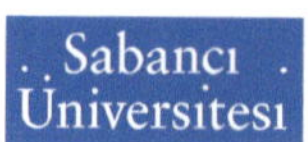
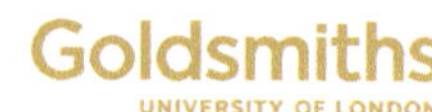
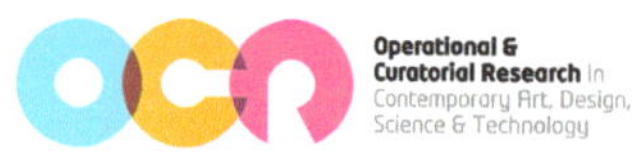
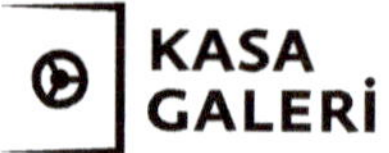

Copyright 2013 ISAST
Leonardo Electronic Almanac
Volume 19 Issue 1
DATE OF PUBLICATION January 15, 2013
ISSN 1071-4391
ISBN 978-1-906897-20-8
The ISBN is provided by Goldsmiths, University of London.

LEA PUBLISHING & SUBSCRIPTION INFORMATION

Editorial Address

Leonardo Electronic Almanac
Sabanci University, Orhanli - Tuzla, 34956
Istanbul, Turkey

Email

info@leoalmanac.org

Web

- www.leoalmanac.org
- www.twitter.com/LEA_twitts
- www.flickr.com/photos/lea_gallery
- www.facebook.com/pages/Leonardo-Electronic-Almanac/209156896252

Leonardo Electronic Almanac is published by:

Leonardo/ISAST
211 Sutter Street, suite 501
San Francisco, CA 94108
USA

Leonardo Electronic Almanac (LEA) is a project of Leonardo/The International Society for the Arts, Sciences and Technology. For more information about Leonardo/ISAST's publications and programs, see http://www.leonardo.info or contact isast@leonardo.info.

Leonardo Electronic Almanac is produced by Passero Productions.

LEONARDO ELECTRONIC ALMANAC, VOLUME 19 ISSUE 1

Not Here Not There

VOLUME EDITORS

LANFRANCO ACETI AND RICHARD RINEHART

EDITORS

ÖZDEN ŞAHİN, JONATHAN MUNRO AND CATHERINE M. WEIR

The Leonardo Electronic Almanac acknowledges the kind support for this issue of

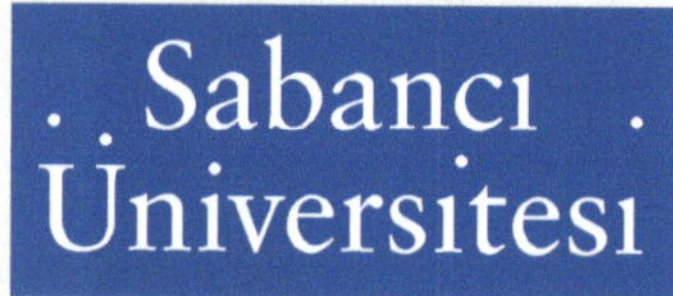

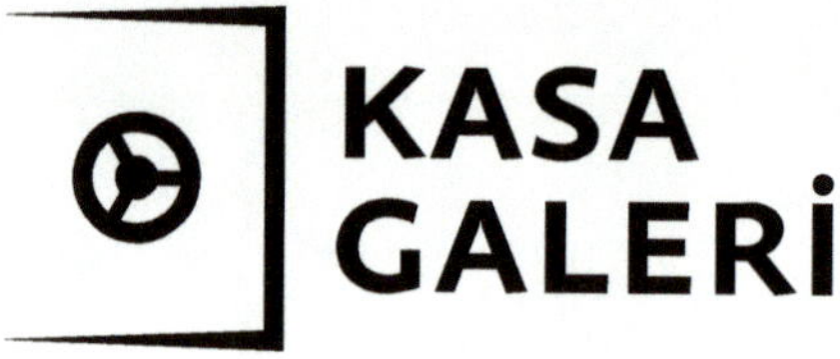

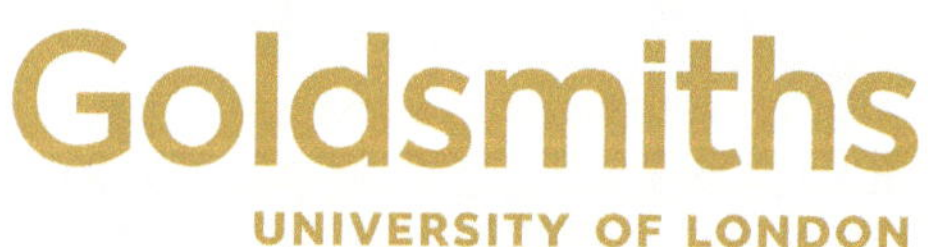

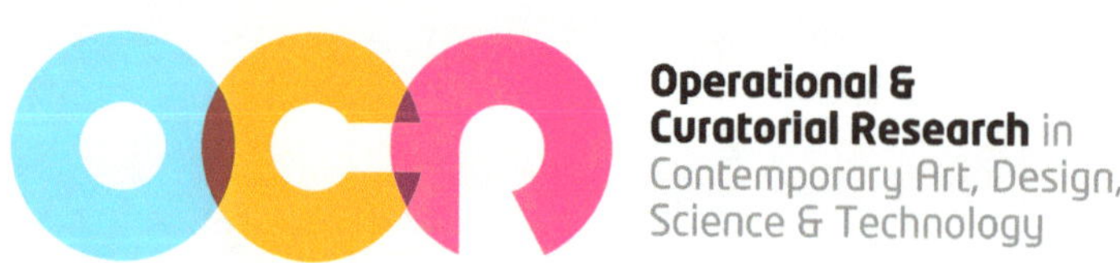

Not Here, Not There: An Analysis Of An International Collaboration To Survey Augmented Reality Art

Every published volume has a reason, a history, a conceptual underpinning as well as an aim that ultimately the editor or editors wish to achieve. There is also something else in the creation of a volume; that is the larger goal shared by the community of authors, artists and critics that take part in it.

This volume of LEA titled *Not Here, Not There* had a simple goal: surveying the current trends in augmented reality artistic interventions. There is no other substantive academic collection currently available, and it is with a certain pride that both, Richard Rinehart and myself, look at this endeavor. Collecting papers and images, answers to interviews as well as images and artists' statements and putting it all together is perhaps a small milestone; nevertheless I believe that this will be a seminal collection which will showcase the trends and dangers that augmented reality as an art form faces in the second decade of the XXIst century.

As editor, I did not want to shy away from more critical essays and opinion pieces, in order to create a documentation that reflects the status of the current thinking. That these different tendencies may or may not be proved right in the future is not the reason for the collection, instead what I believe is important and relevant is to create a historical snapshot by focusing on the artists and authors developing artistic practices and writing on augmented reality. For this reason, Richard and I posed to the contributors a series of questions that in the variegated responses of the artists and authors will evidence and stress similarities and differences, contradictions and behavioral approaches. The interviews add a further layer of documentation which, linked to the artists' statements, provides an overall understanding of the hopes for this new artistic playground or new media extension. What I personally wanted to give relevance to in this volume is the artistic creative process. I also wanted to evidence the challenges faced by the artists in creating artworks and attempting to develop new thinking and innovative aesthetic approaches.

The whole volume started from a conversation that I had with Tamiko Thiel – that was recorded in Istanbul at Kasa Gallery and that lead to a curatorial collaboration with Richard. The first exhibition *Not Here* at the Samek Art Gallery, curated by Richard Reinhart, was juxtaposed to a response from Kasa Gallery with the exhibition *Not There*, in Istanbul. The conversations between Richard and myself produced this final volume – *Not Here, Not There* – which we both envisaged as a collection of authored papers, artists' statements, artworks, documentation and answers to some of the questions that we had as curators. This is the reason why we kept the same questions for all of the interviews – in order to create the basis for a comparative analysis of different aesthetics, approaches and processes of the artists that work in augmented reality.

When creating the conceptual structures for this collection my main personal goal was to develop a link – or better to create the basis for a link – between earlier artistic interventions in the 1960s and the current artistic interventions of artists that use augmented reality.

My historical artist of reference was Yayoi Kusama and the piece that she realized for the Venice Biennial in 1966 titled *Narcissus Garden*. The artwork was a happening and intervention at the Venice Biennial; Kusama was obliged to stop selling her work by the biennial's organizers for 'selling art too cheaply.'

"In 1966 [...] she went uninvited to the Venice Biennale. There, dressed in a golden kimono, she filled the lawn outside the Italian pavilion with 1,500 mirrored balls, which she offered for sale for 1,200 lire apiece. The authorities ordered her to stop, deeming it unacceptable to 'sell art like hot dogs or ice cream cones.'" [1]

The conceptualization and interpretation of this gesture by critics and art historians is that of a guerrilla action that challenged the commercialization of the art system and that involved the audience in a process that revealed the complicit nature and behaviors of the viewers as well as use controversy and publicity as an integral part of the artistic practice.

Kusama's artistic legacy can perhaps be resumed in these four aspects: a) engagement with audience's behaviors, b) issues of art economy and commercialization, c) rogue interventions in public spaces and d) publicity and notoriety.

These are four elements that characterize the work practices and artistic approaches – in a variety of combinations and levels of importance – of contemporary artists that use augmented reality as a medium. Here, is not perhaps the place to focus on the role of 'publicity' in art history and artistic practices, but a few words have to be spent in order to explain that publicity for AR artworks is not solely a way for the artist to gain notoriety, but an integral part of the artwork, which in order to come into existence and generate interactions and engagements with the public has to be communicated to the largest possible audience.

"By then, Kusama was widely assumed to be a publicity hound, who used performance mainly as a way of gaining media exposure." [2] The publicity obsession, or the accusation of being a 'publicity hound' could be easily moved to the contemporary group of artists that use augmented reality. Their invasions of spaces, juxtapositions, infringements could be defined as nothing more than publicity stunts that have little to do with art. These accusations would not be just irrelevant but biased – since – as in the case of Sander Veenhof's analysis in this collection – the linkage between the existence of the artwork as an invisible presence and its physical manifestation and engagement with the audience can only happen through knowledge, through the audience's awareness of the existence of the art piece itself that in order to achieve its impact as an artwork necessitates to be publicized.

Even if, I do not necessarily agree with the idea of a 'necessary manifestation' and audience's knowledge of the artwork – I believe that an artistic practice that is unknown is equally valid – I can nevertheless understand the process, function and relations that have to be established in order to develop a form of engagement and interaction between the AR artwork and the audience. To condemn the artists who seek publicity

1. David Pilling, "The World According to Yayoi Kusama," *The Financial Times*, January 20, 2012, http://www.ft.com/cms/s/2/52ab168a-4188-11e1-8c33-00144feab49a.html#axzz1kDck8rzm (accessed March 1, 2013).

2. Isabelle Loring Wallace and Jennie Hirsh, *Contemporary Art & Classical Myth* (Farnham; Burlington, VT: Ashgate, 2011), 94.

 ISSN 1071-4391 ISBN 978-1-906897-20-8

in order to gather audiences to make the artworks come alive is perhaps a shortsighted approach that does not take into consideration the audience's necessity of knowing that interaction is possible in order for that interaction to take place.

What perhaps should be analyzed in different terms is the evolution of art in the second part of the XXth century, as an activity that is no longer and can no longer be rescinded from publicity, since audience engagement requires audience attendance and attendance can be obtained only through communication / publicity. The existence of the artwork – in particular of the successful AR artwork – is strictly measured in numbers: numbers of visitors, numbers of interviews, numbers of news items, numbers of talks, numbers of interactions, numbers of clicks, and, perhaps in a not too distant future, numbers of coins gained. The issue of being a 'publicity hound' is not a problem that applies to artists alone, from Andy Warhol to Damien Hirst from Banksy to Maurizio Cattelan, it is also a method of evaluation that affects art institutions and museums alike. The accusation moved to AR artists of being media whores – is perhaps contradictory when arriving from institutional art forms, as well as galleries and museums that have celebrated publicity as an element of the performative character of both artists and artworks and an essential element instrumental to the institutions' very survival.

The publicity stunts of the augmented reality interventions today are nothing more than an acquired methodology borrowed from the second part of the XXth century. This is a stable methodology that has already been widely implemented by public and private art institutions in order to promote themselves and their artists.

Publicity and community building have become an artistic methodology that AR artists are playing with by making use of their better knowledge of the AR media. Nevertheless, this is knowledge born out of necessity and scarcity of means, and at times appears to be more effective than the institutional messages arriving from well-established art organizations. I should also add that publicity is functional in AR interventions to the construction of a community – a community of aficionados, similar to the community of 'nudists' that follows Spencer Tunic for his art events / human installation.

I think what is important to remember in the analysis of the effectiveness both in aesthetic and participatory terms of augmented reality artworks – is not their publicity element, not even their sheer numbers (which, by the way, are what has made these artworks successful) but their quality of disruption.

The ability to use – in Marshall McLuhan's terms – the medium as a message in order to impose content bypassing institutional control is the most exciting element of these artworks. It is certainly a victory that a group of artists – by using alternative methodological approaches to what are the structures of the capitalistic system, is able to enter into that very capitalistic system in order to become institutionalized and perhaps – in the near future – be able to make money in order to make art.

Much could be said about the artist's need of fitting within a capitalist system or the artist's moral obligation to reject the basic necessities to ensure an operational professional existence within contemporary capitalistic structures. This becomes, in my opinion, a question of personal ethics, artistic choices and existential social dramas. Let's not forget that the vast majority of artists – and AR artists in particular – do not have large sums and do not impinge upon national budgets as much as banks, financial institutions, militaries and corrupt politicians. They work for years with small salaries, holding multiple jobs and making personal sacrifices; and the vast majority of them does not end up with golden parachutes or golden handshakes upon retirement nor causes billions of damage to society.

The current success of augmented reality interventions is due in small part to the nature of the medium. Museums and galleries are always on the lookout for 'cheap' and efficient systems that deliver art engagement, numbers to satisfy the donors and the national institutions that support them, artworks that deliver visibility for the gallery and the museum, all of it without requiring large production budgets. Forgetting that art is also about business, that curating is also about managing money, it means to gloss over an important element – if not the major element – that an artist has to face in order to deliver a vision.

Augmented reality artworks bypass these financial challenges, like daguerreotypes did by delivering a cheaper form of portraiture than oil painting in the first part of the XIXth century, or like video did in the 1970s and like digital screens and projectors have done in the 1990s until now, offering cheaper systems to display moving as well as static images. AR in this sense has a further advantage from the point of view of the gallery – the gallery has no longer a need to purchase hardware because audiences bring their own hardware: their mobile phones.

The materiality of the medium, its technological revolutionary value, in the case of early augmented reality artworks plays a pivotal role in order to understand its success. It is ubiquitous, can be replicated everywhere in the world, can be installed with minimal hassle and can exist, independently from the audience, institutions and governmental permissions. Capital costs for AR installations are minimal, in the order of a few hundred dollars, and they lend themselves to collaborations based on global networks.

Problems though remain for the continued success of augmented reality interventions. Future challenges are in the materialization of the artworks for sale, to name an important one. Unfortunately, unless the relationship between collectors and the 'object' collected changes in favor of immaterial objects, the problem to overcome for artists that use augmented reality intervention is how and in what modalities to link the AR installations with the process of production of an object to be sold.

Personally I believe that there are enough precedents that AR artists could refer to, from Christo to Marina Abramovich, in order develop methods and frameworks to present AR artworks as collectable and sellable material objects. The artists' ability to do so, to move beyond the fractures and barriers of institutional vs. revolutionary, retaining the edge of their aesthetics and artworks, is what will determine their future success.

These are the reasons why I believe that this collection of essays will prove to be a piece, perhaps a small piece, of future art history, and why in the end it was worth the effort.

Lanfranco Aceti
Editor in Chief, Leonardo Electronic Almanac
Director, Kasa Gallery

 ISSN 1071-4391 ISBN 978-1-906897-20-8

Site, Non-site, and Website

In the 1960's, artist Robert Smithson articulated the strategy of representation summarized by "site vs. non-site" whereby certain artworks were simultaneously abstract and representational and could be site-specific without being sited. A pile of rocks in a gallery is an "abstract" way to represent their site of origin. In the 1990's net.art re-de-materialized the art object and found new ways to suspend the artwork online between website and non-site. In the 21st century, new technologies suggest a reconsideration of the relationship between the virtual and the real. "Hardlinks" such as QR codes attempt to bind a virtual link to our physical environment.

Throughout the 1970's, institutional critique brought political awareness and social intervention to the site of the museum. In the 1980's and 90's, street artist such as Banksy went in the opposite direction, critiquing the museum by siting their art beyond its walls.

Sited art and intervention art meet in the art of the trespass. What is our current relationship to the sites we live in? What representational strategies are contemporary artists using to engage sites? How are sites politically activated? And how are new media framing our consideration of these questions? The contemporary art collective ManifestAR offers one answer,

> *"Whereas the public square was once the quintessential place to air grievances, display solidarity, express difference, celebrate similarity, remember, mourn, and reinforce shared values of right and wrong, it is no longer the only anchor for interactions in the public realm. That geography has been relocated to a novel terrain, one that encourages exploration of mobile location based monuments, and virtual memorials. Moreover, public space is now truly open, as artworks can be placed anywhere in the world, without prior permission from government or private authorities – with profound implications for art in the public sphere and the discourse that surrounds it."*

ManifestAR develops projects using Augmented Reality (AR), a new technology that – like photography before it – allows artists to consider questions like those above in new ways. Unlike Virtual Reality, Augmented Reality is the art of overlaying virtual content on top of physical reality. Using AR apps on smart phones, iPads, and other devices, viewers look at the real world around them through their phone's camera lens, while the app inserts additional images or 3D objects into the scene. For instance, in the work *Signs over Semiconductors* by Will Pappenheimer, a blue sky above a Silicon Valley company that is "in reality" empty contains messages from viewers in skywriting smoke when viewed through an AR-enabled Smartphone.

AR is being used to activate sites ranging from Occupy Wall Street to the art exhibition ManifestAR @ ZERO1 Biennial 2012 – presented by the Samek Art Gallery simultaneously at Bucknell University in Lewisburg, PA and at Silicon Valley in San Jose, CA. From these contemporary non-sites, and through the papers included in this special issue of LEA, artists ask you to reconsider the implications of the simple question *wayn* (where are you now?)

Richard Rinehart
Director, Samek Art Gallery, Bucknell University

Leonardo Electronic Almanac
Volume 19 Issue 1

 ISSN 1071-4391 ISBN 978-1-906897-20-8

The Variable Museum: Off-Topic Art

Augmented reality provides the opportunity to find a balance point between personalized digital content and the shared context of a group of people in a physical room. *Taking advantage of the opportunity requires navigating some significant obstacles though, including the aura associated with traditional art spaces and objects. The Variable Museum provides individuals, in a group, with varying limited experiences of an artwork and asks them to discover what the complete work is by comparing their perspective with the others. The resulting discussion creates a new work specific to the group that participates in it and replaces the illusion of personalization with discourse and social construction.*

by

JOHN BELL

Assistant Professor, Innovative Communication Design
The University of Maine
426 Chadbourne Hall
Orono, ME 04469-5713
john.p.bell@maine.edu
http://www.johnpbell.com/

There are not many hard and fast rules on the Internet, but one thing I have found to be a remarkably consistent truth since the dawn of the web is that the most fascinating part of any forum is its off-topic area. Websites that put a lot of effort into creating focused, topical content to draw people together who like politics, or coding, or 'lolcats' quickly learned that politics, coding, and lolcats were not all their visitors wanted to discuss. Thus was born the off-topic forum, a place for people with a common interest to talk about all the things they do not have in common. On many sites, an off-topic forum fosters a feeling of

 ISSN 1071-4391 ISBN 978-1-906897-20-8

community that mirrors the offline world more closely than purely topical discussions. They are the digital equivalent of town hall dinners or downtown coffee shops, the places where humans – constrained by geography instead of shared interests – get together and talk about the rest of their lives. Sometimes the talks are friendlier than others, but the result is a conversation where everybody learns how they are similar to and different from the people around them. Here, borders are exposed, and new ideas can form from the collisions of old ones.

Creating these liminal spaces between perspectives is one of the goals of my artistic practice. While it is possible to suggest them using traditional media, augmented reality brings a powerful new technique to the table: the ability to personalize and tailor an artwork to different viewers' specificities while still maintaining the viewers' relationships to each other and to the space as a whole. As in the off-topic forum, viewers are brought together by a common aspect – physical proximity – have their own unique perspectives – personalized AR (Augmented Reality) imagery – to smash together and see what they can create. This is the space I tried to create in my installation *The Variable Museum*.

Creating an opportunity for discussion is not enough for many viewers, particularly when they are in the unique state of consciousness that is brought on by entering the art world. In this world, where the inviolability of objects is reinforced by glass cases and security guards, additional prompting is often needed to move visitors from being passive viewers to active creators. AR can remove the physical barriers easily. The cultural barriers, through – the aura of the art object – are more difficult to be overcome, but also provide some unique opportunities for new understandings.

MYTH AND AURA

In Walter Benjamin's 1935 essay, *The Work of Art in the Age of Mechanical Reproduction*, he describes the 'aura' as the sense of authenticity that is conferred upon an original work by "the essence of all that is transmissible from its beginning, ranging from its substantive duration to its testimony to the history which it has experienced." [1]

Colin Lang sums up several characteristics of aura by saying it is not "a singular concept, but rather [a] shifting code for several crucial terms within Benjamin's investigation. In particular, aura stands in for concepts such as tradition, myth, singularity or uniqueness, and beauty, which crop up throughout Benjamin's writings." [2] With the arguable exception of beauty, the common point between each of those characteristics is their reliance on a rhizomatic network of ideas that are external to the artwork itself. Aura can be conceived of as the extrinsic properties of an artwork that give to the artwork itself – to use Benjamin's word – "authority." Given this definition, it seems reasonable to add other similar factors like economic value and referential prestige into the mix of auratic characteristics that Lang supplies.

One key effect of aura is that, upon entering the art world – a museum, gallery, or other space defined as a container of art – a viewer who accepts the aura of the piece believes it to be recondite. The relationship between work and viewer changes putting the viewer into a state of curiosity and receptivity that is not associated with everyday creative acts. Artists who wish to do so may use this mode for any number of interventions that would not be possible in a different context. Roy Ascott describes this state of curiosity and receptivity in his article, *Towards a Field Theory for Post-Modernist Art*. He defines this space as a locus "in which the viewer is actively involved, not in an act of closure, in the sense of completing a discrete message from the artists, (a passive process) but by interrogating and interacting with the system 'artwork' to generate meaning." [3]

BREAKING AURA DOWN

While the aura can be used as an advantage, it is more often damaging to the relationship between artwork and viewer. Benjamin puts forth a strong argument describing the drawbacks of the aura in his original essay on the subject, explaining a process where the aura forces viewers to change how they approach a work of art so that they cannot judge the work on its own merits, beauty, or ideas.

The aura can also have a negative influence on the artwork itself, not just the way in which it is interpreted. When a work is treated as a cult fetish object, it becomes stagnant, with those who are in charge of maintaining it hesitating even to preserve it against natural decay, and totally adverse to make any change to it. As predicted by Benjamin, today's art and artists are becoming more involved in temporal concerns than in the past. When art is anchored in the moment, after that moment passes the art is forced to change from being based upon and having an impact to merely being an interesting product. AR may seem like a way to break down the aura and get around the process of stagnation as virtual objects are harder to fetishize than physical objects. AR occupies a hybrid space that may be closer to an ephemeral work than a painting, but even ephemera can suffer damage from stagnation. One illustrative case is the history of event scores in the Fluxus movement. Designed as a set of open prompts, the aura created around the initial realization of those prompts has turned some of them into effectively fixed performances. For example, when Ben Patterson performed George Brecht's Drip Music in 2002 he noted that Brecht's original instructions allowed for either a single source or multiple sources of dripping water – contrary to his memory and the traditional interpretation of the score. [4]

The notion that there are "traditional interpretations of these works" undermines the premise of a flexible, ever-changing score to be interpreted by the performer, even if Patterson did choose to go back and look at the source for this particular performance. In this case, the aura of the original work has been conflated with the aura of an instance of the work to such a degree that Patterson did not even know the true parameters of the work he intended to perform. The original work has been hidden by its own legacy because the minds of its interpreters are seeking a repeatable, predictable performance; they are trying to make an ephemeral work persist, helping to preserve its aura by attempting to keep the work as close to a static object as is possible.

OFF-TOPIC ART

The dual-edged blade of aura – its necessity in creating Ascott's field and its simultaneous ability to block that field – is a central conundrum for any artist who wants to intervene in the traditional art/viewer relationship and one that I tried to design around *The Variable Museum*. Given the centrality of aura to the modern conception of fine art, it is clear that I could not eliminate aura and still maintain the label of art for my creative output. Instead, I could only seek to minimize its negative effects on the work I produce.

As aura's natural tendency is to cluster around closed, fixed systems, one strategy is to create work that emphasizes the open aspects of art. Umberto Eco describes how art consists of open and closed sides:

> *A work of art, therefore, is a complete and closed form in its uniqueness as a balanced organic whole, while at the same time constituting an open product on account of its susceptibility to countless different interpretations which do not impinge on its unalterable specificity. Hence, every reception of a work of art is both an interpretation and a performance of it, because in every reception the work takes on a fresh perspective for itself.* [5]

 ISSN 1071-4391 ISBN 978-1-906897-20-8

In some ways the clause "which do not impinge on its unalterable specificity" seems to indicate that creating an open work is simply a matter of not creating a closed work or a work that is so regimented as to preclude "countless different interpretations." Ben Patterson's story about Drip Music would seem to indicate that this is not all that is required. There are multiple versions of the Drip Music score, but the simplest version is no more than a single word: "Dripping." [6] If such a vague work is still subject to aura restriction then the answer must be more than simply leaving a work open to interpretation. In order for an off-topic forum to exist, there must be an on-topic forum to ground it.

LEARNING FROM SOFTWARE

Since Eco's constant acts of interpretation and performance are made manifest in many interactive works that cannot function without the user's active involvement, examining them to discover how they are constructed may shed some light on reusable processes that encourage those acts. One key structure is what Lev Manovich refers to as database-narrative opposition. Manovich ascribes to the database the semiological characteristics of paradigm, while narrative takes the role of syntagm. In static works, he finds that the paradigm is implicit while the syntagm is explicit. Interactive works reverse that relationship: "Database (the paradigm) is given material existence, while the narrative (the syntagm) is de-materialised. Paradigm is privileged, syntagm is downplayed." [7]

Using the interactive relationship between paradigm and syntagm is not trivial in a non-interactive work. Following Manovich's path of privileged database/paradigm even further leads to the realm of artificial intelligence (AI). One approach to AI in particular, pursued by a group Warren Sack calls the Neo-Encyclopediaists, is concerned with trying to build intelligent AI by collecting a giant database of "common sense." [8] This database powers an intelligent system by leveraging massive paradigmatic knowledge to produce syntagmatic knowledge. Importantly, however, once the syntagmatic knowledge exists, any one instance of the paradigmatic knowledge can be substituted for another instance within its same paradigmatic set. Translating this process back into the world of art production, I created *The Variable Museum* – a work made up of paradigmatic components held together in a syntagmatic rule set. The individual sees only one component of each set, not enough to define the rule set alone. The rule set can only be defined by discovering other components and reverse engineering the syntagm, forcing Ascott's field to include not just the artist, viewer, and artwork, but the other viewers as well. The expanded field functions as the "off-topic forum" for the artwork, a place where people have been brought together by physical proximity and given explicit license to throw ideas together wih the intention to actulize those ideas.

CREATING THE FIELD

The Variable Museum creates a system that attempts to change the relationship between artwork, curator, and viewer. No physical artifacts exist in *The Variable Museum*; it relies on augmented reality to present digital artifacts to members of its audience. Since these artifacts are presented to an individual viewer instead of an entire group – as would be required in a physical museum – AR fulfills the goal of crafting an exhibition that is tailored to the individual without impinging upon communication within a group.

Such an exhibition operates on a fundamentally different principle than the traditional museum, which is heavily invested in singular objects, performances, or moments in time. *The Variable Museum* replaces a focus on singular objects with a focus on a paradigmatic group of artifacts that are individually fungible. Selection of these artifact groups is the job of a curator-artist whose artwork is the creation of an intangible set of rules.

An active museum visitor's role is also transformed under this system as they seek to discover the invisible thread the curator has produced. Since each visitor has only one piece of the paradigmatic set, the only way to uncover the common thread is to talk to other visitors and discover what they are experiencing. In this way, the true artwork that the artist has created is brought into being by social exchange between visitors whose individual experiences are little different from in a physical museum.

CREATED PARADIGMS AND INVOKED SYNTAGMS

While it might be difficult to imagine how The Variable Museum's system works when applied to artwork, applying it to simpler artifacts demonstrates how it transmits a different impression of an artwork than a traditional museum would do. Consider the example of the playing card in figure 1.

Figure 1. The eight of clubs. Lesser GNU Public License By Brandon Ardient based on SVG-cards by David Bellot.

If asked to identify this card, most likely people would say that it is the eight of clubs. Adding a second card forces the viewer to change their perception of the set:

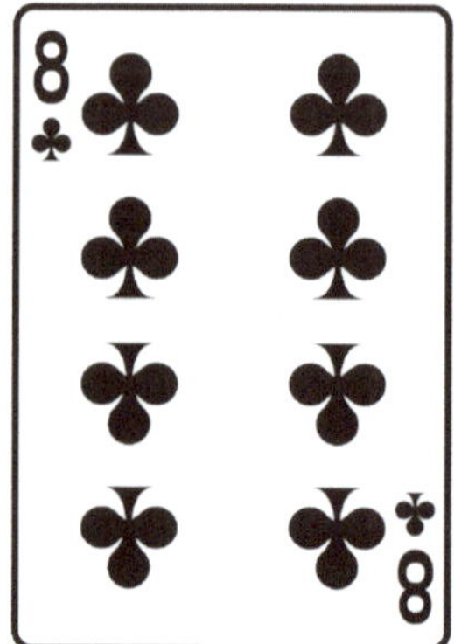
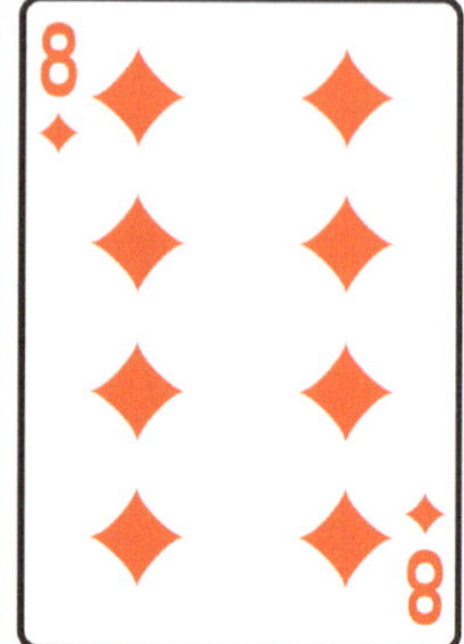

Figure 2. A group identified as "eights." Lesser GNU Public License By Brandon Ardient based on SVG-cards by David Bellot.

As the eight of clubs has now been joined by the eight of diamonds, the paradigmatic description of the cards becomes just "eights." Additional information has forced a definition of the set that includes more cards – four, including two not shown, instead of just one – and also discards the part of the previous definition that no longer fits – "of clubs." A slightly different second card produces not just a different definition, but a new piece of information:

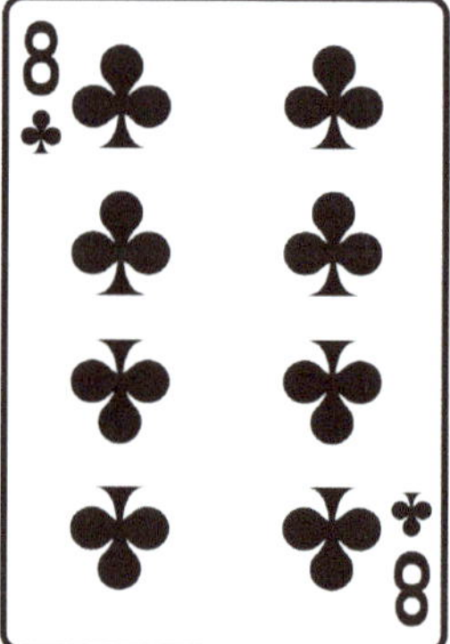
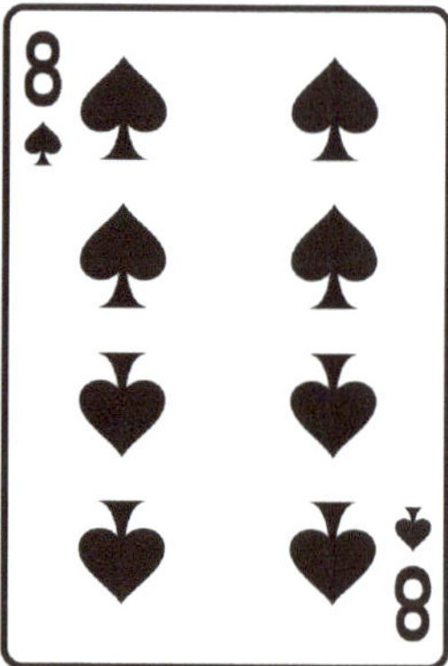

Figure 3. A group identified as "black eights." Lesser GNU Public License By Brandon Ardient based on SVG-cards by David Bellot.

A likely description of the eights of clubs and spades would be "black eights." While these cards fit the definition of the last set because they are both eights, there is also a new similarity between the two that allows us to narrow the definition to fit only these two

 ISSN 1071-4391 ISBN 978-1-906897-20-8

cards. Importantly, it is also a piece of information that did not explicitly exist in the definition of the original single-card set. The eight of clubs may be black, but if asked to name the card it is not usually labeled as black without a point of contrast or similarity that forces the viewer to include it as a parameter for describing the card – in this case provided by a second black eight. In fact, if we want to create a paradigm that is just "black," we would likely have to remove all other points of similarity between the two cards:

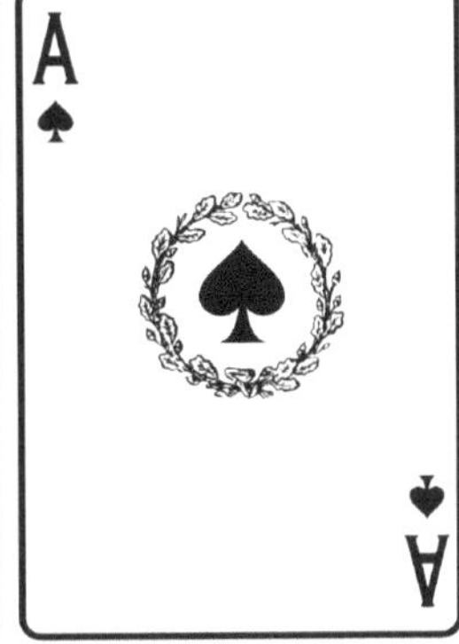

Figure 4. A group identified as "black cards." Lesser GNU Public License By Brandon Ardient based on SVG-cards by David Bellot.

The parameter of "black" is usually a secondary characteristic of the parameter "suit" so the only way to force its primacy is to invalidate a single suit as the descriptor while maintaining the blackness of both cards, as shown here with the eight of clubs and the ace of spades. Of course, "black" is an extremely general characteristic, applying to half the deck. The last example could have been the eight of spades and the ace of clubs without changing the resulting definition.

However, including all four cards triggers a new result for anybody who happens to have the right knowledge base (figure 5).

For somebody who knows a bit of gambling lore, two black eights and two black aces will prompt a new definition of the set: been the cards in the famous "dead-man's hand," named supposedly because it is the hand that Wild Bill Hickok was holding when he was shot while playing poker (though other, less famous, accounts suggest a different origin). Though the previous paradigmatic definitions of the set still apply to these cards, it has now been overridden by a new name. "Dead man's hand" is a syntagmatic description, invoked by the internal relationships between the displayed cards and an external narrative. This description does not explicitly include any data intrinsic to the shown cards at all, relying instead on an extrinsic cultural reference that may not be known to all and may change over time.

With this example, we can see a few of the ways that manipulating the given elements of a set can change that set's definition, adding or removing specificity or even completely changing the label a viewer might apply to it. The single eight of clubs is indeed a black eight that is part of a dead-man's hand, so any of the subsequent set definitions could have been used to describe that single card from the very beginning. However, without the additional artifacts the viewer has no way to know what specific characteristic of

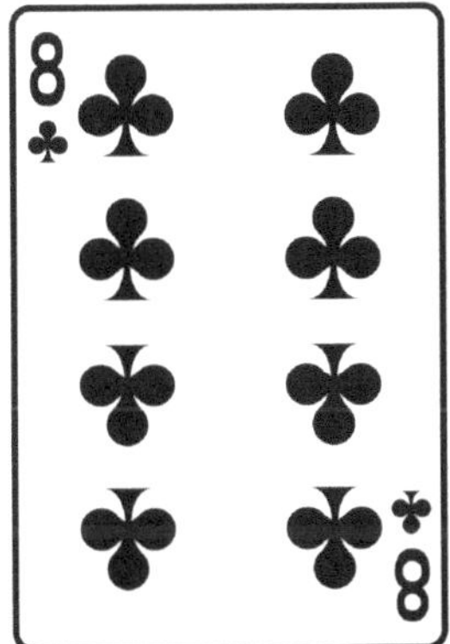
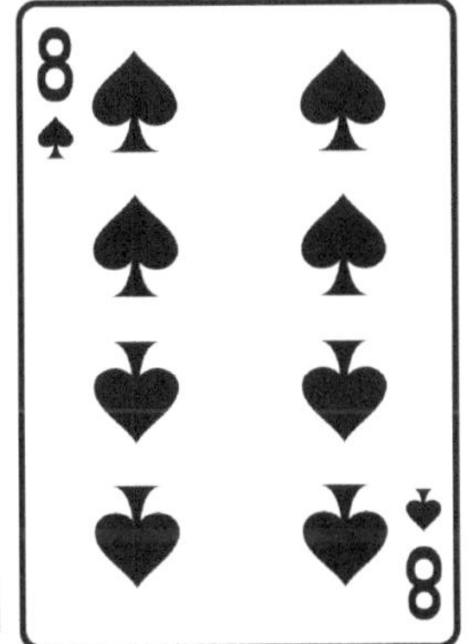
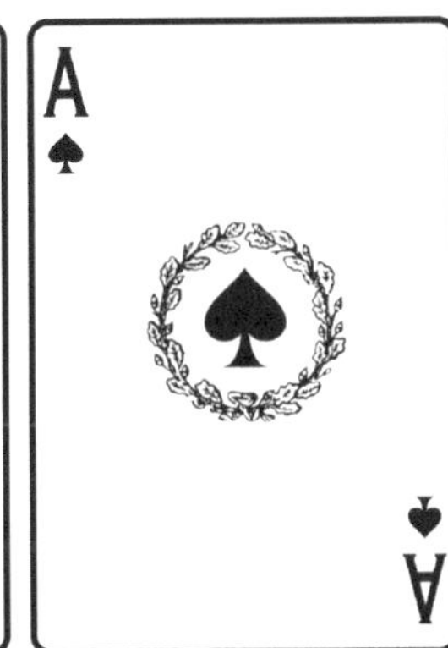
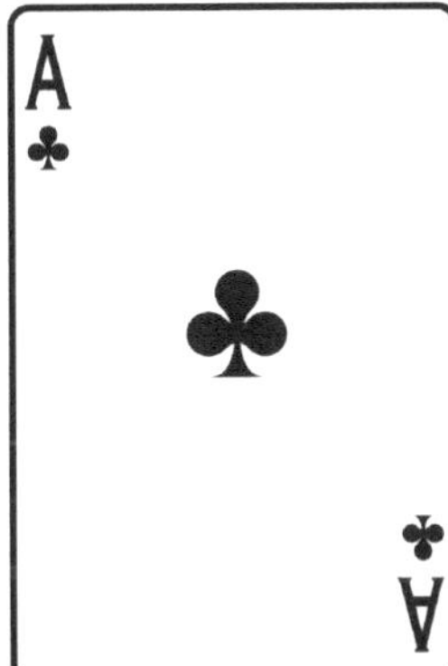

Figure 5. A group identified as a "dead man's hand." Lesser GNU Public License By Brandon Ardient based on SVG-cards by David Bellot.

that card to describe, defaulting to simply stating the most obvious data available: it is the eight of clubs.

COLLABORATIVE CONTEXTUALIZATION

Manipulating the identification of a set is a common feature of art. Recontextualization is, after all, taking an object and putting it in a new setting. If one thinks of setting as just another potential member of the set, on par with the artifact itself, then contextualization defines the identification of the entire set of the artwork.

In museum settings, the role of providing context is usually given to a curator, likely either working with the artist or with respect to the artist's perceived wishes and intentions. Everything from lighting to positioning, and the other works that share a space, can provide context and shape perception of an artwork. In some cases, context is so powerful that the roles of the artist and curator are forced to merge so that an integrated system describing the work and its context can be created.

Often left out of this process are the ultimate consumers of the work, who are expected, simply, to show up and accept what is placed before them. While there is a common understanding that audiences will apply their own contextual history to a piece, the traditional expectation is that this is either a process internal to individual audience members or a transaction between artist and viewer as in Ascott's Field Theory. Third parties often only become involved when critics and historians write about the work, influencing its perception over time and creating an aura around the work.

The Variable Museum makes third party contextualization an integral part of the work. However, doing so requires tweaking the vocabulary of art and coming up with some new definitions:

» Artifact – an individual work, what would usually be called an artwork (e.g., a painting, a sculpture, an installation).
» Set – A collection of multiple artifacts that form a paradigmatic group. For the purposes of The *Variable Museum*, the individual artifacts are fungible.
» Artwork (or piece) – in *The Variable Museum*, an artwork can be understood to be a physical location in the gallery where a set is placed. The artwork is represented to individual visitors as a single artifact. Construction of the final piece is only possible when multiple visitors combine their experiences of the artifacts they perceive in that location.

The Variable Museum is intended to encourage discussion between visitors and thus the construction of the final piece and in fact may be best defined as the rules that are in place to encourage this discussion:

» Visitors must pass through *The Variable Museum* in groups, staying together until they leave. Individuals are not allowed to take in the piece alone.
» Artifacts in sets must be linked in a non-trivial way. Ideally, a balance point should be found where linkages are not so apparent as to be dismissed as obvious and not so obscure as to be easily missed. Defining the paradigm is left to the artist in charge of each instance of *The Variable Museum*.
» Artifacts in an artwork must occupy the same physical space as one another but must also only be perceived by one individual in a group.
» Ideally, the AR implementation should not allow visitors to easily share the artifact assigned to them with other members of their group. Visitors have to come up with their own means of describing or discussing their artifact and creating their artwork. Due to practical concerns, this may not always be possible.
» The AR implementation should not interfere with the ability of the members of a group to communicate with each other. This is a critical point for a work that is trying to promote discussion, and a missing feature from full virtual reality or distributed network-based approaches to digital content.

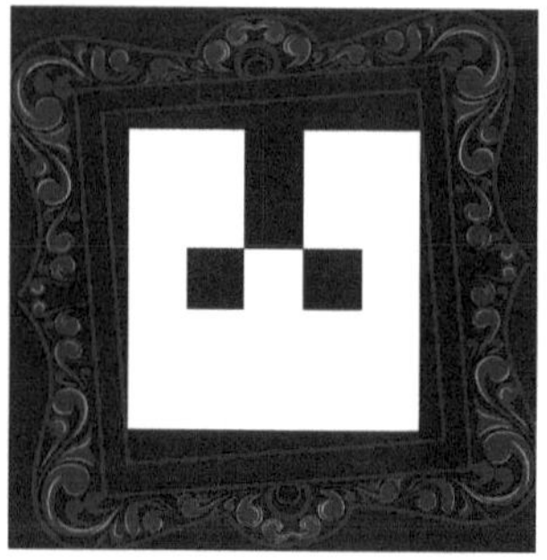

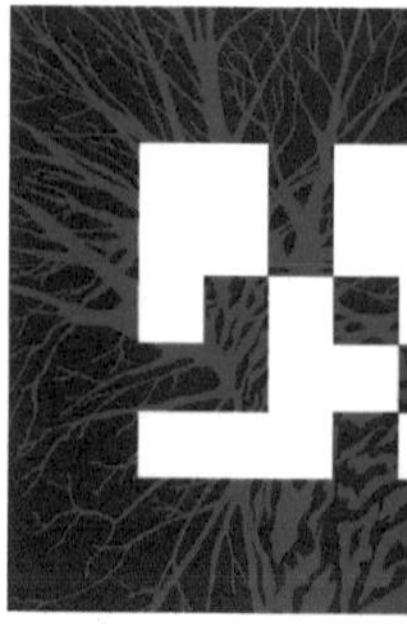

 ISSN 1071-4391 ISBN 978-1-906897-20-8

This set of rules clearly leaves a great deal open to interpretation. Specific means of displaying artifacts, the paradigms and artwork under consideration, and the installation of *The Variable Museum* itself are all left to the artists in charge of each iteration of the piece. Instead, the core of *The Variable Museum* is an idea: when several people in the same space are given partial experiences of an artwork, communication between them will develop a shared connotative meaning that is different from if they were all given the complete experience.

Consider the infrastructure that is necessary to describe an artifact to another person. Herbert Clark calls this process "grounding," describing it as not only the process of description but also the feedback required to be sure that understanding has actually been established between two conversants:

> *We assume that the criterion people try to reach in conversation is as follows (Clark and Schaefer, 1989; Clark & Wilkes-Gibbs, 1986): The contributor and his or her partners mutually believe that the partners have understood what the contributor meant to a criterion sufficient for current purposes. This is called the grounding criterion. Technically, then, grounding is the collective process by which participants try to reach this mutual belief.* [9]

The steps necessary to establish grounding vary considerably depending upon the individuals in a group. Strangers have to do more work because they must establish the background and experiences of their partners before they can begin to discuss actual content. Their respective backgrounds will further influence how an artifact is described: two art historians may be able effectively to communicate an image of a painting by simply stating its name. Two people without that shared background would need to describe the intrinsic properties of the painting itself, recreating it from scratch, within the mind of the listener and strongly inflecting the image with the speaker's biases.

THE VARIABLE MUSEUM

The first instantiation of *The Variable Museum* was installed at *Without Borders VIII* in Orono, Maine, in August 2011. This version of the piece was built around three Vuzix AR920 augmented reality headsets running on three MacBook Pros. Installed in a gallery setting, the augmented reality fiducial markers were framed and placed on the walls to establish a space in which virtual artifacts could be placed. Each marker

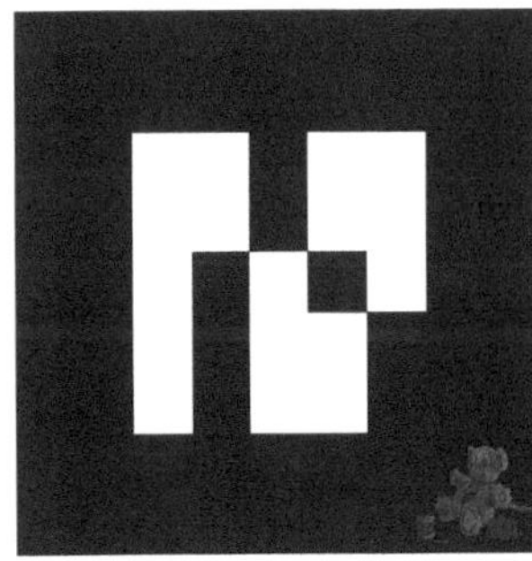

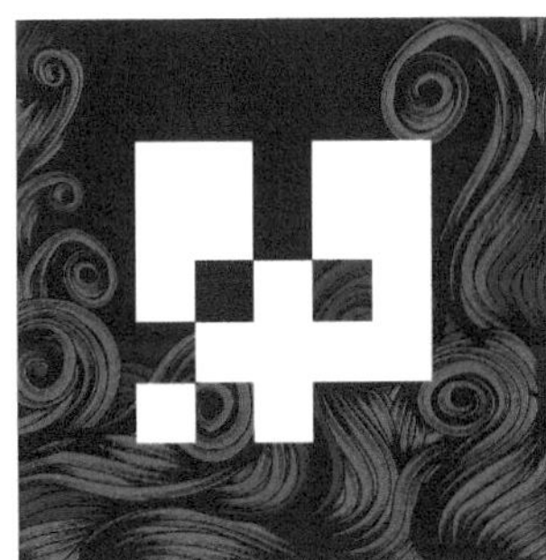

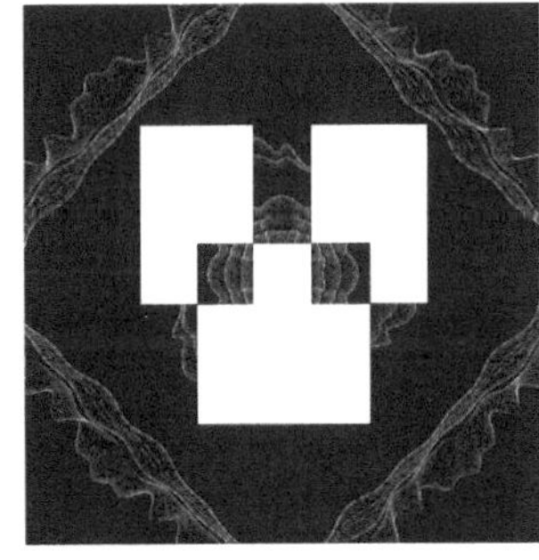

Figure 6. AR markers used in the Without Borders VIII installation of *The Variable Museum*, Orono, ME 2011. © John Bell.

ISSN 1071-4391 ISBN 978-1-906897-20-8

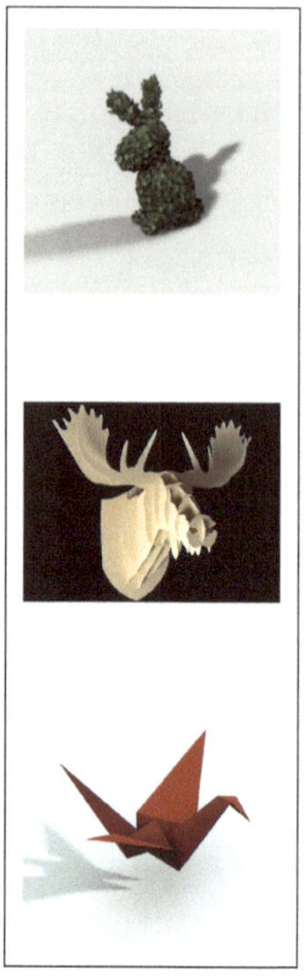

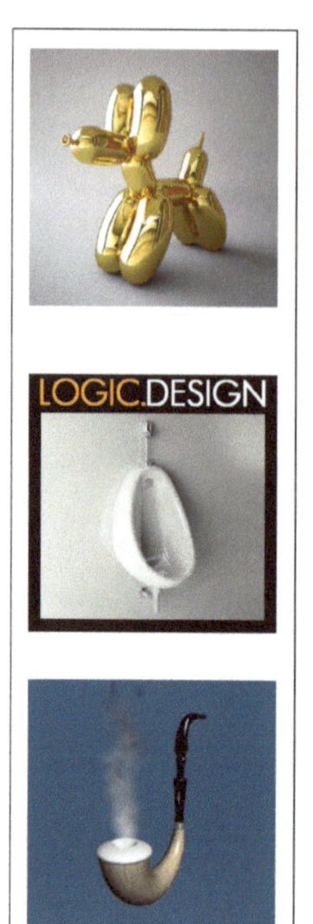

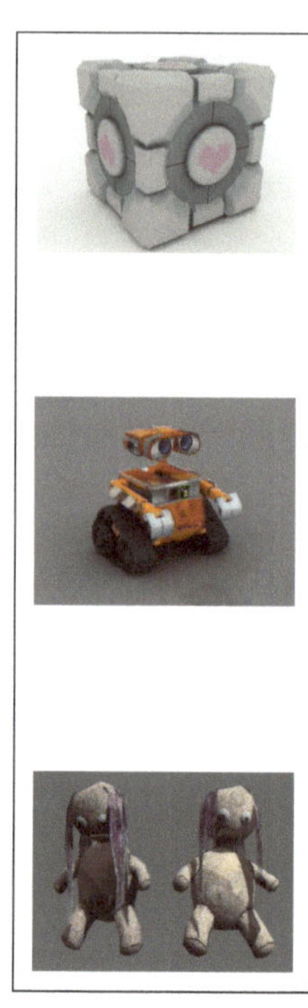

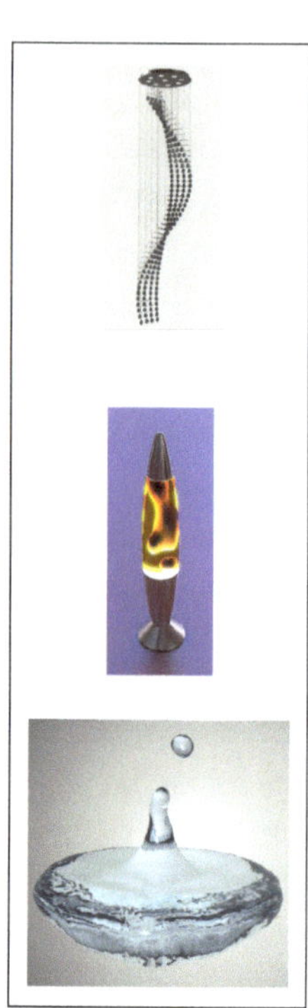

Figure 7. The four artworks in the Without Borders VIII installation of *The Variable Museum*, Orono, ME 2011. Royalty-free licensed images from turbosquid.com.

was modified to add clip art embedded in the images that helped describe the rules of the set at its location.

Each MacBook Pro/AR920 combination presented its wearer with one artifact in each of four artworks as defined previously. To emphasize the fungibility of the individual artifacts clip art was also used for the 3D models. The four artworks each demonstrates different methods of establishing paradigmatic sets that could form the basis of future iterations of *The Variable Museum* including one with a focus on purely auratic properties, one with purely intrinsic aesthetic looks, one that mixes the aesthetic and intellectual, and one with strong extrinsic but non-auratic properties. (The fifth marker was adopted to adapt the installation to the physical space available and did not have an artwork associated with it.)

The second instantiation of *The Variable Museum* was at the Pixxelpoint 2011 exhibition in Gorizia, Italy in December 2011. The artworks shown were the same as the first instance, though the physical layout was different and the extra fiducial could be removed. The key difference, though, was that the Pixxelpoint version did not use the fully immersive headsets from Without Borders; instead, iPod Touches were used to view artifacts. This adaptation was necessary to handle the larger crowds at Pixxelpoint since the AR920s are extremely cumbersome. While the content in both instantiations was identical, it was much easier to show somebody else the screen of an iPod Touch than share the view through a set of AR glasses. This difference led to less crosstalk between viewers and the expansion of Ascott's field was less obvious. Future installations will need to find a better balance point between accessibility and personalization.

PIERCING THE BUBBLE

In 2011, Eli Pariser gave a name to a phenomenon that many media critics had been noticing since the rise of the search engine: The filter bubble. [10] The filter bubble is created by invisible, algorithmic data curation that is customized to individuals and shows them only things in which they are already interested or arguments with which they already agree. It is created when Google, Facebook, or other mediation portals try to be helpful, but as Pariser argues, lack of exposure to alternative viewpoints may be harmful to the discourse necessary to keep a society together. They ensure that the only perspective an individual ever sees is the one they already possess.

Filter bubbles can only exist because they are invisible. As I sit in front of my monitor and see the results of a Google search, the only reason I do not understand it as a bubble is that there is not somebody sitting next to me and getting different results from the same search on their monitor. If the search term is a grounding point, like the fiducials in The Variable Museum, then there is nobody there to provide the second perspective necessary for analysis and discourse. There is no off-topic forum because all results are defined as topical.

Personalization, whether in art or informatics, is not inherently destructive to discourse; in fact, it is necessary. The borders of the individual filter bubble is where all the compelling discussions happen. *The Variable Museum* makes filter bubbles explicit, handing the viewer their own perspective and establishing rules that encourage finding ways to merge them together. If a group of people can burst their individual bubbles and creates a new, shared perspective, then the installation is a success. ■

REFERENCES AND NOTES

1. Walter Benjamin, The Work of Art in the Age of Mechanical Reproduction, 1935, http://www.marxists.org/reference/subject/philosophy/works/ge/benjamin.htm (accessed December 1, 2009).
2. Colin Lang, "After Aura: Re-reading Benjamin's Kunstwerk," Reproducing Art: Walter Benjamin's Work of Art Essay Reconsidered (spec. issue of interculture), 2007, http://interculture.fsu.edu/pdfs/ lang%20colin.pdf (accessed December 2, 2009).
3. Roy Ascott, "Towards a Field Theory for Post-Modernist Art." *Leonardo* 13, no. 1 (1980): 51–52.
4. Co Seegers, "George Brecht | Events and Performances," June 2009, http://members.chello.nl/j.seegers1/flux_files/brecht_performances.html, (accessed December 4, 2009).
5. Umberto Eco, *The Poetics of the Open Work* (Cambridge, MA: Harvard University Press, 1989), 4.
6. Ken Friedman, Owen Smith, and Lauren Sawchyn, "The Fluxus Performance Workbook," 2007, http://www.thing.net/~grist/ld/fluxusworkbook.pdf, (accessed December 8, 2009).
7. Lev Manovich, *The Language of New Media* (Cambridge, MA: MIT Press, 2001), 203.
8. Warren Sack, "Network Aesthetics," in *Database Aesthetics*, ed. Victoria Vesna, 183–210 (Minneapolis, MN: University of Minnesota Press, 2007).
9. Herbert Clark and Susan Brennan, "Grounding in Communication," in *Perspectives on Socially Shared Cognition*, ed. Lauren Resnick, John Levine, and Stephanie Teasley, 127–149 (Washington DC: American Psychological Association, 1991).
10. Eli Pariser, *The Filter Bubble: What the Internet is Hiding From You* (New York: Penguin Press, 2011).

ACKNOWLEDGEMENTS

Special thanks to the University of Maine Intermedia program and Virtual Environments and Multimodal Interaction Laboratory. Card images from Brandon Ardiente's SVG-Z-cards, released under LPGL.

JOHN BELL

interviewed by
Lanfranco Aceti & Richard Rinehart

Is there an 'outside' of the Art World from which to launch critiques and interventions? If so, what is the border that defines outside from inside? If it is not possible to define a border, then what constitutes an intervention and is it possible to be and act as an outsider of the art world? Or are there only different positions within the Art World and a series of positions to take that fulfill ideological parameters and promotional marketing and branding techniques to access the fine art world from an oppositional, and at times confrontational, standpoint?

There is an outside of the art world, but the line of demarcation is not so much a border as a semi-permeable membrane. It selectively allows in only those pieces that are tagged with the label of 'art.' Interventions will inevitably either be assimilated and tagged as 'art' or rejected and cast back out into reality. For the pieces that are accepted, aura begins to accumulate as soon as they are tagged and any claim of being an outsider is rendered moot.

There is a brief window in the time between acceptance and assimilation where work can be done, and that is what intervention should aim for. The only hope is that the assimilation process changes the art world as much as it changes the artwork during this time. Certainly there is precedent for that, and occasionally it can even be said that the change is the intentional result of an intervention. The ratio of interventions causing shifts in the art world to the art world causing shifts in would-be interventionists is not encouraging for those who are after systemic change, and yes, the result often boils down to marketing and branding.

The more successful art interventions take ideas and methodology from art and apply it elsewhere, creating artistic works that do not get through the membrane until somebody inside the art world goes out and

 ISSN 1071-4391 ISBN 978-1-906897-20-8

grabs them. These pieces, whether labelled technology, or industry, or craft are what drives art world change and what art interventions seek to emulate. The intervention itself is often an attempt to artificially accelerate this process, since the art world as an institution is slower to see these changes than individual artists.

"In *The Truth in Painting*, Derrida describes the *parergon* (*par-*, around; *ergon*, the work), the boundaries or limits of a work of art. Philosophers from Plato to Hegel, Kant, Husserl, and Heidegger debated the limits of the intrinsic and extrinsic, the inside and outside of the art object." (Anne Friedberg, *The Virtual Window: From Alberti to Microsoft* (Cambridge, MA: MIT Press, 2009), 13.) Where then is the inside and outside of the virtual artwork? Is the artist's 'hand' still inside the artistic process in the production of virtual art or has it become an irrelevant concept abandoned outside the creative process of virtual artworks?

I do not see virtual artworks as being any different than any other kind of artwork for these purposes. What intrinsic property of a virtual artwork would move that line-wherever it may be-compared to a painting, or sculpture, or performance? The artist is still setting a stage, and the viewer is still interrogating it to extract whatever they may find. Both are still contextualizing everything they see with their outside experiences and knowledge. If I push bits instead of paint, it just means that I am manipulating a different set of tools to get ideas, images, and environments out of my head and into some setting where others can take a look.

The break point here is not between intrinsic and extrinsic; it is between different sets of extrinsic properties. Virtual artworks, particularly augmented reality because of its personal relationship to the viewer, make it possible to present varying experiences to multiple viewers. One person may look at a particular spot on the wall and see a flower, while another may see a gun. The artist has defined this ahead of time, so while there are two separate images they are still manifestations of the same intrinsic property of the work. However, since they are going to prompt very different reactions in the two viewers, there is an opportunity for the externalities to access entirely different rhizomatic networks of ideas and thus change the perception of the piece.

Of course, this happens with interpretation of all artwork, so it is a difference of degree, not type. Augmented reality provides a second feature that can be exploited here though: personalization. Personalization is different than customization. In my example of the gun and the flower, that effect could be achieved physically by using lenticular printing so that there are two different "customized" images depending on where the viewer stands. To see the other image all one has to do is shuffle a few feet to the side and look from a different angle, providing the viewer with all the information the artwork has to offer.

Augmented artworks – at least once the technology reaches the point the industry is racing toward, with glasses- or contact lens-based displays – are personalized. One viewer cannot trivially discover what another viewer is seeing. To extract all intrinsic properties from the artwork requires talking to other viewers to discover what their personalized display is showing them, and in the process the viewer is forced to take on the externalities of everybody they talk to. Here, the artist's hand becomes supplemented by the viewers'–though certainly not replaced – and the final impact of the piece is the result of collaboration and negotiation between all the players.

Virtual interventions appear to be the contemporary inheritance of Fluxus' artistic practices. Artists like Peter Weibel, Yayoi Kusama and Valie Export subverted traditional concepts of space and media through artistic interventions. What are the sources of inspiration and who are the artistic predecessors that you draw from for the conceptual and aesthetic frameworks of contemporary augmented reality interventions?

I think Fluxus is a good place to start, particularly scores by Dick Higgins, George Brecht, or Ken Friedman, among many others. These are pieces that highlight the collaborative space between artist and viewer (I'd prefer to use the word 'consumer' here since that is less medium-specific, but will stick with 'viewer' because it lacks commercial overtones that I do not intend). My work attempts to get to a similar place, though I try to provide more of a supporting structure and direction than a Fluxus score.

It may sound somewhat strange, but my background as a programmer strongly influences my conceptual framework for art. Programming decisions, particularly object-oriented programming, are often motivated by the idea of separation of concerns – that is, making sure that different parts of a program carry out specific functionality. A program is an assembly of these specific modules of functionality that work together toward a certain goal. My artwork tends to be assembled in a similar way, by first determining what my overall goal is, then constructing the individual pieces necessary to meet it and assembling them into a cohesive whole. This is particularly important for personalized augmented reality interventions where individual viewers only have partial information about the piece. What modules are necessary for everybody? Which ones can I supply as an artist, and what does the viewer have to bring to the table? How can they be compiled into a solution for the problem I'm trying to solve? These are the same kinds of issues that programmers think about when designing software architecture.

I first started to apply these ideas to the art world with work on the Variable Media Questionnaire, a preservation tool focusing on ways to maintain ephemeral or media-dependent artwork that has a short natural life span. Within those works, I saw the same kind of modules that I see in software: a CRT that takes on the functionality of displaying video, but might have to be replaced with an LCD of similar functionality when the original dies. Augmented reality allows a new way to import these modules and connect them together. I've recently been referring to my work as 'born variable,' designed from the outset to be a field of modules that can be replaced as necessary so long as the overall core remains intact. If there is a slippery slope involved in variable media preservation, 'born variable' creation unapologetically roams at the bottom of the gully to see if there is anything interesting waiting to be brought up.

In the representation and presentation of your artworks as being 'outside of' and 'extrinsic to' contemporary aesthetics why is it important that your projects are identified as Art?

The label of 'art' expands the possibilities of interaction and impact for artists who take advantage of it. Art, particularly contemporary fine art, has a social standing that prompts viewers to look below the surface for deeper insight, meaning, or emotion. Once a viewer believes an artwork to be recondite, the relationship between the two changes and the viewer is put into a state of curiosity and receptivity that is not associated with everyday creative acts. Artists who wish to do so may use this mode for any number of interventions that would not be possible in a different

 ISSN 1071-4391 ISBN 978-1-906897-20-8

context. I like Roy Ascott's description of this state in his article *Towards a Field Theory for Post-Modernist Art*:

> *Art does not reside in the artwork alone, nor in the activity of the artist alone, but is understood as a field of psychic probability, highly entropic, in which the viewer is actively involved, not in an act of closure in the sense of completing a discrete message from the artists (a passive process) but by interrogating and interacting with the system 'artwork' to generate meaning. This field provides for transactions to take place between the psychic system 'artist' and the psychic system 'viewer' where both are, to use Umberto Eco's phrase, 'gambling on the possibility of semiosis'. Thus the viewer/observer must be a participator and is of operational importance in the total behavior of the system.* (Roy Ascott, "Towards a Field Theory for Post-Modernist Art ." *Leonardo* 13, no. 1 (1980): 51–52.)

What has most surprised you about your recent artworks? What has occurred in your work that was outside of your intent, yet has since become an intrinsic part of the work?

I think the lack of intent or determinacy has been surprising for me. Originally, my artistic practice was all about finding a way to get an idea out of my head, transmit it intact through whatever medium was most useful, and convince the viewer to reconstruct it in their mind. Even when that works it can only happen to a limited extent, and most people do not like to be lectured to by art in any case, so the result was an overall state of disengagement between the viewer and the work.

In trying to get more engagement out of viewers, I started to build interactive hooks into my work. Sometimes these were aggressive – a web site that sends you an email every few minutes comes to mind – and other times it was about giving incentives to the viewer – interact with this artwork and you get a copy for free! But what I eventually ended up doing is creating half of an artwork; pieces and prompts that encourage the viewers to be creative and complete the other half, either physically or mentally. In augmented reality pieces like *The Variable Museum*, I can go even further and just create a space where two viewers supply each other with the missing halves of their own creations. That is incredibly far away from the simple communication model that I started with, but I find watching the results to be fascinating and inspirational. ■

JOHN BELL

statement & artwork

The Variable Museum is an experiment in the relationship between the creators, curators, and consumers of art.

The pictures on the wall are not the artwork: they are augmented reality markers, used to position a head mounted display in space. When looking through the display a visitor sees 3D artifacts inserted into the physical museum space; these, though, are not the artwork either. Visitors are only allowed to use the displays in groups where each member of the group experiences different artifacts occupying the same physical space. While visitors cannot experience each other's artifacts, if they describe the artifacts to each other they will find common threads among each set. The sets of artifacts that groups of visitors experience, along with the descriptions of the individual artifacts that they give each other, is the actual artwork.

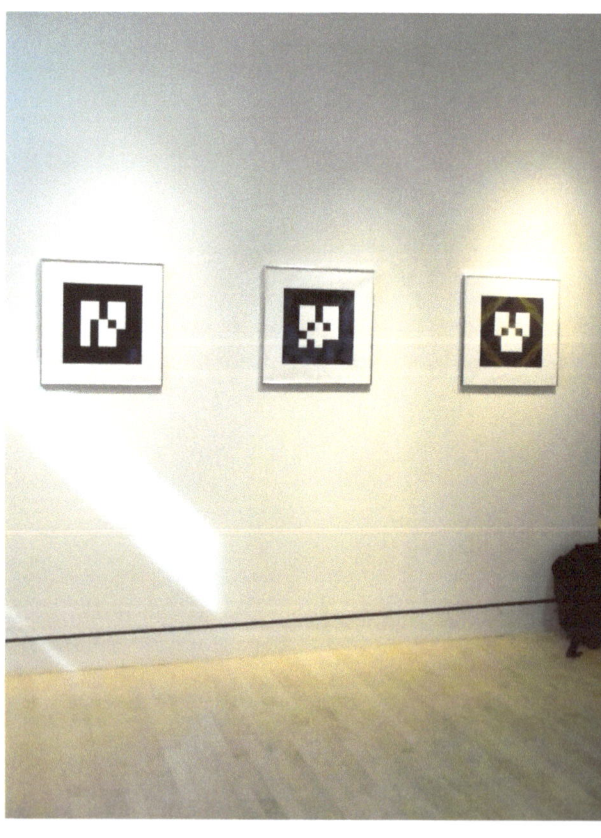

One of my major goals for my work is that everything I make should be valid across multiple disciplines, with the only difference between them being the perspective taken by the work's consumer. If a project I create is shown in a gallery or museum it can be art; if it is discussed in writing it might be concept or theory; if it is used to accomplish a task it is an application. While one perspective may be the primary one for a given work, in order to be complete my work must balance conceptual, perceptual, and technical aspects to produce a whole that is greater than the sum of its parts. ■

 ISSN 1071-4391 ISBN 978-1-906897-20-8

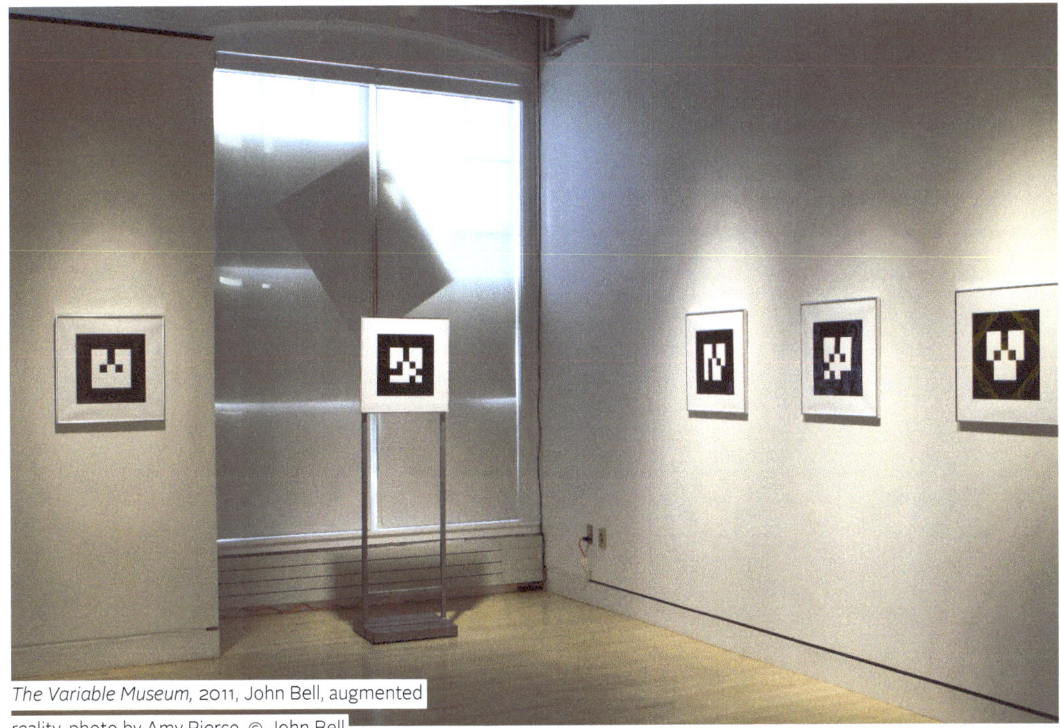

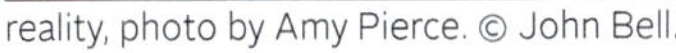

The Variable Museum, 2011, John Bell, augmented reality, photo by Amy Pierce. © John Bell.

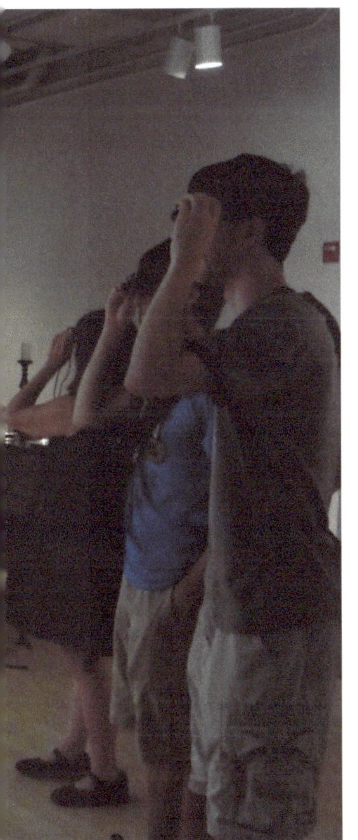

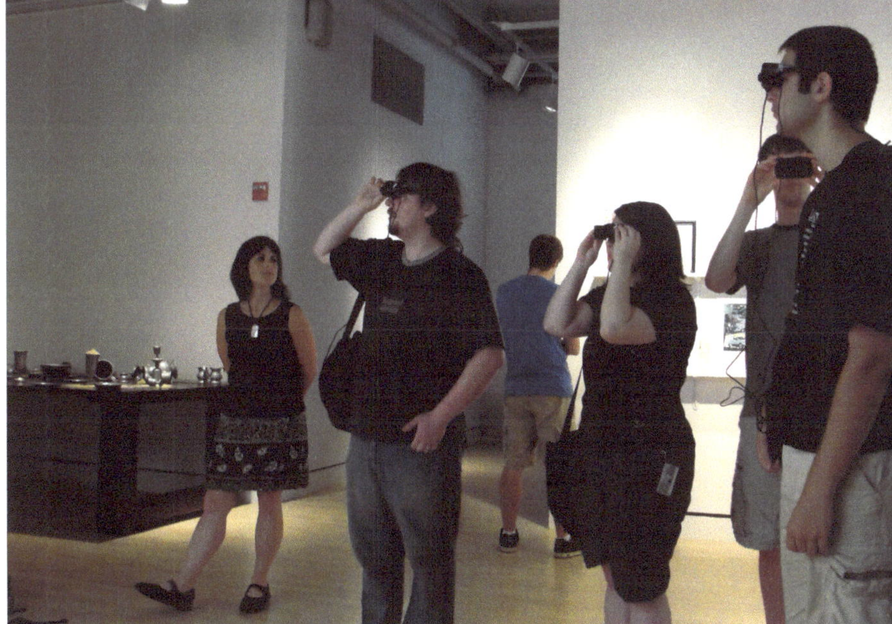

The Variable Museum, 2011, John Bell, augmented reality, photo by Jon Ippolito. © John Bell.

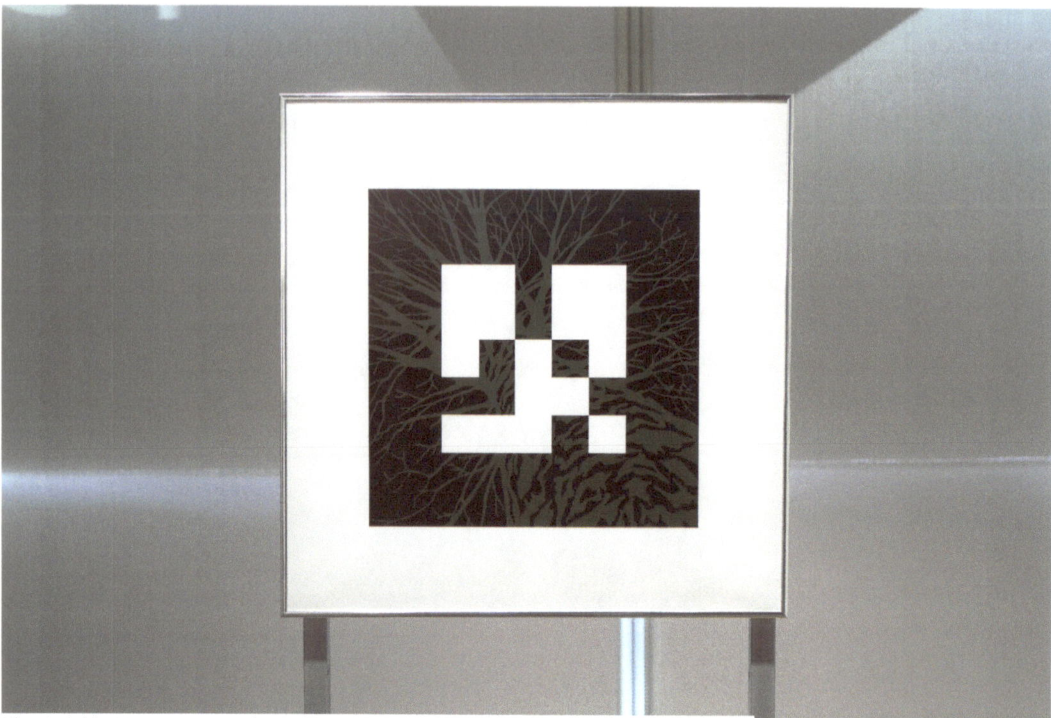

The Variable Museum, 2011, John Bell, augmented reality, photo by Amy Pierce. © John Bell.

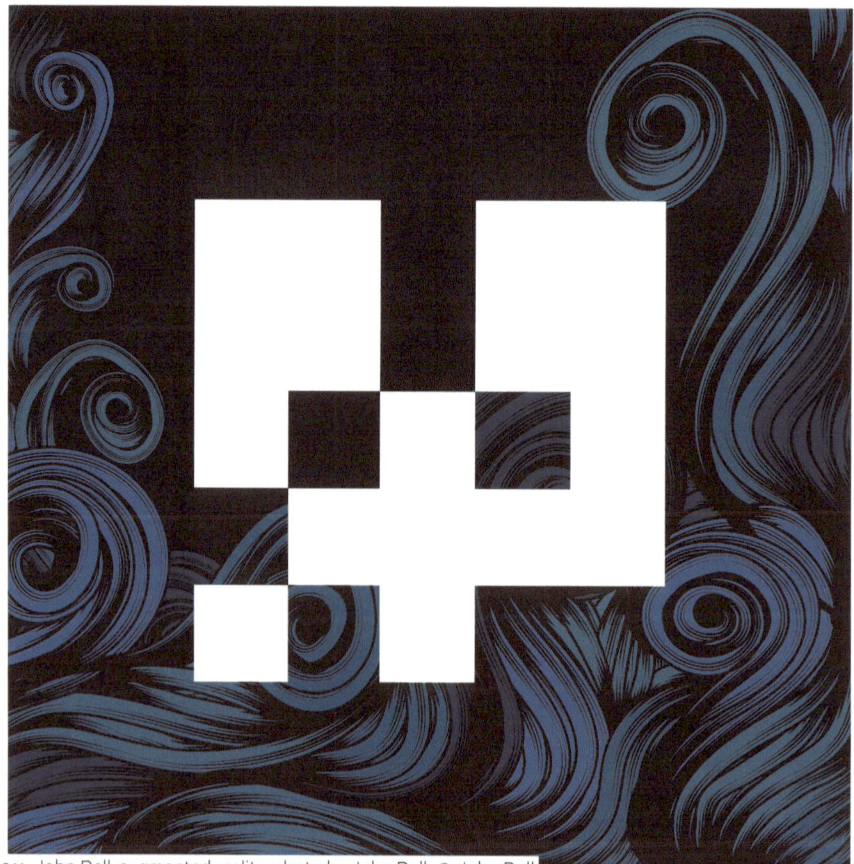

The Variable Museum, 2011, John Bell, augmented reality, photo by John Bell. © John Bell.

 ISSN 1071-4391 ISBN 978-1-906897-20-8

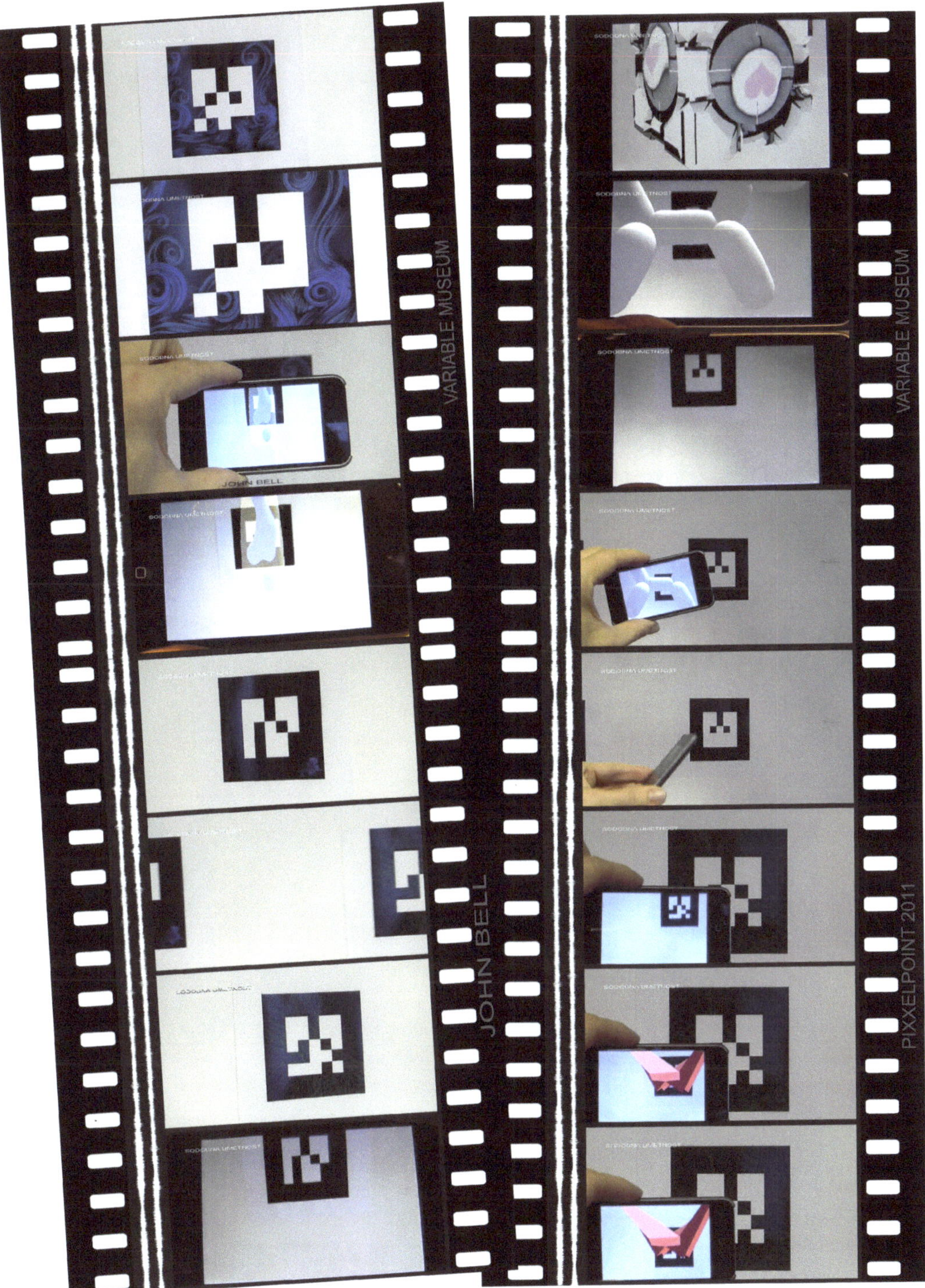

The Variable Museum, 2011, John Bell, augmented reality, image by John Bell, video frames from *PIXXELPOINT 2011* by Aljoša Abrahamsberg. © John Bell.

Translocated Boundaries

by

JACOB GARBE

Digital Arts New Media MFA Program
UC Santa Cruz
jgarbe@ucsc.edu
http://danm.ucsc.edu
http://www.jacobgarbe.com

The challenge of new media interactive artwork is becoming more and more familiar to the conversation of exhibition practice. While these works are radical in many ways, for the most part they still establish their interactivity within a statically delineated physical space: a gallery, an installation, or an area created through the formulation of specific environmental parameters. They break down the fourth wall of passive experience through interactivity, but still – for the most part – partake of traditional exhibition space, and leverage that to provide boundaries for acceptable behavior. In many cases, they are in active dialogue with that space, and are engaging, co-opting, or subverting those spaces and their accompanying expectations. However, they remain concerned with a specific physical location.

Augmented reality (AR) art, however, distinguishes itself through its particular mechanics of exhibition and performative re-contextualization. This allows the artist to translocate the borders and constraints of experience from physical to virtual, expressing the piece onto spaces in a way that is independent of physical constraint. This practice of anchoring virtual assets to the physical world allows artists to make use of mutability and replication, while engaging with issues of embodiment, performance, and presence. In this way AR pieces, such as *From Closed Rooms, Soft Whispers,* show themselves as dynamic both in content due to their performativity, and in a physical location of experience due to their mediation.

 ISSN 1071-4391 ISBN 978-1-906897-20-8

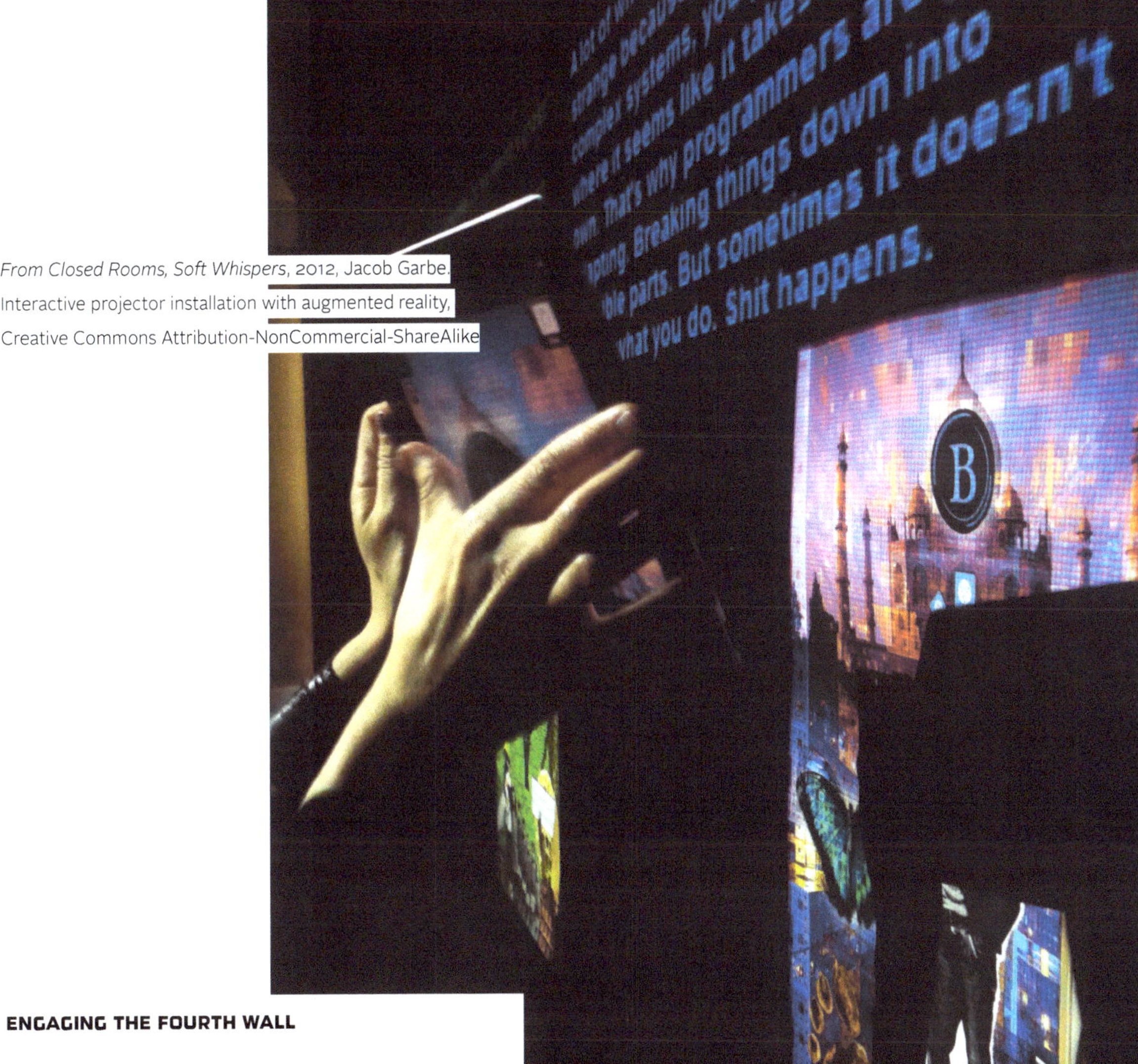

From Closed Rooms, Soft Whispers, 2012, Jacob Garbe. Interactive projector installation with augmented reality, Creative Commons Attribution-NonCommercial-ShareAlike

ENGAGING THE FOURTH WALL

Engagement of the fourth wall occurs when the observed piece changes or speaks directly to the audience. New media interactive artworks in general already violate our notion of the fourth wall insofar as the viewer's participation is an integral part of the performativity of the piece. Artworks for their part are concerned with perlocutionary acts, which is to say acts described from the vantage point of their effect on the viewer: scaring, angering, beguiling. Specifically, perlocutionary is also a useful term in describing the actions required from the viewers of the pieces of artwork – and the performances the pieces respond with – and how this process can create an emotional effect in the viewer. The perlocutionary qualities of certain new media pieces create a feedback loop of continual engagement, which is only broken when the participant has exhausted the piece's ability to perform, or the engagement offered cannot compete with their diminished attention span. Dourish explored this in his investigation of 'engaged interaction.' [4]

How is this different from experiencing a non-interactive piece of artwork? While a painting or sculpture may seem different to a viewer who steps closer or spends longer with the piece, the critical point is that the artwork asks nothing from them in terms of embodied action. All demands are perceptual, ones they can comfortably respond to, from their position behind the passive fourth wall. In this method too one can consider a non-interactive work conceptually complete when sitting in a gallery space unobserved. Interactive works, however, have a critical component missing that robs them of their expressive voice when they are sitting unengaged within an exhibition space.

AR complicates this even further by adding intermediary devices into the interpretive and experiential mix. Augmented reality artworks provide a way in which the fourth wall of passive viewing is enriched, at the most basic level, by technology which is appended to the senses of the viewer. The 'performances' or 'texts' of the piece are first mediated through a device, usually a video feed computationally modified and then displayed. This can take the form of a computer connected to a gallery's display, or in the case of locationally diffuse works, the ever more ubiquitous smart phone.

The most passive level of interaction takes place purely on the level of the machine, which provides a virtual frame for interaction, with the viewer then moving or changing the view/focus of the machine, but not interacting with the primary components. The viewing device for the user becomes a digital prosthesis which allows them to 'sense' artwork in a variety of ways invisible to others. However, they do not actively take part in the piece, such that it effects change for other viewers. They are performative observers who can be affected by the piece, and even be receptive to it in a perlocutionary way, but when physical action or participation is demanded of them they will opt instead for a passive role.

There are many works of augmented reality which take advantage of the fact that most audience members are comfortable with having their perceptions challenged, but are less likely to engage with concepts of interactivity being challenged in a performative way. One of the sub-genres of augmented artworks that take advantage of those proclivities are locative literature pieces, such as those authored by StoryTrek software.

In one such piece, entitled *Crisis 22*, viewers experience a story spatially, tied in a physical location to a street in Ottawa, Canada. Viewers use a mobile device as a prosthesis for the communication of narrative, and exhibit agency in the story through an exploratory framework. Retracing their steps reveals backstory, while heeling off into an alleyway provokes narrative digression. In this way the piece leverages augmented reality for an artistic experience that is closely tied to place yet whose borders of experience are not clearly defined to the participant. However, nothing more is being asked of the participant other than the exploration of physical space to yield narrative. They change nothing in the work for others through their interactions. They have agency only as far as their own experience and interpretation of the work goes – much like a viewer of a non-interactive work in a gallery. What makes *Crisis 22* interesting is its engaging use of space, which at once seems delineated, yet open to ambiguity.

Another good example is Camille Scherrer's *The Haunted Book*. [9] Through the experience of this piece viewers see what amounts to short movies that correspond to the different pages of the narrative. It is a beguiling piece that provokes a whimsical state of interaction with the viewer – one that is focused on the aspect of hidden content revealed through the appropriate digital prosthesis. However, we see here again that while people interact with the book by turning the pages, they are not performatively engaged as co-producers of the piece. The singularity of its experience is mirrored in the singular experience of static artwork exhibited in a gallery or museum.

 ISSN 1071-4391 ISBN 978-1-906897-20-8

A more involved level of interaction occurs when the viewer participates in some mediated way with the objects which provide "hooks" or liminal intersection points between the realms of the digital and physical. These sorts of engaged interactions call for the artist to leverage predictive dramaturgical skills in order to craft a piece in which the performance resulting from it is both rich and communicative – a sort of "performative design." [6] Artists who craft these sorts of interactive works must strike a fine balance between planning and crafting responses within the artwork to a normative set of interactions, whilst also leaving room enough that the participants feel they have space to explore and possess a sense of agency (whether that is co-opted / subverted or not) in their own experience. An example of such a work is the Blast Theory collective's *Uncle Roy All Around You,* which uses mobile devices and website interaction to stitch together an experience that feels custom-tailored to each person, dramatizing a city space. [12]

EXPERIENCE AS PERFORMANCE

Central to this performance, and intrinsic to the unbound physical locatively unique to certain forms of AR, is the concept of perceptual re-contextualization. For example, in works such as Manifest.AR's gallery interventions [2] or Phoenix Toews' sculptural app *Pyrite,* [8] the artistic interface becomes invasive in its deployment. Participants are engaging the real world through a mediated context which dramatizes spaces that are otherwise mundane. Not only breaking down the 'fourth wall' in terms of active participation, it also eliminates the boundaries in which this art is experienced. *Pyrite* allows viewers to create and find persistent sculptures anywhere, turning the most mundane of locations into opportunities for artistic display. Manifest.AR's interventions allow visitors to their website the ability to submit art and have it virtually displayed in any number of galleries worldwide. Thus the performative approach that artists foster contextually redefines not just the conventional interactive spaces, but potentially any part of the real world.

It is tempting then to see the medium as one that is breaking down or eliminating the privileged space of the gallery in favor of more pervasive and revolutionary implementation. Arguably however, when considering AR, the blurring of lines for exhibition space is not so much the removal of the wall, but the translocation of it. Explanation or revelation of the experience's border parameters is always deferred, until the performative and perlocutionary components of the piece are exhausted. Only then do viewers, if they engage for an appropriate period of time, grasp the borders of what the piece can offer.

Even then the underlying architecture, the operational logic of the piece remains implicit, not explicit, to the viewer. [10] There is a body of code, one could even argue language; that is just as valenced and proscriptive as the visual language of curation in a physical exhibition. Compiled programs can only be explored experientially, in a virtual manner. Thus, through the lens of software development, works which in terms of physical space seem limitless and inexhaustible are actually very clearly delineated. They have acceptable, supported forms of interaction (with all the affordances those entail) even if only visible to the artist. Indeed, there's much to be said about the parallels between gallery art installation – resulting from the configuration of elements in precise manners for an intended aesthetic effect – and art software installation – the arrangement of device physical states into precise configurations for an intended aesthetic functionality. What confuses the perception of AR borders is that it is a medium seeking (or in dialogue with) embodiment. It inscribes from the riot of virtual expressive possibilities a specific domain, touching the physical world. And it asks of its audience that they engage these virtual elements in an embodied way.

PRIVATE INTERACTION, COLLABORATIVE PARTICIPATION

Espen Aarseth coined the term "ergodic literature" to refer to written works that require significant effort by the reader to decode in order to experience. [1] I would argue AR too is especially ergodic in nature – requiring real work from the viewers (usually technical proficiency) that can mean some succeed and others fail in grasping its embodied rules, and thus exploring the piece to full expressivity. This challenge set before viewers gives rise to another layer of consideration when thinking about the performativity of AR pieces.

In non-interactive artworks, there is generally one level of engagement the audience participates in. The differing layers and contexts of analysis each person brings to a piece of artwork may differentiate them when they are placed in dialogue, but for the most part the experience is a uniform level of engagement, even if there are different times and styles of attention and engagement on that level. The varying valences of content can go privately unresolved while the only thing made public within the exhibition space is the piece of the artwork itself.

For viewers of participative interactive artwork, however, interaction can change the perception of the piece for other viewers. Those who come forward to impact the work through interaction become part of the display, and their ability to tease out the performative, perlocutionary subtleties of the work can open them to critique from other viewers, giving rise to performance anxiety. This segments viewers into groups based on their willingness to interact, their willingness to perform the piece. [7] Thus, there's an undeniably relational aesthetic element to these projects, especially since the mediation through a technological framing device demands – as a base requirement – perceptual performance from its audience. Holding the device just so, downloading this app, scanning that QR code, knowing to perform a specific sequence of actions, even outside a gallery setting, creates a Bourriaudian "state of encounter." [8] While at an installation there's a sense of being part of a group, but even in one's home or outside a physical gallery, when accessing AR there's an element of being privy to secret knowledge, a hidden virtual world, that creates a sense of being "in the know." There's a feeling of membership in a distinct group of people, accented by the very fact that AR viewers literally see the world differently than those unaware of the virtual content anchored around them.

How can one get out of the gallery without going completely virtual in the artwork? One of the quirks of much exhibited new media art, especially installation work, is its inherent difficulties to mechanically reproduce. However, certain forms of augmented reality can overcome this through composition of virtual assets overlaid on physical objects, which in themselves can be very straightforward, such as the collages in *From Closed Rooms, Soft Whispers*. [11] Thus, you can have an art print – easily reproduced – which acts as an anchor for a extremely complicated configuration of virtual objects, allowing freedom from the limitations of physical configuration of interactive work, yet retaining a vestige of physicality in that they can only be triggered by the art object. This opens up a further realm of inquiry for the blending of the digital and the real.

 ISSN 1071-4391 ISBN 978-1-906897-20-8

CASE STUDY

From Closed Rooms, Soft Whispers [11] premiered at the Open Studio exhibition at the UC Santa Cruz Digital Arts Research Center in 2011, and featured physical collages used as interfaces through which viewers could activate the display of narrative. The initial context was collaborative, via cell phones and iPads which changed projections of text on the gallery's wall. However, prints of the collages could also be purchased by viewers. As an art object, they function in a traditional manner, static and straightforward, but their function as a marker, a hook for AR elements hosted on the artist's web server (a digital space under constant revision) allows the modification of their virtual components. This means the story elements, the virtual visual artifacts which must be accounted for when speaking of the piece as a whole, are dynamic and subject to change.

When *Whispers* is exhibited in a gallery with an installed projector, the piece is a collage of narrative fragments displayed on the space surrounding the collages. Passive viewers of the piece may have decidedly different experiences depending on the level of interaction the piece is currently experiencing in that space. Lexias may vanish before they are read when another viewer triggers a different part of the story. However, prints displayed at home or in another area are interacted with on a solo level, allowing the viewer to experience the display of text with no one else to usurp interaction or judge them based on individual proficiency. Its ability to perform both in the gallery as a public collaboration of text and image, and privately as a less performative, deeper interactive piece, with artistic content provided from a singular source, make it multi-valent and dynamic on several levels.

Whispers can take place in locations all around the world, simultaneously in multiple settings, but the artist can change one aspect on the server and impact the experience of viewers and interactors in multiple venues. Museums, homes, offices, from the most formal of gallery space to the most informal. The text can be changed, the behaviors of its appearance and availability can be impacted, and the story and imagery presented can change over time.

Additionally, the piece's use of databased location awareness opens a host of tools to the artist in both

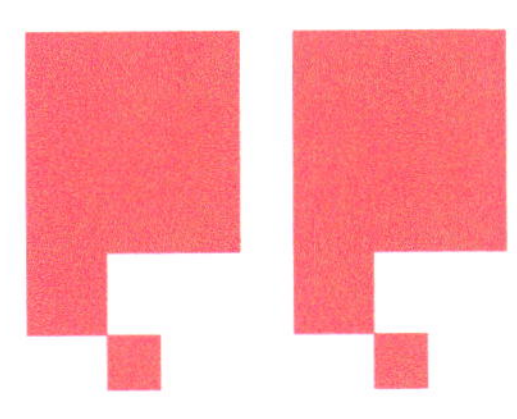

But how can one get out of the gallery without going completely virtual in the artwork?

tracking an audience, gauging the depth and breadth of interaction, and changing or modifying the virtual artwork tied to a specific instantiation of a physical object. In this way the artifact of the art print becomes more than just a static mechanical reproduction. It becomes a subscription, an open channel that can be dynamic, novel, and eminently re-configurable. The database capabilities, while raising clear issues of privacy, also mean the interaction with an artwork can become further grist for the mill in an extremely concrete fashion. Data-based works can be driven by previous interactions with other pieces, and thus the double gesture of presentation and reception, vision and re-vision, is made digitally possible.

CONCLUSION

Interactive new media works challenge traditional interpretive methods in many ways – their exceptions and special cases are as variegated as the artists and mediums used in their composition. The addition of interaction complicates audience reception and segments viewers into active participants, or passive receivers of the perlocutionary actions enacted by the piece. Augmented reality artworks, situated as pieces re-contextualizing the perceptions of the viewers through intermediary devices, further show themselves as challenges – in the perception of the viewer if not in actuality – to not only the fourth wall of audience passivity, but to the borders and accepted limits of interaction. They accomplish this by translocating those borders into the more numinous virtual world, whose affordances provide a bewildering array of compelling expressions to artists. Although in the content they partake of the digital, there is always an element of the physical to augmented reality artwork, something to tie it to the viewer and their embodied experience of the piece. In this way AR art invites a model of the world as not one in which art happens, but one which is conditionally defined and experienced as an integrative work of art. ■

REFERENCES AND NOTES

1. Espen J. Aarseth, *Cybertext: Perspectives on Ergodic Literature* (Baltimore, MD: Johns Hopkins UP, 1997).
2. Sander Veenhof and Mark Skwarek, "Augmented Reality Art Exhibition MoMA NYC (guerrilla intervention)," http://www.sndrv.nl/moma/ (accessed April 25, 2012).
3. Nicolas Bourriaud, *Relational Aesthetics* (Dijon: Leses Du Réel, 2009).
4. Paul Dourish, *Where the Action Is: The Foundations of Embodied Interaction* (Cambridge, MA: MIT Press, 2001).
5. Brian Greenspan, "The New Place of Reading: Locative Media and the Future of Narrative," in *Digital Humanities Quarterly* 5, no. 3 (2011).
6. Andrew Morrison, "Designing Performativity for Mixed Reality Installations." *FORMakademisk* 3, no. 1 (2010). Online version: November 11, 2011, https://journals.hioa.no/index.php/formakademisk/article/view/187/182 (last accessed March 19, 2013).
7. Stuart Reeves, Steve Benford, Claire O'Malley and Mike Fraser, "Designing the Spectator Experience," in *Proceedings of 2005 SIGCHI Conference on Human Factors in Computing Systems*, New York, New York, 741–750.
8. Phoenix Toews. "Augmented Mountain- Pyrite," http://www.augmentedmountain.com/pyrite/ (accessed April 25, 2012).
9. Camille Scherrer, Julien Pilet, Pascal Fua, and Vincent Lepetit, "The Haunted Book," in *Proceedings of the 7th IEEE/ACM International Symposium on Mixed and Augmented Reality* (ISMAR '08), 2008.
10. Noah Wardrip-Fruin and Michael Mateas, "Defining Operational Logics," in DiGRA 2009 – *Breaking New Ground: Innovation in Games, Play, Practice and Theory*, Brunel University, Brunel University, 2009.
11. Jacob Garbe, "From Closed Rooms, Soft Whispers," http://www.jacobgarbe.com/whispers (accessed April 25, 2012).
12. Blast Theory, "Uncle Roy All Around You," http://www.blasttheory.co.uk/bt/work_uncleroy.html (accessed April 25, 2012).

 ISSN 1071-4391 ISBN 978-1-906897-20-8

JACOB GARBE

interviewed by
Lanfranco Aceti & Richard Rinehart

Is there an 'outside' of the Art World from which to launch critiques and interventions? If so, what is the border that defines outside from inside? If it is not possible to define a border, then what constitutes an intervention and is it possible to be and act as an outsider of the art world? Or are there only different positions within the Art World and a series of positions to take that fulfill ideological parameters and promotional marketing and branding techniques to access the fine art world from an oppositional, and at times confrontational, standpoint?

Conceptually, I feel there are always subjects, methodologies, and approaches that can be considered outside a given field of practice. Drawing distinctions from which we establish an "art world" necessitates an outside to define itself against. That said, I feel the borders are fluid and conditional upon the form in question and the analytical context. For example, the art world for traditional figurative paintings encapsulates a different space than Fluxus event scores. Therefore, there's always room to intervene. I do not feel transgressing those boundaries is an act necessarily in dialogue with marketing or commercially motivated branding strategies. Also I do not characterize intervention as something oppositional, so much as playful. In my own practice, I'm concerned with expanding and perforating borders with intent towards hybridization and mutation, with the hope that it can expose new opportunities and affordances to viewers. I'm not concerned with the commercial or branding success of my pieces, or challenging some institution, abstract or concrete. What is important to me is the creation of a novel expression, something that challenges the viewer from a perceptual standpoint, and others in the art world from a conceptual standpoint.

"In *The Truth in Painting*, Derrida describes the *parergon* (*par-*, around; *ergon*, the work), the boundaries or limits of a work of art. Philosophers from Plato to Hegel, Kant, Husserl, and Heidegger debated the limits of the intrinsic and extrinsic, the inside and outside of the art object." (Anne Friedberg, *The Virtual Window: From Alberti to Microsoft* (Cambridge, MA: MIT Press, 2009), 13.) Where then is the inside and outside of the virtual artwork? Is the artist's 'hand' still inside the artistic process in the production of virtual art or has it become an irrelevant concept abandoned outside the creative process of virtual artworks?

I like to describe digital artwork as works that inhabit digital space. There's a lot that goes into the construction and curation of that space by the artist, and in programming and configuring installations (and having them break down). As a matter of fact, there's arguably quite a few similarities between installing a piece in a gallery, and installing a program on a computer. The thing to keep in mind is that the materials of virtual artwork can be fluid and dynamic--such as data streams or reactive sensors--but what is typically explicitly coded is a piece's functionality. With augmented reality artwork, one can have different assets mapped onto physical spaces or objects that seem incongruous or mash-up. So to the viewer it may appear that the parergon of the piece is highly nebulous, and the digital/virtual nature of it complicates the framing in an inscrutable way. However if you talk to the artist and the person that programmed those routines and methodologies, they will have unusually clear descriptions of what behaviors and functions are possible. The generative nature of its performance may make the end result unpredictable, but the performance of the technology itself something explicit. In my own work, I've found that the functional space is very clearly delineated. Pragmatically speaking, for non-installation AR work you are typically starting up an app on a mobile device. Expressively speaking, who knows where the limits of the correlation and mapping of that piece – interventionist or not – will be? Within that context, it may not be known or may be non-existent, but from a functional standpoint, I believe pressing the button on the device – starting that app, entering that channel, scanning that QR code – is a perceptual move to inside the frame. It is entering a curated, deliberated digital space.

Virtual interventions appear to be the contemporary inheritance of Fluxus' artistic practices. Artists like Peter Weibel, Yayoi Kusama and Valie Export subverted traditional concepts of space and media through artistic interventions. What are the sources of inspiration and who are the artistic predecessors that you draw from for the conceptual and aesthetic frameworks of contemporary augmented reality interventions?

In my work, I'm still focused mostly on creation and technical proficiency, so the main sources of my inspiration have tended towards the conceptual and the technological, rather than interventionist. Wardrip-Fruin and Carroll's piece *Screen* was one of the first VR pieces I saw that drove home the possibilities of digital interactive narrative. Visually I also find the installation work of John Campbell compelling, as well as what artists like Klaus Obermaier and Gideon Obarzaneks are currently doing with interactive projection.

My pieces all contain narrative elements, in writing those stories I've been inspired by people like Mark Amerika, John Crowley, Angela Carter and William Gibson. I still dream of some day making a Young Lady's Illustrated Primer. A piece I'm currently working on is much more embedded in the social arena, I find ARG's and social engineering projects such as those done by 42 Entertainment and No Mimes Media really compelling, although I'd be more comfortable if they didn't have commercial underwriting. I find myself doing most of my conceptual work by watching tech

 ISSN 1071-4391 ISBN 978-1-906897-20-8

demos and reading research articles from labs in academic journals, and figuring out how to de-couple the concepts from the commercial or research domain and appropriate them as an artistic medium.

In the representation and presentation of your artworks as being 'outside of' and 'extrinsic to' contemporary aesthetics why is it important that your projects are identified as art?

In working with augmented reality and other cutting-edge technologies, there's the risk of pieces always being perceived as not much more than glorified tech demos – something gimmicky that is not making a genuine statement, aesthetic or otherwise. For many viewers, it is their first experience with the medium (be that AR, projection mapping, body-responsive pieces, etc). That usually means an initial moment of acclimatization, an interaction learning curve. The revelation of a novel expressive space is where some people sign off. They feel that in understanding the instantiation of the medium, they've grasped the full content of the piece. So what I find myself struggling to achieve is not only getting people to engage my pieces on a "material" or medium level, but also giving honest time to explore what the piece is trying to say. Coming from my background as a writer, there's a narrativity to all my work, that takes time to express. It is important to me that my pieces are cast in an artistic context so that--operating within that space--viewers are more likely to take that time, and dig deeper than surface issues of technology.

Also, if it is identified as art, then people are more likely to look for the aesthetic reasoning that went into its production. As an artist, I ask myself constantly "why are you using this particular technology for this piece?" I feel there has to be a justification for my choice of medium, especially given new media's breadth of materials and techniques. Having my pieces identified as art makes it more likely viewers will continue the conversation to that aesthetic level, and that is where I want the deeper engagement to occur.

What has most surprised you about your recent artworks? What has occurred in your work that was outside of your intent, yet has since become an intrinsic part of the work?

Originally I thought my art practice would center around purely digital constructions, and the exhibition and installation of them would be incidental to pieces as a whole. I saw myself more as a net artist. However, once I started working with spaces and seeing how one could overlay digital assets onto physical surfaces, I was really beguiled. Additionally, modifying a space so that physical actions of viewers are required to explore the expression of an artwork sets up some truly intriguing affordances. I've found that when viewers are asked to physically participate, even when it is something as simple as moving viewing devices over the surface of the work, you get unexpected, emergent behavior. I think it is exciting when people collaborate on interaction, and I love watching them share their approaches to interaction with others. That is a great energy.

I do not want to get heavy into the installation because I like the ubiquity of the net, and do not like the idea of something I've worked on only being experienced for a specific time in a specific place, I attempt to achieve both. I would certainly say that installation is now an intrinsic consideration in my conceptual process. There are just too many good opportunities to explore to pass that up. What I'm hoping to straddle with pieces like *From Closed Rooms, Soft Whispers* is the presentation or extrusion of virtual pieces into an exhibition space, so I can tap into that collaborative interaction energy, but preserve the piece's activity through the expressive capabilities of AR-enabled prints outside the gallery. ■

JACOB GARBE

statement & artwork

From Closed Rooms, Soft Whispers is an interactive narrative concerning loss and the passage of time, utilizing augmented reality as its medium.

It humanizes a high-technology concept through interaction with real world objects, blurring the border between the physical media and the digital media overlaid upon it. It focuses on how memories and feelings are triggered and re-experienced through objects all around us, providing a symbolic afterlife for the people and events they evoke long after the passage of time has removed them from our lives. You can find out more at jacobgarbe.com/whispers ■

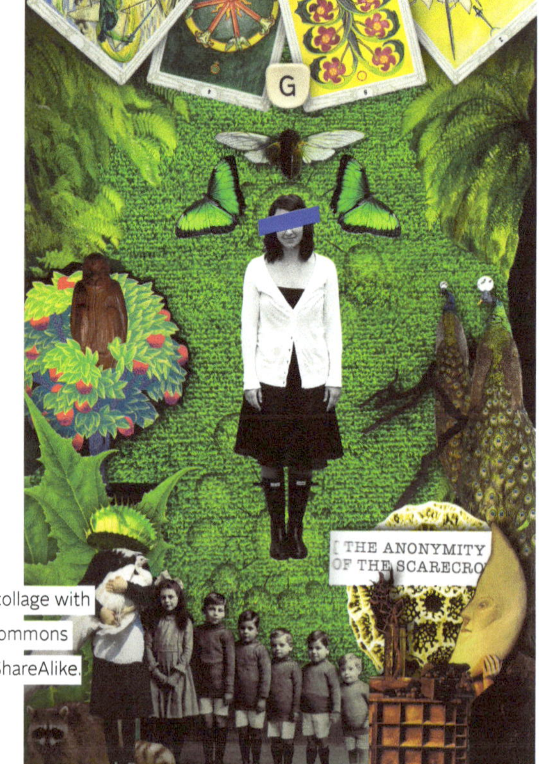

G, 2012, Jacob Garbe, digital collage with augmented reality.

 ISSN 1071-4391 ISBN 978-1-906897-20-8

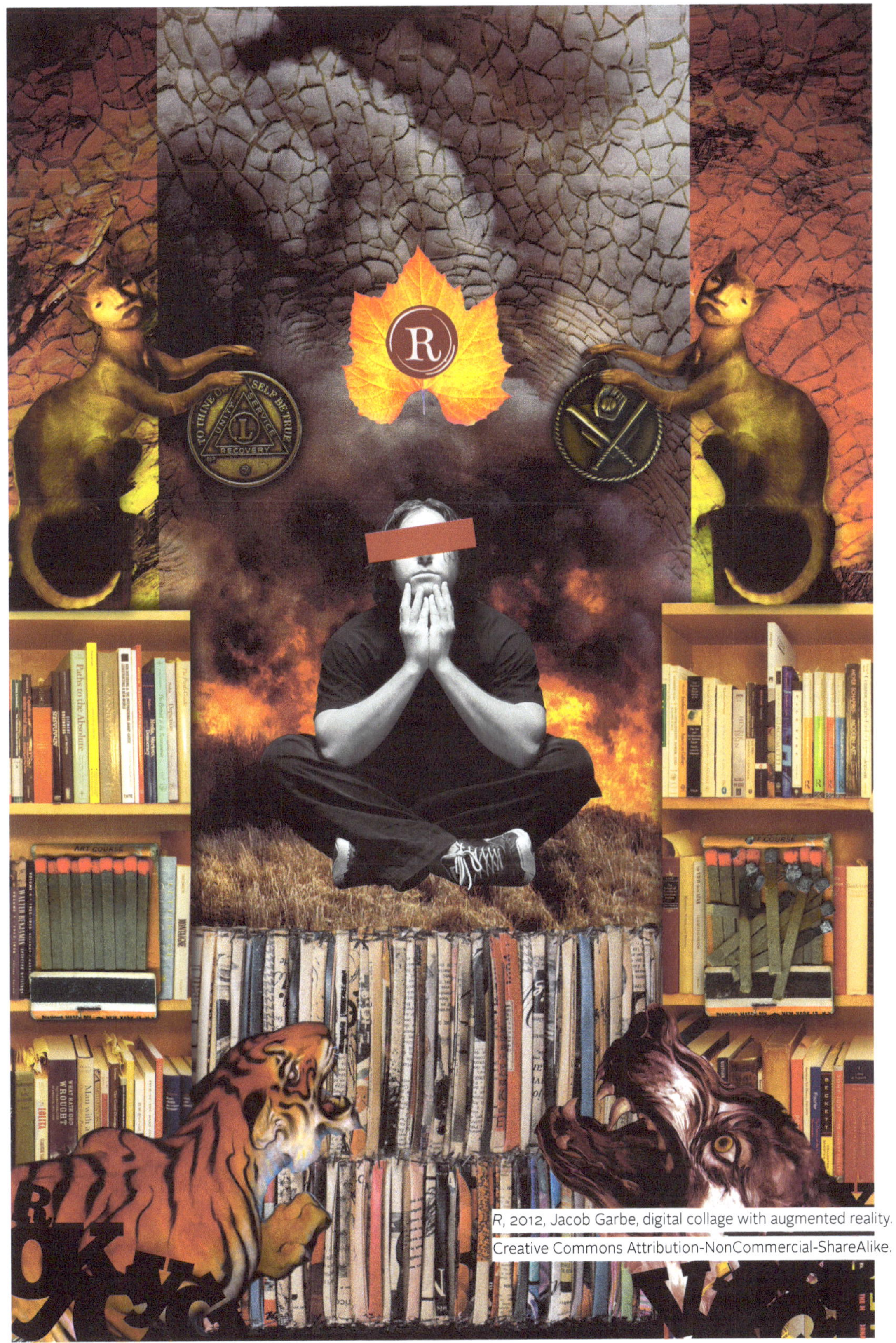

R, 2012, Jacob Garbe, digital collage with augmented reality.

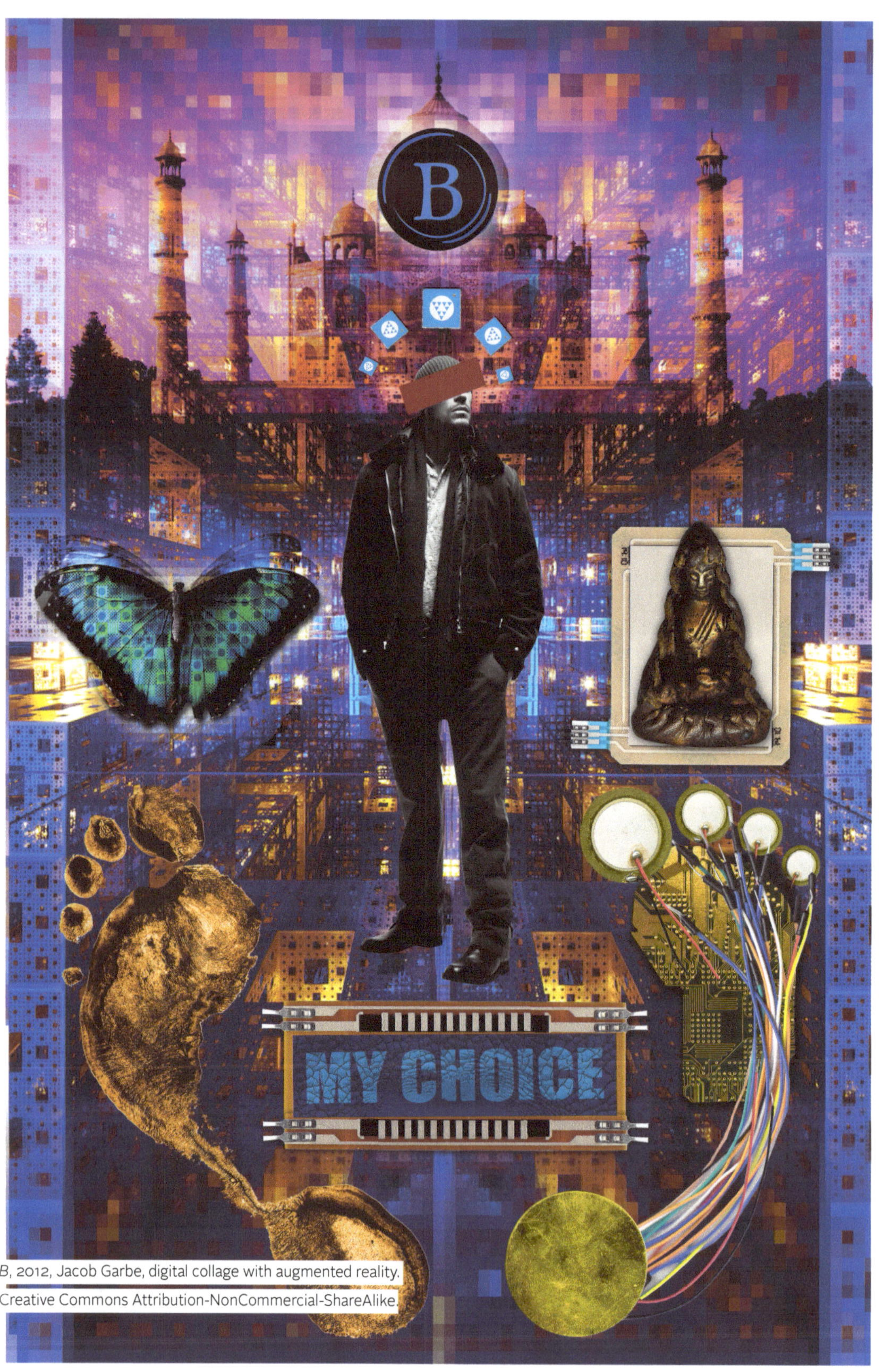

B, 2012, Jacob Garbe, digital collage with augmented reality.

 ISSN 1071-4391 ISBN 978-1-906897-20-8

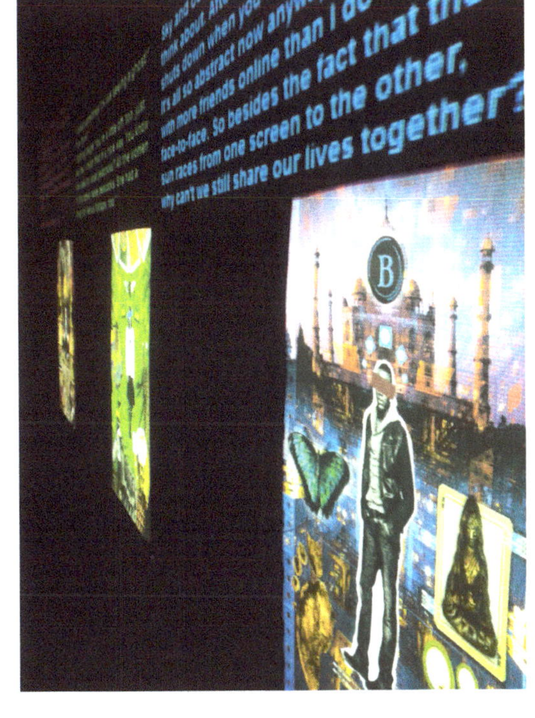

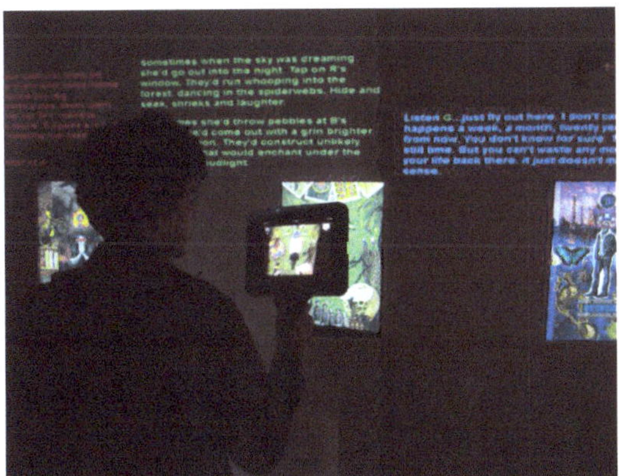

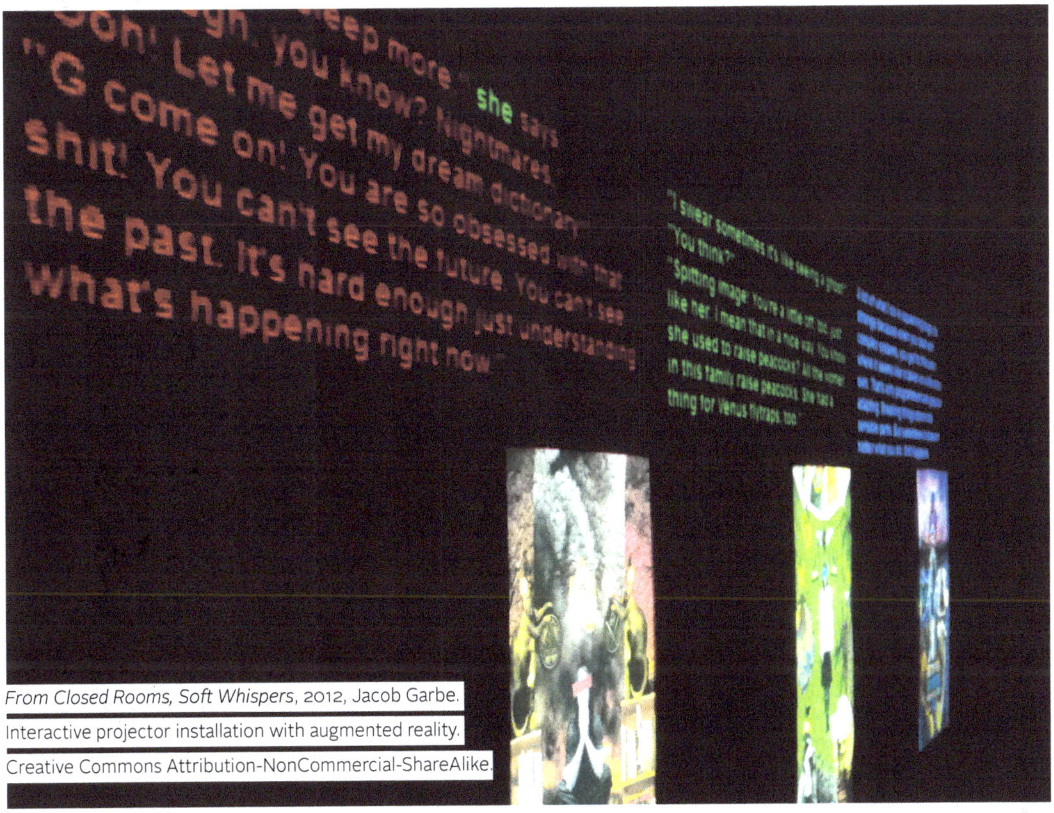

From Closed Rooms, Soft Whispers, 2012, Jacob Garbe.
Interactive projector installation with augmented reality.

In Between: Experiencing Liminality

The present paper is a study of rituality in art and daily life; *its main subject is the detailed analysis of the rites of passage which de-contextualise the individual when s/he enters in contact with traditional architectural spaces. Therefore, the paper proposes a close reading of the discontinuities of the spaces experienced by the individual, realised by means of art and Augmented Reality (AR). The authors intend (by means of relating the creative act to digital technology) to put the spectator in a position of awareness of the physical and psychological discontinuity of a ritual space, which situates the viewer not here, not there in a stage of* liminality.

by

DRAGOŞ GHEORGHIU & LIVIA ŞTEFAN

Dragoş Gheorghiu
National University of Arts – Bucharest
gheorghiu_dragos@yahoo.com

Livia Ştefan
ITC Institute – Bucharest
livia.stefan@itc.ro

INTRODUCTION

The two authors of this article are a visual artist / cultural anthropologist and an IT expert who collaborated on the transfer of artistic and anthropologic works in the contemporary digital space. The joint effort resulted in the development of a mobile application, which allows the observer to perform an urban exploration, both aesthetically and anthropologically.

We intend (by relating the creative act to digital technology) to position the observer in a liminal position which situates him/her not here, not there, yet aware of the physical and psychological discontinuities of the

 ISSN 1071-4391 ISBN 978-1-906897-20-8

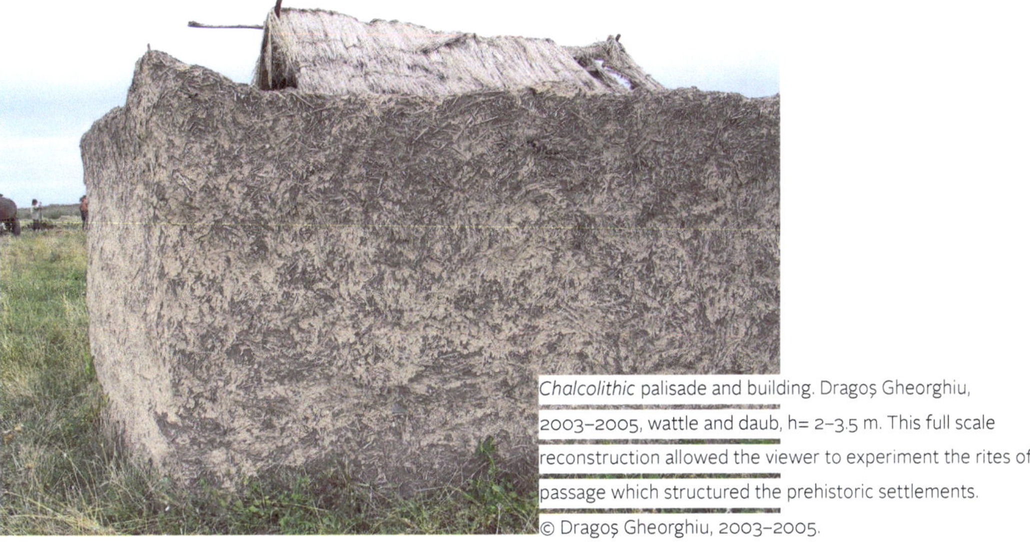

Chalcolithic palisade and building. Dragoş Gheorghiu, 2003–2005, wattle and daub, h= 2–3.5 m. This full scale reconstruction allowed the viewer to experiment the rites of passage which structured the prehistoric settlements. © Dragoş Gheorghiu, 2003–2005.

space. Such a transition from the role of spectator to that of actor (even if only at the level of mental experience) is the result of the immersion into a real-virtual collage.

Thus, one can visualise the immateriality of past and present *liminal* zones which de-contextualise the viewer, and experience the *in-between state* transmitted by the productions of the past, with the help of contemporary art.

ABOUT ART AND RITUALS (GHEORGHIU)

Although the rites of passage (with their tripartite structure: separation, liminality and reintegration) [1] [2] play an important role in humans' lives, [3] they seem to have been overlooked by contemporary art. One cannot ignore the significance of everyday rituality in traditional societies, with emphasis on corporeality and structured actions. [4]

Positioned between art and science (for this liminal state see Calzadilla and Marcus 2006), [5] and practicing art-chaeology (i.e. the use of metaphors to stimulate the archaeological imagination), [6] I was preoccupied by this phenomenological aspect of the human body in space, both from the artistic and anthropological points of view.

As an experimentalist, I am aware that no space is homogenous, and I have attempted through my theoretical and artistic work to put this idea into evidence. Among the three stages forming a rite of passage, the liminal stage is the most interesting because of its special, symbolic character, being situated between the phase of dis-membering and re-membering. [7] A liminal phase makes one aware of the space where you come from, and of the space you are entering. In a liminal space, there is no here, no there; but an in-between. [8] This is the reason why a liminal phase may appear to threaten. In some of my artworks such as the reconstructions of the palisades of the prehistoric Danube settlements, [9] [10] or of the prehistoric strongholds in the mountains of Portugal [11] (https://www.youtube.com/watch?v=Eyq8FZUyB8E&feature=relmfu), I imagined these liminal phases as spaces of tense expectations.

In my analysis liminal spaces can be perceived not only in the real world, by means of the materialization of metaphors with the help of art installations and land art works, but also as a hybrid space, liminally positioned between real and virtual. [12]

After having used digital technologies to record artworks and scientific experiments I started to exploit their poetic [13] [14] and modelling [15] potential, and added a new dimension to my works, with digital mapping [16] (http://www.panoramio.com/photo/45692516).

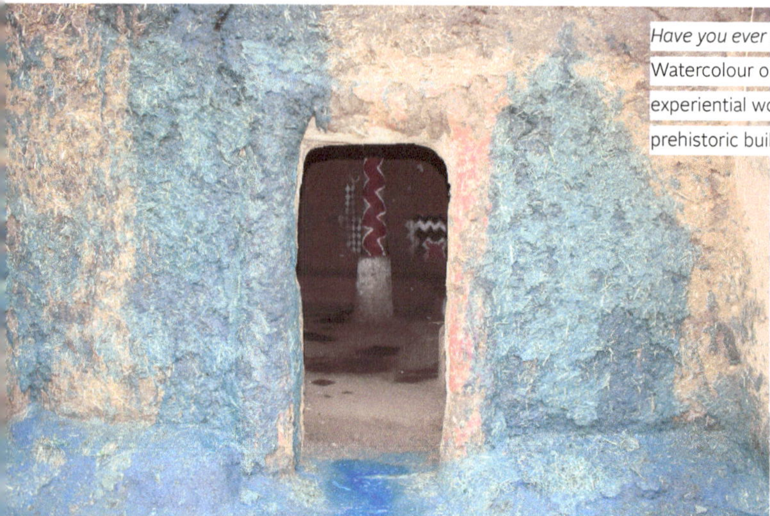

Have you ever seen the Rain?, 2007, Dragoş Gheorghiu. Watercolour on wattle and daub facade, h= 3 m. An experiential work to perceive the rite of passage in a prehistoric building. © Dragoş Gheorghiu, 2007.

The entrance of Manuc Inn, Bucharest. Early 19th century. One of the rarest examples left of vernacular architecture specific for the South Eastern Europe. © Dragoş Gheorghiu.

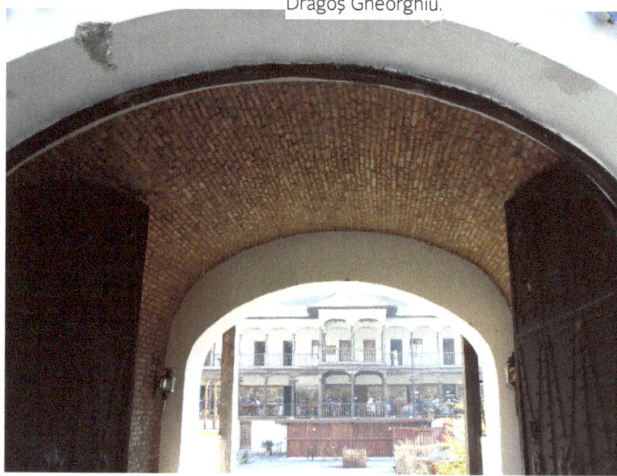

By overlapping metaphors on real contexts with AR technology, one can create a state of liminality, the spectator's psyche situating itself for a brief moment between the real and the virtual, before proceeding to their synthesis, and immersing into the hybrid space thus created.

Through the study of the protective strategies of prehistoric settlements which implied the existence of a series of rites of passage, [17] as well as of the vernacular architecture, [18] [19] I approached the traditional rituality and symbolism materialised under the form of solid metaphors. [20] Through the experience of the process of construction of the traditional buildings I approached the rituality of the human body [21] in relationship with the materiality of architecture.

An important aspect of my current research is the experience of materials, [22] and the extent to which the material itself can transmit information. [23]
In this perspective the present paper tries to approach the following topic: the presentation of architectural space as a discontinuous state, with liminal zones, whose experience of their own materiality creates a special state of mind.

Because architecture is structured on a dual principle, with an interior and exterior space, [24] [25] thus implying the existence of a rite of passage, the experience of a liminal space can be embodied, like any other body experience. [26]

For the last decade I have worked towards laying the foundations of an archaeology of the ancient architecture's ritual spaces, which collected and studied the phenomenological and artistic features of the ancient spaces. [27] [28]

With the help of Livia Ştefan's IT expertise, within a research grant aimed at the preservation of immaterial heritage, [29] I started using Augmented Reality (AR), to highlight the rituality of architectural spaces, the present paper being a continuation of this research.

The smartphone application we propose is designed to approach a rite of passage with the help of a hybrid space, combining real and virtual elements. This augmented space, which is generated by visual metaphors intended to evoke into the spectator's mind the liminal phase of the rite of passage, is geo-coded, and

 ISSN 1071-4391 ISBN 978-1-906897-20-8

geographically determines the human experience. As metaphors I designed images to evoke one of the antique principles in architecture (i.e. *soliditas* or resistance), which could be experienced when passing through the portico of an ancient building. This augmentation is realised with freehand drawings and 3D reconstructions of scaffolding, which make visible the immense pressure of the ceiling and the thick walls. The investigation site selected was Bucharest's old city centre, one of the most fascinating parts of the capital. To emphasize the ritual entrances, and the materiality of the liminal stages of this site, the most suitable example is Manuc's Inn, a splendid example of the local architecture dating from the beginning of the 19th century. [30]

The visitor approaching the arched entrance of the building will be visually notified of the existence of a rite of passage by a coloured threshold, and when stepping in beneath the entrance's vault, namely when stepping into the liminal zone, s/he will be faced with the metaphorical images of the invisible forces of the building, and thus become aware of the liminal space.

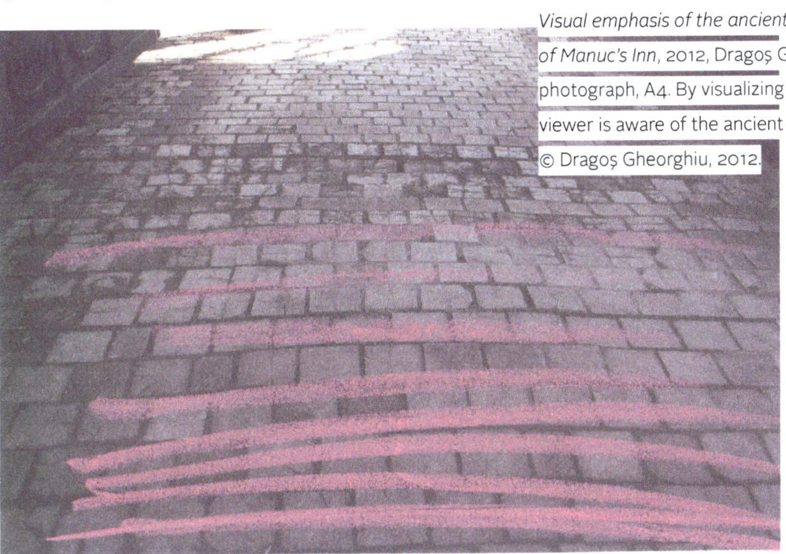

Visual emphasis of the ancient threshold of the entrance of Manuc's Inn, 2012, Dragoş Gheorghiu. Coloured chalk on photograph, A4. By visualizing the now invisible threshold the viewer is aware of the ancient liminal space of the passage. © Dragoş Gheorghiu, 2012.

Line drawing evoking the forces of pressing in Manuc's Inn entrance's vault, 2012, Dragoş Gheorghiu. Coloured chalk on photograph, A4. The aim of this image is to warn the viewer about the invisible forces existing within the vault and walls of the liminal space of the passage inside the old building. The drawing suggests simultaneously a scaffold to support the vault, and the fracture of a structure supporting it. © Dragoş Gheorghiu, 2012.

MOBILE AUGMENTED REALITY (STEFAN)

In order to illustrate the artistic concept elaborated in this paper, the authors have chosen to use the technology of Augmented Reality on mobile devices (called mobile AR or MAR), which implements AR on smart phones and Tablet PCs. We created a content layer called LIMIN-AR which targets Manuc's Inn and can be visualized on the video live stream by means of a commercially available mobile application for Android devices, called Layar AR browser. This "AR browser" [31] allows users either to automatically see an augmentation of the targeted reality, or to browse through available augmentations, presented as POIS (Points of Interest) in a surrounding area. An activated mobile Internet connection (3G or Wi-Fi) is required.

Even if not a recent technology, it is only in the last few years that the concepts and the uses of Augmented Reality have been oriented towards ordinary users, by means of every-day purpose applications. At its beginnings, AR was mainly used in academic laboratories and research projects, [32] and needed highly specialized equipment, such as HMDs (Head Mounted Devices). [33] [34] Currently the availability and the expected user-centered success of the technology, mainly by means of educational and cultural applications, [35] are made possible by the rapid advancements in the mobile device industry which have led to "smart" and "wearable" devices. [36] To cite just a few of these facilitation factors: the miniaturization techniques which allowed several sensors (such as compass, accelerometer and GPS) to be integrated in one piece of equipment; the increase in mobile processing power; the improvements made in the mobile display size and quality; and last but not least, the improved financial affordability.

The hardware elements which make the smartphone, or a Tablet PC, an ideal AR platform are: [37] the GPS (Global Positioning System) receiver, the WiFi/3G, the cell tower radio receiver/A-GPS, the video camera, the solid-state compass and the accelerometer. The reality is perceived by means of a video live stream, on which digital content is overlaid. [38] Predefined conditions trigger the augmentations.

The mobile AR (MAR) supplements the AR technology by allowing users to be mobile and to discover places and information. [39] MAR facilitates the provision of contextual [40] or "situated" information based on a combination of geographic position and user behavior. The "behavior" is expressed in device movements on the 6 degrees of freedom (6 DOF), translated by the accelerometer sensor, and in direction changes, translated by the compass sensor.

The AR applications fall under 2 main categories: [41] geographic/sensory AR and computer-vision AR. The latter can be either marker-based / marker-based / image tracking, which uses "helper" or fiducial images for augmentation triggering, or marker-less / image recognition and tracking, which uses advanced natural feature recognition.

The marker-based AR would not be appropriate for our paper (having the target buildings environmentally distributed), as we wish to leave users to discover them based on "indices" offered by the AR application by means of POIS (Points of Interest) [42] and not by making any changes. On the other hand, the triggering only based on geographic localization it is not possible, due to the imprecision of the GPS satellites. The localization accuracy has to be improved with additional information from the other device sensors and/or with different techniques such as computer vision algorithms.

Although a "state-of-the art" technology, Augmented Reality has not yet reached a mature developmental stage, [43] as has its counterpart, the Virtual Reality technology, because AR algorithms need to be further

 ISSN 1071-4391 ISBN 978-1-906897-20-8

Description of the LIMIN-AR *Layar layer, publisher Dragoş Gheorghiu*. Download the LAYAR AR Browser from the play store (if not already installed); Activate an Internet connection; Launch the LAYAR AR Browser; Select Layers/Categories: Architecture and Buildings: LIMIN-AR-Dragos Gheorghiu Or copy the link http:/layar.it.lxrea3 in the address bar of a mobile Internet browser and select "open with Layar." © Dragoş Gheorghiu.

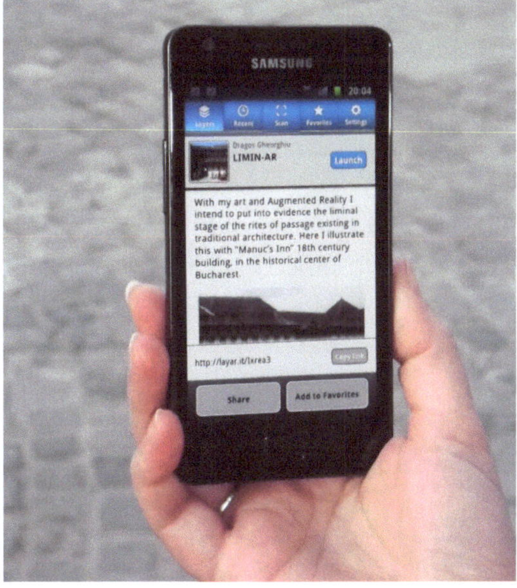

improved, significant applications are yet to be developed, and user content created. The potential of AR for knowledge development and mediated perception is proven, due to its capacity to naturally add and interact with digital content, in various formats (simple text, images, audio, video, 3D graphics), thus creating a new kind of sensory immersion. [44]

The difficulties faced by an AR developer arise from the fact that there are no standards. [45] There are several development tools and environments, which offer proprietary AR algorithms, each offering different technical advantages.

Of course, as expected, the authors of the paper encountered some of these difficulties in selecting the appropriate development tools, but ultimately decided that AR, as an IT technology, would serve the artistic and cultural ideas of the paper. The reasons behind the decision lie in the very specific characteristics of AR, which integrates / juxtaposes the real and the virtual, in real time, in a 3D space and in an interactive manner. [46] The highest objective of an AR application, besides the obvious one of enriching reality with additional information, is to dissolve the line between the real and the virtual, and that was what the artist (Gheorghiu) needed in order to express his idea of liminality.

THE APPLICATION DESIGN

The AR application was designed to use both mobile device's sensors and image recognition.

An additional requirement was that the application be accessible from Android smart phones and Tablet PC, which are not equipped with GPS receivers but can be a better AR application platform due to their larger screen and rapid processing.

Finally, we selected the *Layar platform*, [47] a major commercially available AR platform from a Dutch software company. The reasons for this choice were: the functional flexibility which allows the development of both geographic AR applications and image recognition application (by means of Layar-Vision component); good product documentation; the fact that it is open to third-party partners for content storage (publicly available), and thus allows the automatic updating of content; and the compatibility with iOS, Android and Bada based smart phones. [48] The front-end application i.e. the mobile application, the Layar AR *browser*, is pre-installed on most Android/iOS smart phones.

As the content storage and delivering platform we chose the *Hoppala Augmentation* platform, [49] developed by a German IT specialist, due to it being recognized as a stable platform and its free of charge services. It also has the advantage of being able to deliver content to all 3 major AR platforms.

Our AR application is based on an "AR layer" in the concept of the Layar platforms, [50] [51] or a channel with the cultural target, the augmented content evoking the idea of liminality. This layer was segmented in

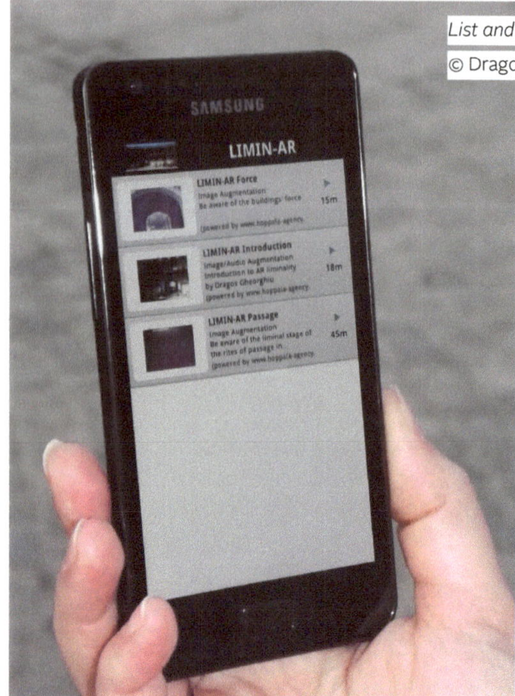

List and description of the 3 LIMIN-AR's augmentations, provided as POIS. © Dragoş Gheorghiu.

3 POIS, corresponding to the different passage stages: one *close to the target*, one evoking the *idea of ritual passage*, and one evoking the *idea of force*. Each POI is defined by geographic coordinates, a Google Maps address and the augmentation content, represented by processed art images.

The development of the AR application has undergone the following stages:

1. Identification of the interest areas; photo shoots using geo-tagging facility; the photos were taken in front and from 15–20 degree angles;
2. Verification and correction of the raw geographic positions for POIS using Google Maps;
3. Image processing in order to illustrate the idea of liminality;
4. Creation and definition of the LIMIN-AR layer on the Layar platform, activating the Layar-Vision feature;
5. Selection, processing and loading on the Layar platform of the reference images for target building recognition;
6. Definition and load on the Hoppala Augmentation Platform of the POIS, which contains our augmentations; association of each POI with the reference images and a set of Layar "actions" which can be audio, video, access of a web site, SMS or email;
7. Save on the Layar platform of the web address to Hoppala Platform, which is a connection between the two;
8. Application tests using the Layar AR browser, verification of the visualization of the POIS and of the augmentations;
9. Several functional adjustments in the LIMIN-AR layer and in the position of the augmentations in order to correspond to the user view field as interpreted by the Layar browser.

On the Android platform a possible application flow can be as follows:

1. The user launches the Layar browser from the Android applications (pre-installed or downloaded from the Play Store).
2. The camera is activated.
3. The user selects and launches the LIMIN-AR layer from a list of Layar layers.
4. The user can adjust the search area for the POIS.
5. Upon entering the geographic area, the LIMIN-AR POIS are overlaid on the camera view.
6. The user selects a POI and a predefined action associated with each POI (e.g. to hear an audio record; to write a tweet).
7. When the user position coincides with the POI's position or the referenced image is recognized i.e. the user is in front of the building or within an angle of +/- 15 degrees, the image augmentation, evoking the idea of liminality, is triggered. [Photo 8 and Photo 9 near here]

CONCLUSIONS

The project we propose is a hybrid of real spaces and art interventions with the purpose of recovering the rituality and sensoriality of the past. By accessing the IT application one can experience an immersion [52] into the materiality and rituality of ancient architec-

 ISSN 1071-4391 ISBN 978-1-906897-20-8

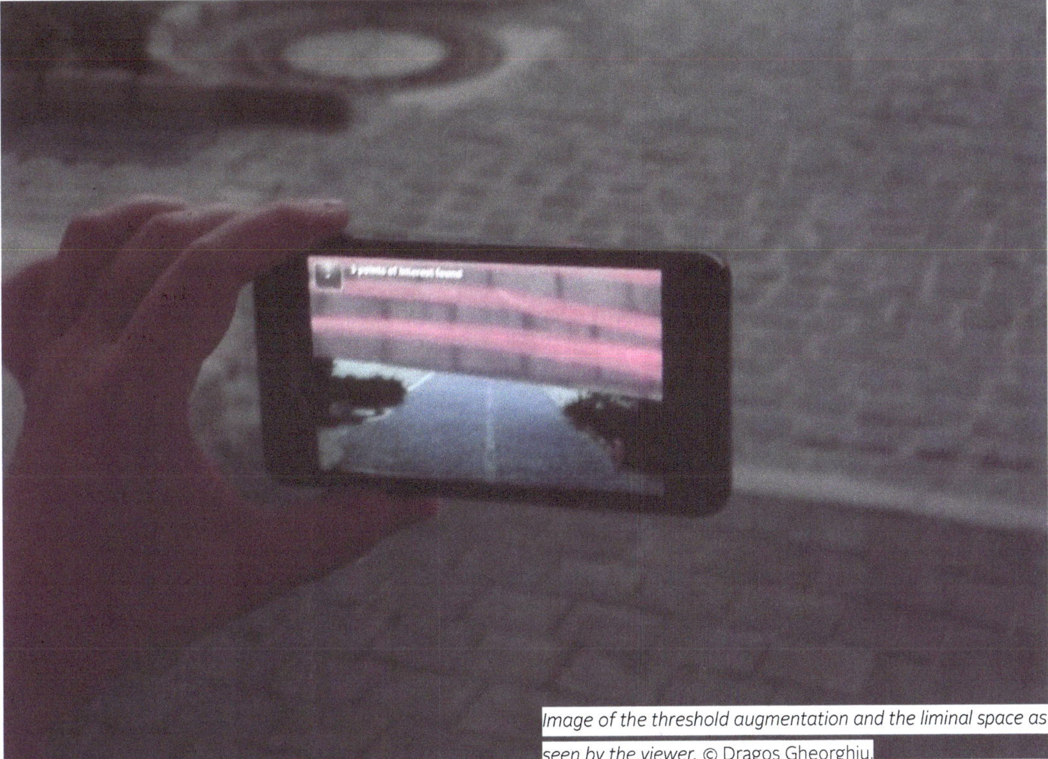

Image of the threshold augmentation and the liminal space as seen by the viewer. © Dragoş Gheorghiu.

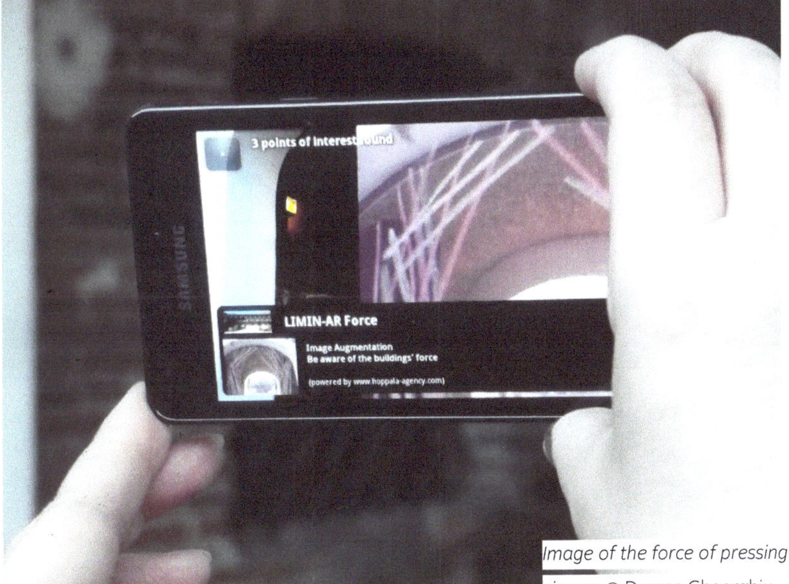

Image of the force of pressing augmentation as seen by the viewer. © Dragoş Gheorghiu.

ture, and develop a virtual archaeological approach based on experientiality. A result of this process could be the re-ritualization of the human body and the re-materialisation of space and of buildings.

The use of mobile phones makes the simultaneous access to art and archaeology available to a broad public, thus the project achieving a sort of in situ exhibition. At the same time, the m-Learning [53] [54] potential of the AR application will function as an educational element by displaying the immaterial heritage we identified to the public. ■

GLOSSARY

AUGMENTED REALITY: a set of advanced IT technologies by means of which the perception of the surrounding reality is augmented with digital objects (images, video, sound files, 3D models), overlaid on a specialized display, or on the camera view. The augmentation is triggered based on real time tracking and recognition of specific markers, or natural features, or landmarks.

AR BROWSER: a type of Augmented Reality application similar to a web application, designed for mobile devices, through which the user can be shown, on a camera stream, different augmentations, and can also browse through a set of information associated with the objects, usually displayed as POIs. The AR browser also serves as a user interface.

COMPUTER VISION: a general term describing image recognition; advanced computer techniques and mathematical algorithms by which a software program can recognize real and complex images and perform automated actions.

IMMERSION: a simulated user presence in a complete virtual reality or in an augmented/mixed reality.

LIMINALITY: a special, symbolic, stage of a rite of passage, representing the moment between the rite of separation and the rite of incorporation.

M-LEARNING: also mobile learning: e-learning using mobile devices like smartphone and Tablet PC.

POI (POINT OF INTEREST): geographical locations associated with meaningful information which can be presented to a user based on his/her position and within a pre-defined search area (e.g. in a search circle of 50m). This information is offered by certain service providers and is a kind of augmentation used in AR browsers.

RITE OF PASSAGE: ritual, which marks the stages of human life, or a physical passage, and is related to time and space.

REFERENCES AND NOTES

1. Victor Turner, *The ritual process. Structure and anti-structure* (New York, NY: Aldine, 1969).
2. Victor Turner, "Frame. Flow and Reflection: Ritual and drama as public liminality," in *Performance in Postmodern culture,* eds. Michel Benamo and Charles Caramello, 33–55 (Madison, WI: Coda Press, 1977).
3. Susan Merill Squier, *Liminal lives – Imagining the human at the frontiers of medicine* (Durham and London: Duke University Press, 2004).
4. Ronald, L. Grimes, "Ritual theory and the environment," in *Nature performed: Environment, culture and performance, eds.* Bronislaw Szerszynski, Wallace Heim, and Claire Waterton, 32–45 (Oxford: Blackwell, 2003).
5. Fernando Calzadilla and George E. Marcus, "Artists in the field: between art and anthropology," in *Contemporary art and anthropology, eds.* Arnd Schneider and Christopher Wright, 95–116 (Oxford and New York: Berg, 2006).
6. Dragoş Gheorghiu, *Artchaeology. A sensorial approach to the materiality of the past* (Bucharest: UNArte, 2009).
7. Turner, *The ritual process.*
8. Jens Hauser, "Who's afraid of the in-Between?," in *Sk-Interfaces. Exploring borders – creating membranes in art, technologies and science*, ed. Jens Hauser, 6–16 (Fact & Liverpool University Press, 2008).
9. Gheorghiu, *Artchaeology.*
10. Dragoş Gheorghiu, "Experimenting with prehistoric spaces (Performance, experience, evocation)," in *The Archaeology of People and Territoriality,* eds. G. Nash and D. Gheorghiu, 343 – 371 (Budapest: Archaeolingua, 2009).
11. Dragoş Gheorghiu, "eARTh Vision (Art-chaeology and digital mapping)," *World Art* 2, no. 2 (2012): 211–217.
12. Steve Benford and Gabriella Giannachi, *Performing mixed reality* (Cambridge, MA: The MIT Press, 2011), 27.
13. Lev Manovich, The Poetics of Augmented Space, in *Visual Communication* 5, no. 2 (2006): 219–240.
14. Hao-Chiang Koong Lin, Min-Chai Hsieh, Eric Zhi-Feng Liu and Tsung-Yen Chuang, "Interacting with Visual Poems Through Ar-Based Digital Artwork," in *The Turkish Online Journal of Educational Technology* 11, no. 1 (January 2012): 123–137.
15. Valery Adzhiev, Peter Comninos and Alexander Pasko, "Augmented Sculpture: Computer Ghosts of Physical Artifacts," in *Leonardo* 36, no. 3 (2002): 211–219.
16. Gheorghiu, "eARTh Vision," 211–217.
17. Dragoş Gheorghiu, "Cultural landscapes in the lower Danube area. Experimenting tell settlements," in *Documenta Praehistorica* XXXV (2008): 167- 178.

 ISSN 1071-4391 ISBN 978-1-906897-20-8

18. Dragoş Gheorghiu, "The archaeology of space: ritual and metaphor," in *Archaeology and Buildings*, papers from a session held at the European Association of Archaeologists Fifth Annual Meeting in Bournemouth 1999, ed. Gunilla Malm (Oxford: Archeopress, 2001): 25–31.

19. Dragoş Gheorghiu, "Brancusi's Gates and Columns: Nineteenth-Century Rites of Passage in Twentieth-Century Art and Architecture," in *Nineteenth-Century Contexts* 21, no. 1 (1999).

20. Suzanne Preston Blier, *The Anatomy of architecture, Ontology and metaphor in Batammaliba architectural expression* (Chicago and London: Chicago University Press, 1987).

21. Catherine Bell, *Ritual theory, ritual practice* (New York & Oxford: Oxford University Press 1992).

22. Linda Hurcombe, *Archaeological artefacts as material culture* (London & New York: Routledge, 2007), 112.

23. Michael B. Schiffer and Andrea R. Miller, *The material life of human beings. Artifacts, behavior, and communication* (London & New York, Routledge, 1999).

24. Arnold van Gennep, *Les rites de passage* (Paris: Librarie critique Emile Nourry, 1909).

25. Christian Norbert-Schultz, *Genius Loci. Towards a phenomenology of architecture* (New York: Rizzoli, 1991).

26. Paul Graves-Brown, "Introduction," *Matter, materiality and modern culture, ed.* Paul Graves-Brown, 1–9 (London and New York: Routledge, 2000), 3.

27. Gheorghiu, "Experimenting with prehistoric spaces," 343–371.

28. Gheorghiu, "Cultural landscapes in the lower Danube area," 167- 178.

29. *The Maps of Time. Real communities, virtual worlds, experimented pasts.* PN-II-ID-PCE- 2011-3-0245, IDEI, Grant No. 185, Director Professor Dragoş Gheorghiu.

30. Grigore Ionesco, *Histoire de l'architecture en Roumanie. De la préhistorie à nos jours*, (Bucharest: Academia RSR, 1972).

31. Jens de Smit, *Towards building augmented reality web applications*, (SURFnet, W3C Augmented Reality on the Web Workshop, Barcelona, 2010).

32. Steven Feiner, Blair MacIntyre, Tobias Höllerer, and Anthony Webster, "A Touring Machine: Prototyping 3D Mobile Augmented Reality Systems for Exploring the Urban Environment," in *Proceeding ISWC '97 Proceedings of the 1st IEEE International Symposium on Wearable Computers*, IEEE Computer Society Washington, DC, USA, 1997.

33. Paul Milgram, Haruo Takemura, Akira Utsumi, and Fumio Kishino, "Augmented Reality: A class of displays on the reality-virtuality continuum," *SPIE* 2351, Telemanipulator and Telepresence Technologies, 1994.

34. Feiner et al., "A Touring Machine."

35. Gerhard Reitmayr and Dieter Schmalstieg, "Collaborative Augmented Reality for Outdoor Navigation and Information Browsing," in *Proceedings ISAR 2001*, New York, USA, Oct. 2001.

36. Albrecht Schmidt, Michael Beigl and Hans-W. Gellersen, "There is more to Context than Location," in *Computers & Graphics Journal* 23, no. 6 (December 1999): 893–902.

37. Clemens Arth and Dieter Schmalstieg, "Challenges of Large-Scale Augmented Reality on Smartphones," in *ISMAR Conference*, 2011, Graz University of Technology, Austria, and Workshop at *Mobile HCI* 2011, 7–10, Stockholm, Sweden, August 2011.

38. Feiner et al., "A Touring Machine."

39. Jayashree Karlekar, Steven ZhiYing Zhou,Weiquan Lu, Yuta Nakayama, and Daniel Hii, "Mixed Reality on Mobile Devices," in *Users Interfaces*, ed. Rita Mátrai, 191–204 (Croatia: INTECH, 2010)

40. Albrecht Schmidt, Michael Beigl and Hans-W. Gellersen, "There is more to Context than Location."

41. Karlekar *et al.* [30]

42. de Smit [31]

43. Arth and Schmalstieg [37]

44. Ivan Poupyrev, *Advanced topics in 3D User Interface Design*, (Interaction Lab, Sony CSL, SIGGRAPH 2001).

45. Arth and Schmalstieg [37]

46. Robert T. Azuma, *A Survey of Augmented Reality* (Hughes Research Laboratories, 1997).

47. de Smit [31]

48. Arth and Schmalstieg [37]

49. Hoppala web page http://www.hoppala-agency.com/

50. de Smit [31]

51. Layar web page, http://www.layar.com

52. Steve Dixon, *Digital performance. A history of new media in theatre, dance, performance art, and installation* (Cambridge, MA: The MIT Press, 2007), 363 and ff.

53. Minjuan Wang and Ruimin Shen, "Message design for mobile learning: Learning theories, human cognition and design principles," *British Journal of Educational Technology* (2011): 1–15.

54. Tobias H. Höllerer and Steven K. Feiner, "Mobile Augmented Reality," in *Telegeoinformatics: Location-Based Computing and Services*, eds. H. Karimi and A. Hammad, 1–39 (London: Taylor & Francis Books Ltd, 2004).

DRAGOŞ GHEORGHIU

interviewed by

Lanfranco Aceti & Richard Rinehart

Is there an 'outside' of the Art World from which to launch critiques and interventions? If so, what is the border that defines outside from inside? If it is not possible to define a border, then what constitutes an intervention and is it possible to be and act as an outsider of the art world? Or are there only different positions within the Art World and a series of positions to take that fulfill ideological parameters and promotional marketing and branding techniques to access the fine art world from an oppositional, and at times confrontational, standpoint?

I always perceived art and science as being two analogous facets, more or less subjective, of human knowledge. The analogy existing between the two represents for me what ancient Greeks labeled *techné*. This is why I cannot imagine a look from "outside" the art field, because I do not know where its limits are. For example, I use artistic metaphors to improve the archaeological imagination, a method, which for me represents a way to augment reality. As experimentalist, I try to use the scientific experiment and the phenomenological experience as well. For example, when studying the architectural structures of a prehistoric settlement I tried to express them at full scale or as art installations, with the aim to embody their material form. It is only after this process of corporal experience of the built forms, which is an augmentation of the archaeological record with my personal experience that I return to their scientific study.

For me, art and science are not two different entities positioned side by side (and therefore which create borders), but each entity is the avatar of the other, existing simultaneously on the same place.

"In *The Truth in Painting*, Derrida describes the *parergon* (*par-*, around; *ergon*, the work), the boundaries or limits of a work of art. Philosophers from Plato to Hegel, Kant, Husserl, and Heidegger debated the limits of the intrinsic and extrinsic, the inside and outside of the art object." (Anne Friedberg, *The Virtual Window: From Alberti to Microsoft* (Cambridge, MA: MIT Press, 2009), 13.) Where then is the inside and outside of the virtual artwork? Is the artist's 'hand' still inside the artistic process in the production of virtual art or has it become an irrelevant concept abandoned outside the creative process of virtual artworks?

To the question if in virtual artworks one can still discern the authority of its creator, one can answer that this depends from case to case (whether a style is preserved in time, and whether this style is observable). A virtual artwork differs from the other art productions by its immateriality. This advantage confers an infinite plasticity to the artwork, but also the risk to lose the identity of its creator.

Virtual art cannot exist outside a high tech instrumental support, and even when the haptic technology will be mass produced, it will continue to maintain the artistic emotion of human sensibility inside a technical device.

I believe the common element of materiality and immateriality is the symbolic thinking of the creator. Finally it is the symbol which allows the immersion, and the generation of emotions; because one shall make a difference between media activism and the work of art which creates emotion. This psychological state is the one which keeps us in the human zone, in spite of the (naïve) trend which believes that if one can put prosthesis into the human body this means a passage to a post-human state.

Therefore, I perceive the world of art as having a borderline, this representing the edge where emotions cease.

Virtual interventions appear to be the contemporary inheritance of Fluxus' artistic practices. Artists like Peter Weibel, Yayoi Kusama and Valie Export subverted traditional concepts of space and media through artistic interventions. What are the sources of inspiration and who are the artistic predecessors that you draw from for the conceptual and aesthetic frameworks of contemporary augmented reality interventions?

 ISSN 1071-4391 ISBN 978-1-906897-20-8

In this case technology was for me a source of inspiration. During the eighties, I used the technologies of the epoch: the slide projector. So I overlapped the slide images and worked on film images, i.e. I augmented the art process to be perceived as a palimpsest. At that time, we did not need high tech digital instruments to create immersion because we relied on the artistic imagination, and because we perceived the real, as Baudrillard stressed, as a form of simulation, therefore being a layer that could be augmented.

The palimpsest became more significant for my world vision when I approached art-chaeology; from that moment I perceived the world as being a stratigraphy. A part of the exhibitions of my archaeological experiments were under the form of overlapped transparent images containing different information, which were perceived simultaneously, as a palimpsest. I continued this technique of overlapping different plans when I decided to visualize the invisible data in the archaeological record with the help of art metaphors. For me, Augmented Reality meant an instrument to visualize vague concepts from science, like 'space,' 'ritual,' or 'landscape,' which I tried to reveal by overlapping different layers of information.

The first time I learned about Augmented Reality from an IT perspective was in 1992, when I read Michael Benedikt's *Cyberspace: First steps* (MIT Press), where the concept was presented more for improving design than art, but I stayed away from this technique for a decade because I wanted to express myself using traditional techniques.

In the representation and presentation of your artworks as being 'outside of' and 'extrinsic to' contemporary aesthetics why is it important that your projects are identified as Art?

A long time ago I renounced calling the result of my work as being purely 'artistic.' While working with ancient technologies I discovered astonishing esthetical qualities, which did not belong to works of art. This is the reason why I do not situate myself in the area of science (i.e. archaeology) nor in the area of art, but in a synthesis of the two which is archaeology. Thus, the difficulty of the reception of my work: archaeologists perceive it as art or experimental archaeology, depending of the ideology of the group. For example, a radical group of archaeologists sees my land-art as an experiential approach of the spirituality of the past (Pleistocene Coalition News, vol. 4, issue 2, March-April 2012, p. 16), and an academic journal like Antiquity (March 2010: 278) sees them as being "sensorial experiments depicted in vivid colours."

Therefore, it depends on the receptor of the work to decide the proportion of art and science in each piece of work.

What has most surprised you about your recent artworks? What has occurred in your work that was outside of your intent, yet has since become an intrinsic part of the work?

The period when I began to activate as a visual artist was the one of the emergence of the site -oriented concept. In my archaeology studies, I realized the decisive importance of context to understand material culture, but it was only recently that I began to present it to the public using digital maps as instruments for visualization of the position of the artworks. Working with digital maps I locate my artwork in a real and a virtual space at the same time (http://www.panoramio.com/photo/58368794?source=wapi&referrer=kh.google.com), in this way offering a global perspective to the work of art.

Probably the most surprising event related to my recent artwork was the acceptance in pop culture of a land-art as part of Nature's geomorphs: a Portuguese website for weather forecast: http://www.meteo-europ.com/en/pt/santarem/zimbreira-pictures.html which presents a collage of the specific images of the local landscape, mixed with the images of a land art I carried in the Zimbreira area to evoke the walls of an ancient castro (prehistoric stronghold). These images were collected from Google Earth and repositioned in a different configuration, together with geographical views, in such a way as to evoke roads or waterfalls.

The recycling of my artwork on the Internet is an example of the current status of contemporary digital art, which may become the rough material for an anonymous and global work. ■

DRAGOŞ GHEORGHIU

statement & artwork

With my art I intend to reveal two great mysteries: Earth and the Past.

Both possess two common traits: space and rites, two concepts, which elude scientific approaches. The rites determine space and space creates the rites, and both cannot be represented but only evoked since they elude quantitative methods.

I try to evoke the rites of passage to show that space is not homogenous that it is structured with liminal zones where one is neither here nor there. My objects shall be perceived more as instructions for the different movements of the body of the receptor, to reproduce the ancient paths of the past. From a phenomenological perspective, they embody space and rituals. By posting these visual instructions on digital maps I intend to reveal, at a global level, the corporal experiences of ancient people.

Being minimalist, my art does not represent but evokes, leaving to the mind and body of the viewer to create the image of the whole. Therefore, my objects situate themselves in a complex liminality, between art and science, local and global, real and virtual. ■

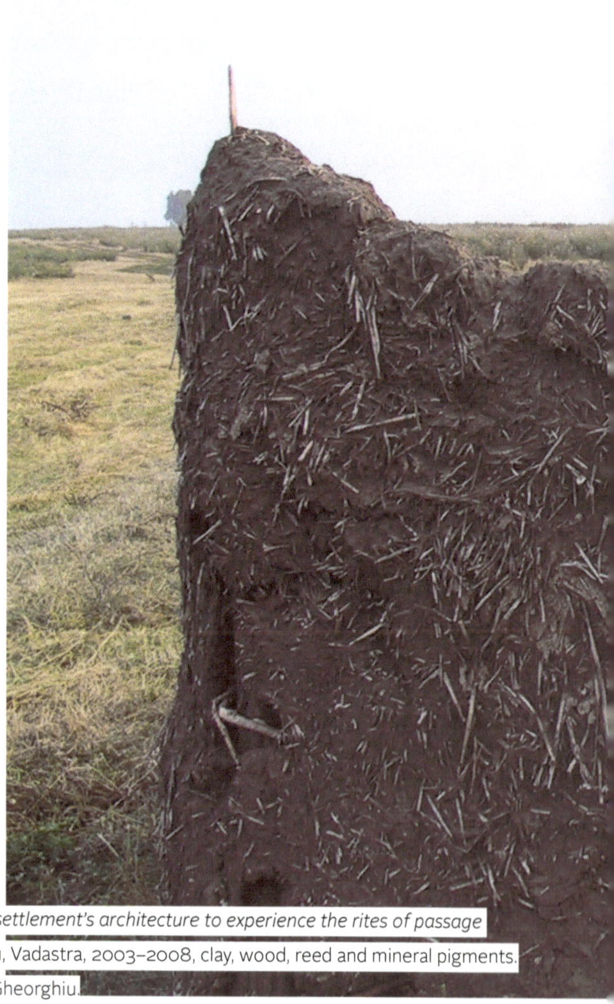

Reconstruction of a prehistoric settlement's architecture to experience the rites of passage and liminality. Dragoş Gheorghiu, Vadastra, 2003–2008, clay, wood, reed and mineral pigments. Photo D. Gheorghiu, © Dragoş Gheorghiu.

 ISSN 1071-4391 ISBN 978-1-906897-20-8

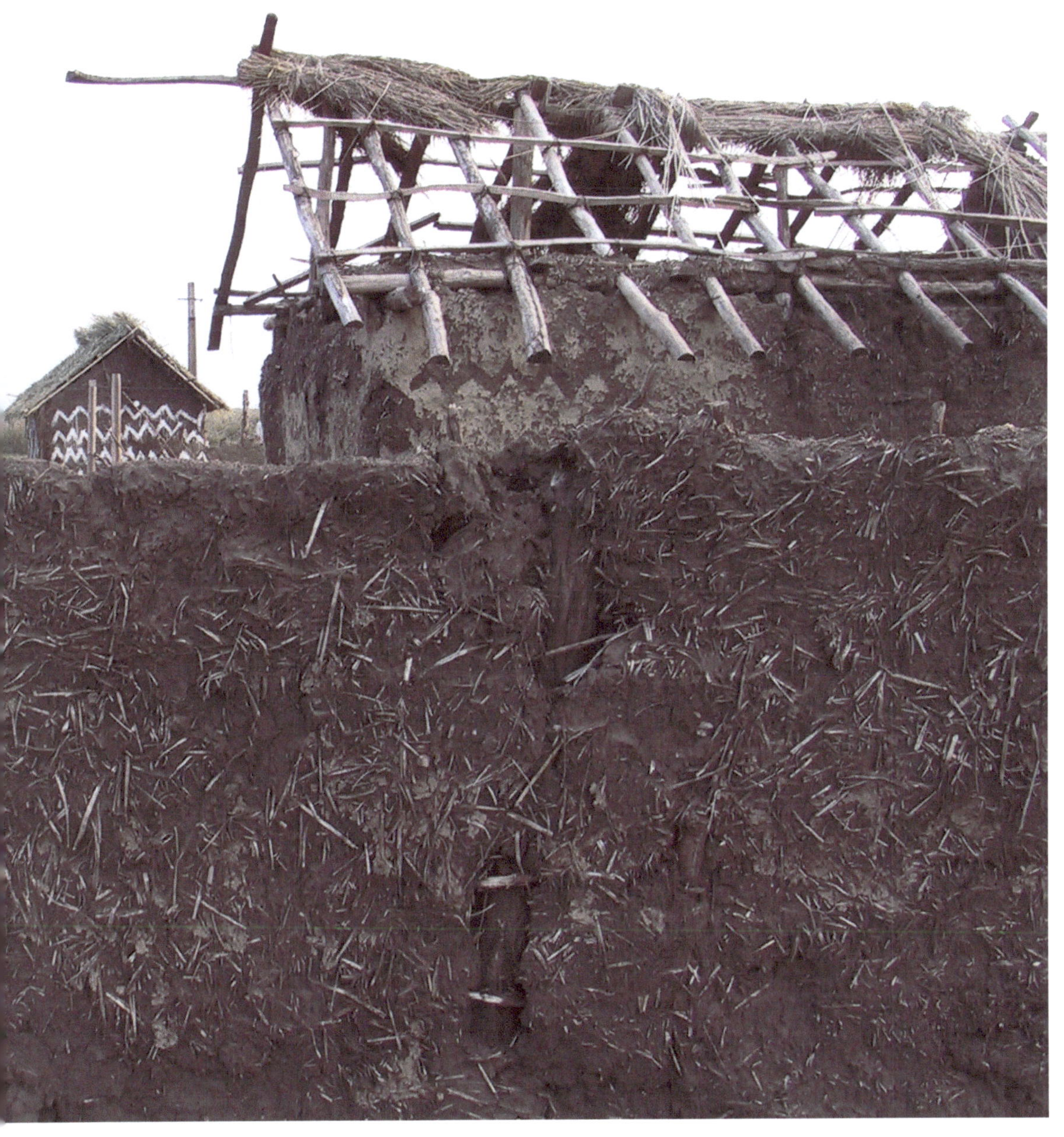

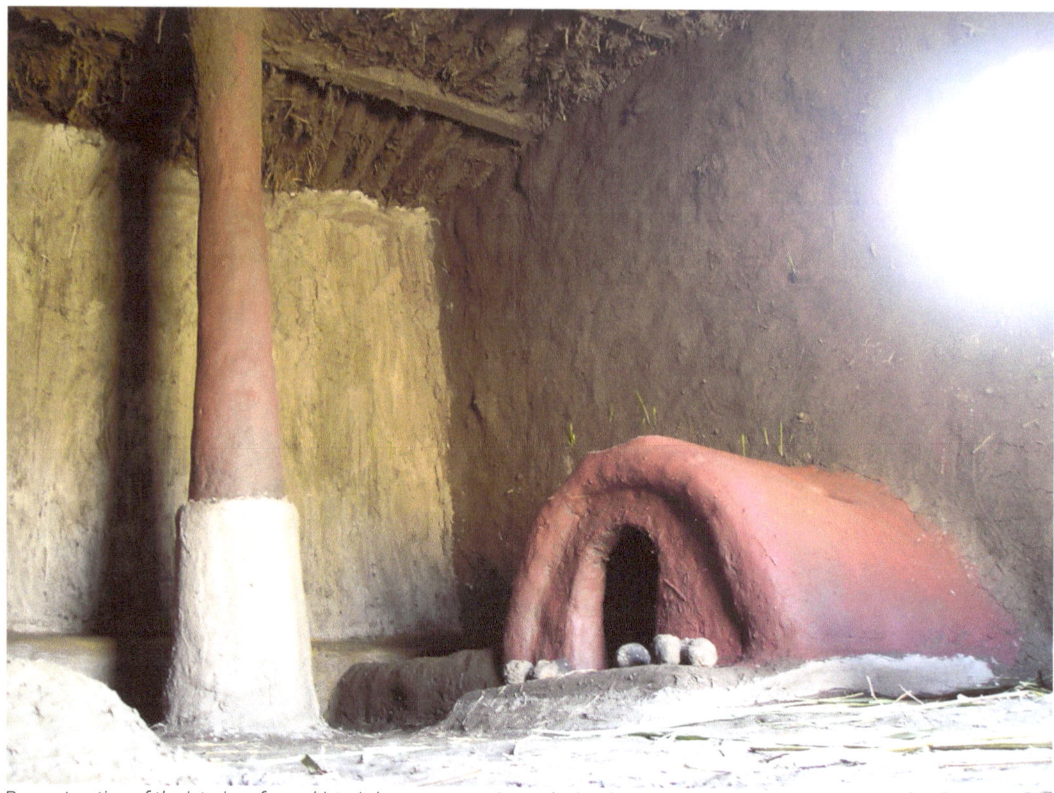

Reconstruction of the interior of a prehistoric house to experience the lived space. Dragoş Gheorghiu, Vadastra, 2003, clay and mineral pigments. Photo D. Gheorghiu. © Dragoş Gheorghiu.

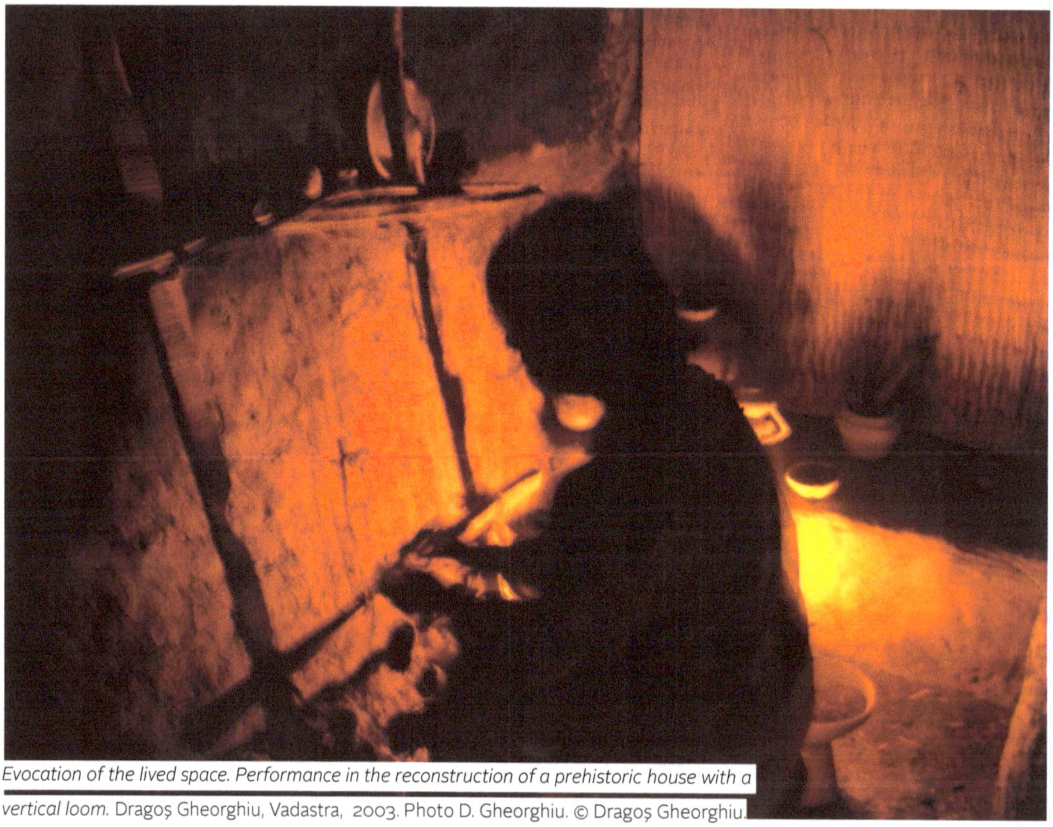

Evocation of the lived space. Performance in the reconstruction of a prehistoric house with a vertical loom. Dragoş Gheorghiu, Vadastra, 2003. Photo D. Gheorghiu. © Dragoş Gheorghiu.

 ISSN 1071-4391 ISBN 978-1-906897-20-8

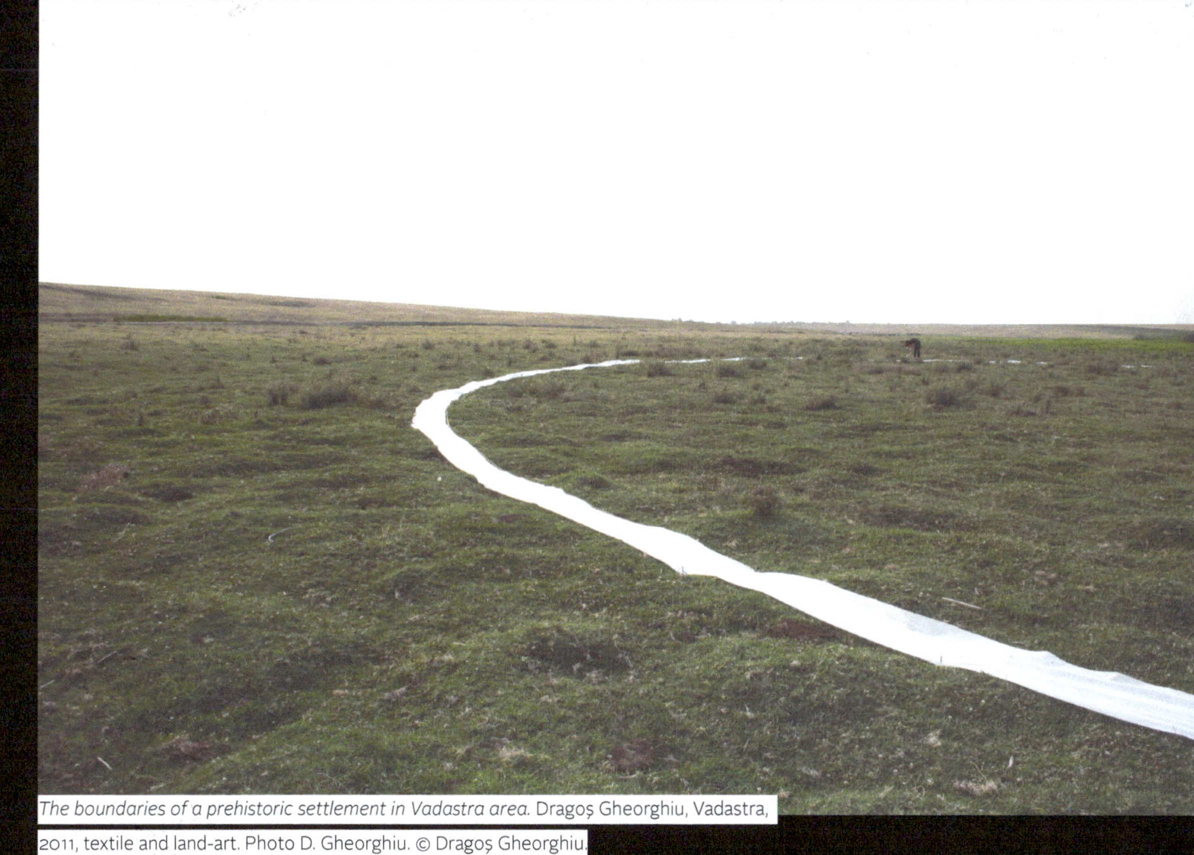

The boundaries of a prehistoric settlement in Vadastra area. Dragoş Gheorghiu, Vadastra, 2011, textile and land-art. Photo D. Gheorghiu. © Dragoş Gheorghiu.

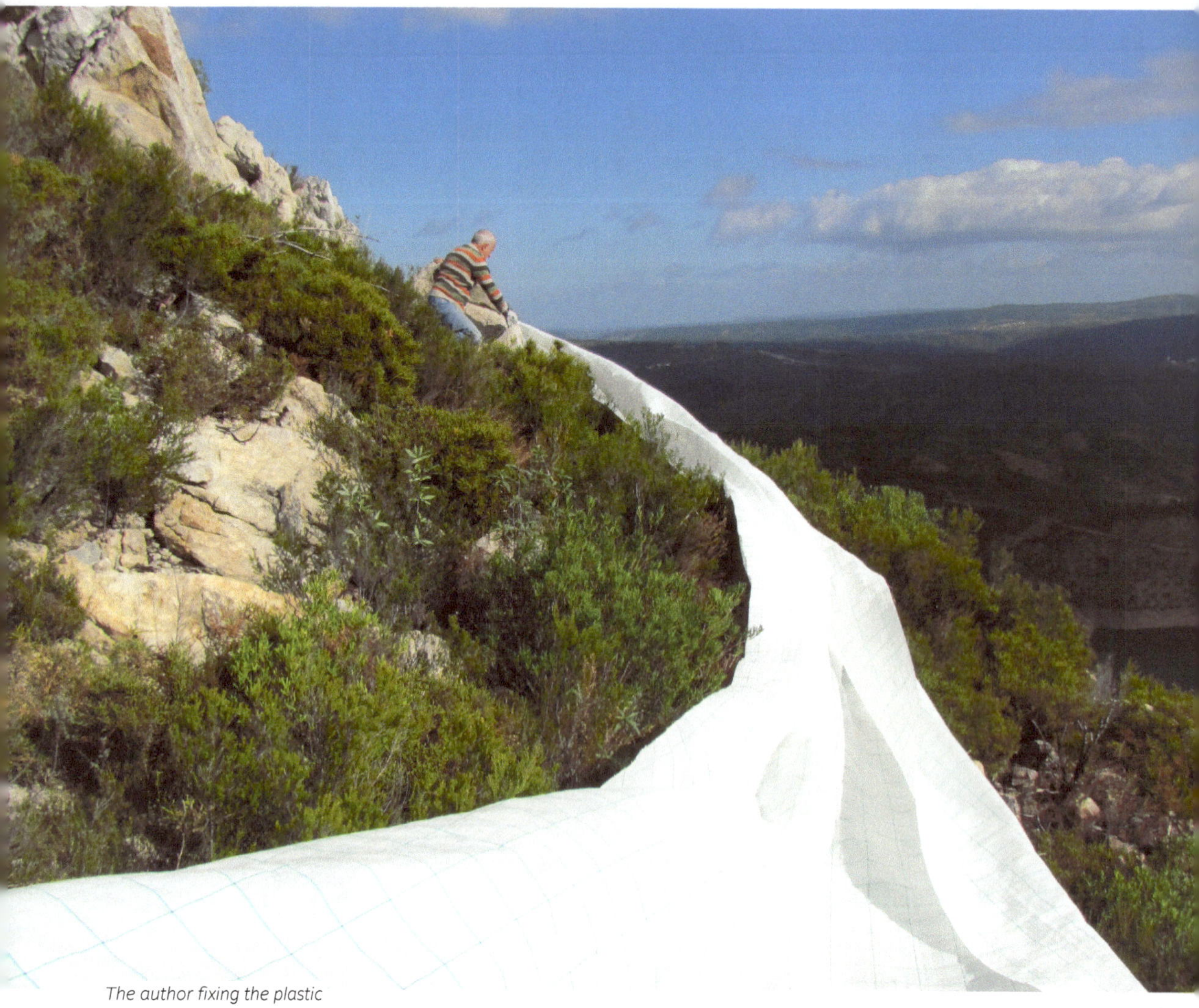

The author fixing the plastic foil on Monte Velho. Land-art on Monte Velho, 2010. Dragoş Gheorghiu, plastic foil fixed with plastic ropes and iron nails. Photo R. Damian. © Radu Damian.

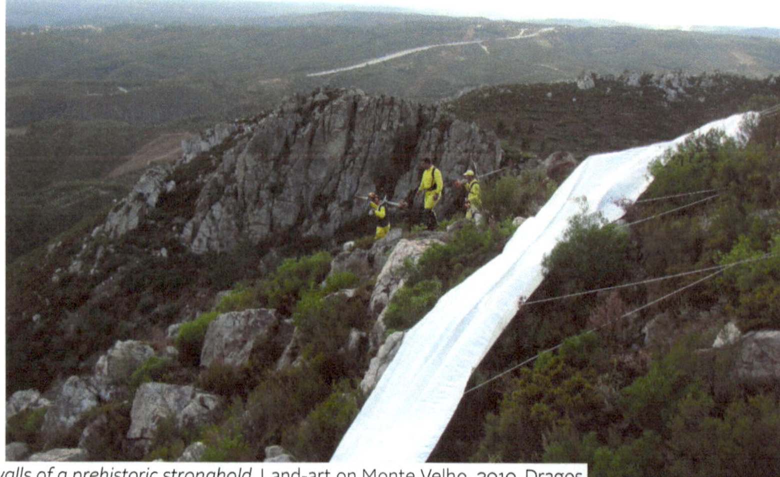

Delimiting the perimeter of the walls of a prehistoric stronghold. Land-art on Monte Velho, 2010. Dragoş Gheorghiu, plastic foil fixed with plastic ropes and iron nails. Photo R. Damian. © Radu Damian.

 ISSN 1071-4391 ISBN 978-1-906897-20-8

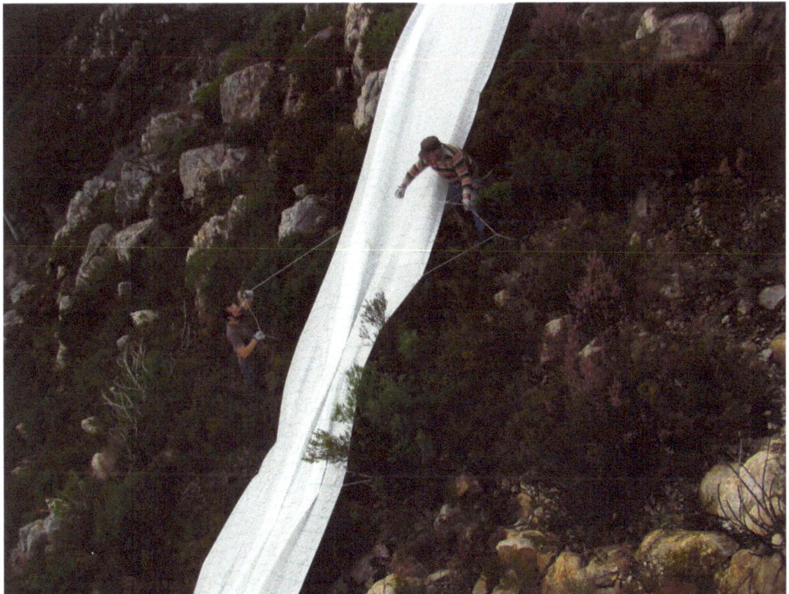

The author with the help of experimentalist Pedro Cura fixing the plastic foil on Monte Velho. Land-art on Monte Velho, 2010. Dragoş Gheorghiu, plastic foil fixed with plastic ropes and iron nails. Photo R. Damian. © Radu Damian.

Brazilian archaeology students helping to fix the plastic foil on Monte Velho. Land-art on Monte Velho, 2010. Dragoş Gheorghiu, plastic foil fixed with plastic ropes and iron nails. Photo R. Damian. © Radu Damian.

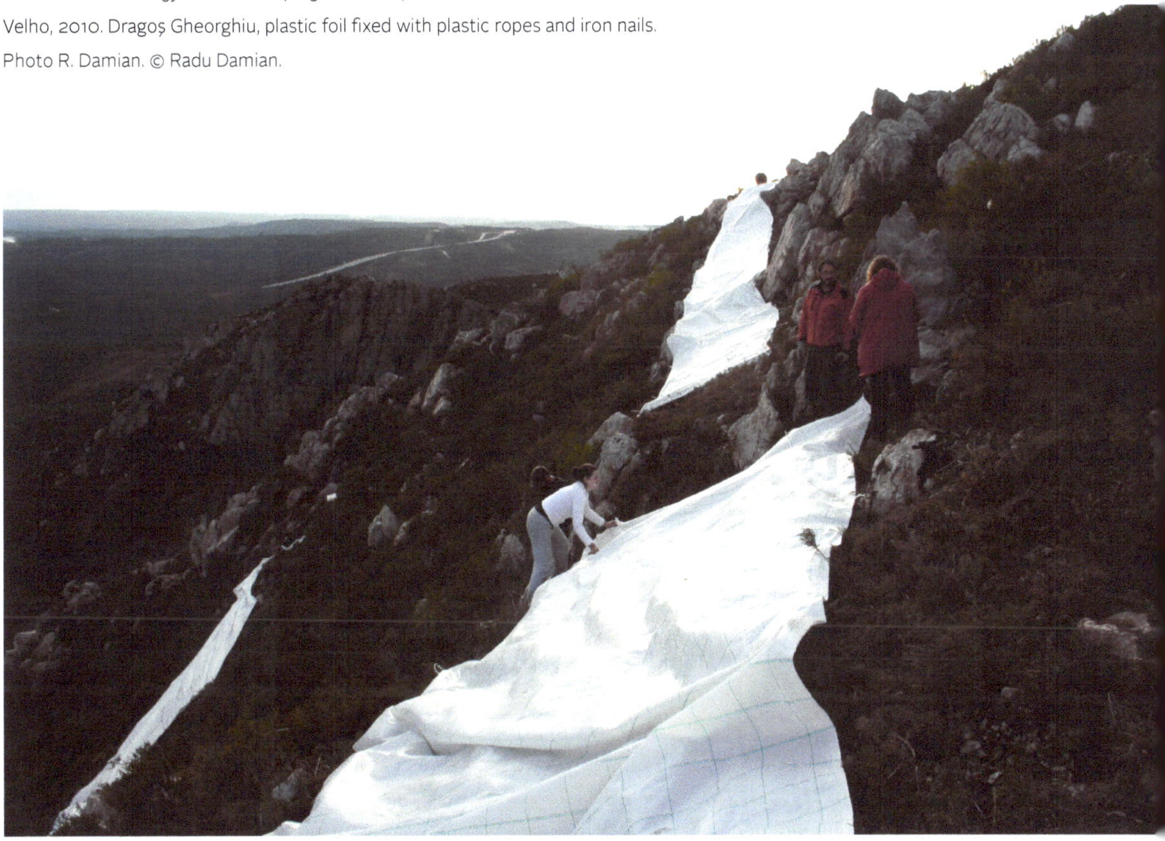

Hacking: A new political and cultural practice

CHRISTINA GRAMMATIKOPOULOU

MSc, Ph.D. Candidate
Universitat de Barcelona, Facultat de Filosofia, Geografia i Història, Departament d'Història de l'Art
xtna@interartive.org
http://www.interartive.org

> *"Hackers create the possibility of new things entering the world. [..] In art, in science, in philosophy and culture, in any production of knowledge where data can be gathered, where information can be extracted from it, and where in that information new possibilities for the world are produced, there are hackers hacking the new out of the old."*
>
> — McKenzie Wark, *A Hacker Manifesto* [1]

INTRODUCTION

The era that started with the massive revelations of classified documents by Wikileaks culminated in the Arab spring and has since caused multiple social and political vibrations. It revealed the potential of the Internet as a revolutionary tool and prepared the ground for the subsequent outburst of a guerilla information war between Internet activists and multinational companies or governments over freedom on the Internet. In this context a range of initiatives in social networks to raise awareness and to motivate people politically have marked a period of constant political and cultural change.

From the shady depths of the web and the complex world of programming, hacking has risen to the surface as an everyday practice that is awakening a new sense of citizenship; instead of following the news passively, people gather in online groups, share information and take substantial political action. Any individual can become part of these groups, from any part of the world, without any particular skills or 'weapons,' simply by expressing ideas online and participating

 ISSN 1071-4391 ISBN 978-1-906897-20-8

Hacking and file sharing are daily acts that have come to constitute cultural practices. *There is a significant political dimension in downloading and transforming files, joining virtual communities and online protests, that is easily detectible in recent developments regarding government transparency and open access to information. This mentality is reflected on contemporary culture, where the participation of the public in the creative act and the 'remixing' of existing forms are standard practices. As examples that substantiate the concept of cultural hacking, the article presents the works of artists that focus on hacking, hacktivism and piracy, either as acts that bring the artwork into existence or as ways of initiating the public into these practices. Through the examples of artworks that belong in different spheres –the virtual, the hybrid or the urban space- hacking emerges as the common thread that links software-based art, augmented reality art and street art.*

in collaborative actions. Hacking and hacktivism have thus gained the force of cultural and political phenomena; and these two aspects will be the main focus of this paper, following an interdisciplinary analysis that expands through the fields of art, Internet and politics.

Contemporary artistic practice often encourages people to undertake political action online or to expand their cultural knowledge by hacking. This is evident in diverse artworks that are based on hacking as an artistic medium, as a cultural practice or a subject; these examples reflect the emergence of alternative ways of (re)acting within the social frame and outline a different future for art and politics.

Beyond art spaces, the idea of 'hacking' as a means of intervening in a space and expanding the experience of reality has gained the force of a cultural phenomenon. Street art, artistic actions in the urban space, as well as artworks based on augmented reality, could be considered as a form of hacking in the urban matrix. It is, therefore, interesting to see how the idea of intervening in a system has changed the perception of reality and art. By looking into a range of examples of 'cultural hacking' –street art and augmented reality art- one can track the evolution of these phenomena and see how the interest has shifted from the 'sacred art object' to art as an everyday experience and from the 'solid world' to an immaterial and fluid space, where the intervention of the public is a vital element of the process.

In this paper we shall focus on how the discourse about free information flow has had an impact on artistic practices, and how artists, in turn, have sought to initiate the public in this ideology through specific artworks and actions. Therefore, after noting how the public is initiated into the process of file sharing, hacking and hacktivism on an everyday level, we shall see how these actions are used as artistic tools within the virtual and the real space.

Deeply politicized but inherently playful, the artistic practices described here can easily grab the attention of the people and stimulate their intention to protest and intervene on a political level.

HACKING AND INFORMATION SHARING AS COMMON AND REVOLUTIONARY PRACTICES

During the past decades, the advent of information technologies has changed drastically the 'materiality' of everyday life. Communication, entertainment and education are continually being distanced from their previous connection to paper, celluloid, vinyl and other materials. Turning into digital files, that can be easily shared, altered, copied or erased. [2] A digital file is based on matter as well: tiny particles, electrodes. However, this minimal matter needs to go through a set of complex codes and technologies in order to be transformed into a world of fleeting images, words and sounds, which have a different impact than their 'solid' counterparts. Hence, an interdisciplinary discourse about this phenomenon has arisen to analyze multiple aspects –sociological, artistic, psychological and other- of what is being called 'immaterial,' 'dematerialized' or 'hypermaterialized' space. [3] The point of convergence among the different analyses and definitions is that within this space, matter is an ensemble of information, interaction and perception.

This state of minimal matter loaded with data creates a fluid environment, where a new socio-political balance is created as new controversies take place. Although these controversies reflect already existent competitive forces, they are further intensified by the dynamic introduced of an information society, which constantly changes the coordinates of contemporary reality.

One of the important parameters of this new balance is a significant differentiation in the traditional roles of the consumer and the producer, the public and the artist, which has shaken the foundations of the financial, political and cultural system. Nowadays, such dipoles are being rendered meaningless since the public takes part in the creative process, whereas the producers or artists base a significant part of their work on crowdsourcing and participation. In other words, we are dealing with two-way interactions. On one hand, the actions of the Internet users –their preferences, their emails and their networks- are being registered and analysed in order to maximise the impact of advertisement campaigns or product launches; on the other hand, the users share, alter and download content, participating thus actively in the dissemination of information and playing a decisive role in the reception of cultural products. [4]

Within a reality where personal pages and networks allow any user to produce and disseminate data, information is becoming disassociated from the established cultural and media networks, such as museums, official institutions and newspapers, whereas the public becomes an active agent in artistic and political developments. The doctrine beneath this development is "information wants to be free." [5] People defend the right to freedom on the Internet by reacting against any law or technical implementation that tries to restrict it; their counteractions frequently include hacking, hacktivism and piracy.

Although the three terms are often used within the same breath or interchangeably, there are certain differences between them. Originally used for journalism based on unorthodox methods, the term 'hack' was adopted by the early programmers to describe a creative solution reached through detours and reworking of existing systems. [6] In this sense, hacking is synonymous with evolution in information technologies since each development is based on the hacking of previous ones. A hacker is someone who enters a system, explores and manipulates its tools, so as to learn how it works and alter it. When this method is used as part of a political action, in order to increase political transparency and raise awareness, we are talking about hacktivism (a neologism created from the words 'hack'

 ISSN 1071-4391 ISBN 978-1-906897-20-8

and 'activism'). Although piracy simply refers to the act of leaking and sharing content illegally, the motives can also be political.

Despite the differences between the terms, they often imply one another –for example, 'hacktivism' could include entering a system and disseminating information illegally.

From the controversy of the trial of the Pirate Bay, to the foundation of the Pirate Party International, which defends the right to free distribution of information online, from the protests against laws that enforce copyright to the Wikileaks case and the Arab spring, one can see that the discourse about hacking, hacktivism and piracy expands beyond the limits of the Internet. This is mainly because these acts question the existing distribution of information and power.

Hence, under the same political umbrella of freedom online, one can find diverse ideologies, with elements from libertarianism, anarchist thought, the free culture movement –rebaptized nowadays into 'open source,' so as to remove any political connotations- and hacker culture. In all, these political currents are described as "information age ideologies." [7]

People that share the information age ideologies "talk about Internet as communication" [8] –whereas for the entertainment industry and other producers, online data are copyrighted or protected content. Additionally, they defend their right to have access to any kind of information, whether it is relevant to culture or political actions.

During the past two years the information age ideologies have contributed significantly to the shaping of political events. The United States diplomatic cables leak by Wikileaks and the Arab Spring are examples that illustrate how political awareness can be raised online and how technological development can lead to political changes. These developments presupposed an online fight for freedom of information that went through blogs and social networks, media networks that are controlled by people. Moreover, when the authorities tried to confront this digital revolution by cutting access to the Internet –in the case of the Arab world-, or blocking funds sustaining the whistleblowers –in the case of Wikileaks-, hackers and online communities counterattacked. Their means of defence and the attack were providing numbers of international Internet Service Providers, in the first case, to enable Internet access for the Egyptian protesters, and unleash denial of service attacks against the websites of the enterprises that supported the blockage of Wikileaks funds in the second case. [9]

One should note that the conflicts mentioned above still have the same roots as the ones in the pre-Internet age. What is more, the 'digital revolution' still needed to be combined with traditional forms of protest in the streets; as Athina Karatzogianni notes, "the groups engaging in cyberconflicts are still fighting for power, participation, democracy but are using an accelerated process and a postmodern medium that enables asymmetries, empowering the previously marginalised or repressed [...] to foster unprecedented social and political change." [10] An old battle with new, downloadable weapons.

The public can easily become involved in the online battle, since they are already used to the idea of acquiring, altering and sharing data. One could say that, after Beuys' affirmation "every person is an artist" and Warhol's promise that "anyone can be famous," the current revelation is that *anyone can become a hacker.*

The 'information age ideologies' are not always aimed directly at political causes; they encompass different manifestations of our lives, including contemporary art. The idea of 'hacking' is transferred onto the cultural field as a medium of creation and as an autonomous artistic practice.

CULTURAL HACKING: CREATION AS AN ACT OF TRANSFORMATION

In order to see how the idea of hacking has fostered a new cultural paradigm, it is useful to have a look into the artistic and ideological background that preceded this evolution.

During the twentieth century artists began to expand their vision beyond the creation of the one and only *sanctified* art object. By engaging in time-specific actions and counting on the interaction with the public, they opened up a new road, where the public was called upon to form part of the artistic *ritual,* and to take part in the creative process.

In a way, the public has always had a substantial role in the creation of an artwork; for receiving is also a form of producing. According to Michel de Certeau, daily life is a collective production of all the people that use cultural products, ideas, spaces; a reader 'inhabits' a text, in a similar way to someone who inhabits a room. [11] In this sense, those who receive an artwork can be viewed as active producers, not as passive consumers.

Their role is even more crucial in interactive art. The idea of interaction, although it's nowadays primarily linked to digital art, began with Dadaism and its 1960s offsprings, like the Fluxus movement. Thus the public became gradually accustomed to the notion that they could contribute to an open artwork by acting and deciding.

With the advent of digital technology, the interactive dimension of art came to the fore in a more prominent way. The "distributed authorship" [12] of the artwork is a realization of Roy Ascott's vision that technology would enable the cooperation among different authors and the collaboration between the author and the audience. [13]

This implies not only participating during the creative process, but also reusing already existing cultural forms as 'prime matter' for the artwork. Dadaist actions like drawing a moustache over Mona Lisa –as well as most of Duchamp's art- are a way of remixing and reusing known images in a new context: they are a form of 'cultural hacking.' Similarly, the Situationist concept of 'détournement,' which encouraged a subversive attitude towards the capitalist system, by reinterpreting and decontextualizing its logos and images, [14] as well as the appropriation and alteration of marketing strategies by the culture jammers of the 1980s could also be viewed as forms of 'hacking.' [15]

These ideas prevailed once the 'tyranny' of originality was rejected –the modernist notion that one needs to start with a blank canvas or a raw material, and create something unique. Instead, nowadays "the artistic question is no longer: "what can we make that is new?" but "how can we make do with what we have?" [16]

Rather than seeking to create new images, artists take ready ones and rework on them; the act of reworking on digital files, subverting previous uses of an object or injecting images arbitrarily on the surface of the city via augmented reality and street art could be viewed as a hacking of cultural forms.

Even though artists have always had a wide range of forms to work with –images from art history or everyday objects- information technologies have multiplied these sources and their transformative potential. Within the Internet, one can find an endless array of images and sounds, which can be digitally transformed

 ISSN 1071-4391 ISBN 978-1-906897-20-8

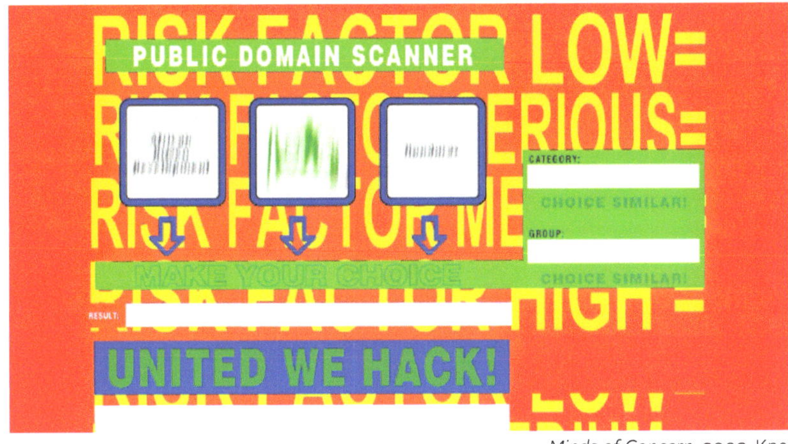

Minds of Concern, 2002, Knowbotic Research, (screen print). Software Installation. Variable dimensions. Installation at the Museum of Contemporary Art of New York, Exhibition 'Open Source Art Hack.' Image courtesy of Knowbotic Research. © Knowbotic Research, 2002.

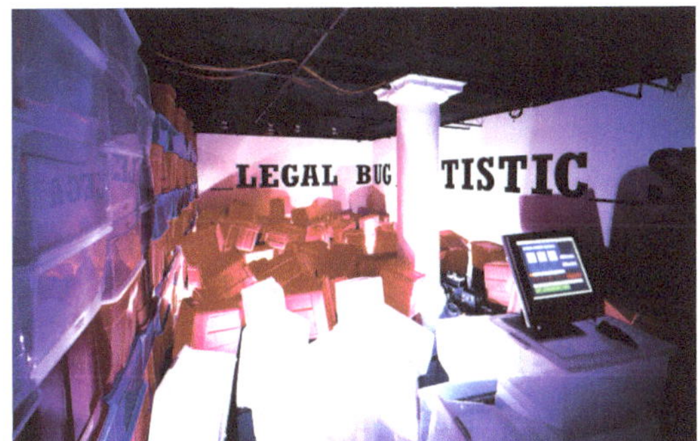

Minds of Concern, 2002, Knowbotic Research, (installation view). Software Installation. Variable dimensions. Installation at the Museum of Contemporary Art of New York, Exhibition 'Open Source Art Hack.' Image courtesy of Knowbotic Research. © Knowbotic Research, 2002.

through software by the artist or the public –roles that are interchangeable and shared.

The act of downloading is a means of producing culture; by browsing, selecting, downloading and sharing one creates a 'digital footprint' and a new association between the items selected, a personal viewpoint that constitutes a 'profile' of one's cultural preferences. So, downloading is not about appropriating –defying ownership or taking something someone else owns- but about helping ideas and cultural objects circulate. As Bourriaud notes, "artists' intuitive relationship with art history is now going beyond what we call 'the art of appropriation', which naturally infers an ideology of ownership, and moving toward a culture of the use of forms, a culture of constant activity of signs based on a collective ideal: sharing." [17]

'Cultural hacking,' in parallel to the generalized use of the term, implies entering a system, understanding how it works and creating something new out of it. Summing up its features, Franz Liebl, Thomas Düllo and Martin Kiel noted that it is about orientation and deorientation, seriousness and playfulness, bricolage and experimentation, radicalization of the original idea, intervention onto a system and dissemination. [18]

These features will be illustrated more analytically below, through the examples mentioned as forms of cultural hacking, within three different dimensions: artworks of hacking online, where the public is initiated into information age ideologies and subversive actions, hacking within a hybrid space –the real space viewed through augmented reality- and hacking within the urban matrix by means of street art.

SPREADING HACKER ETHICS AND DATA SHARING IDEALS THROUGH ART

Hacking has recently become a significant source of inspiration for artists who use software and the Internet as a basic element of their work. By using hacker methods, piracy and hacktivism, these artists not only reflect the political events and social currents of our time, but also create an environment where the public can get personal experience of these processes.

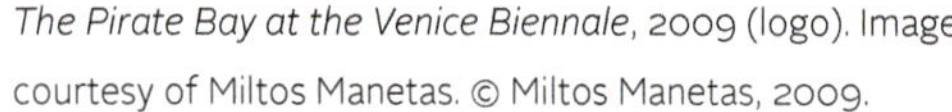

The Pirate Bay at the Venice Biennale, 2009 (logo). Image courtesy of Miltos Manetas. © Miltos Manetas, 2009.

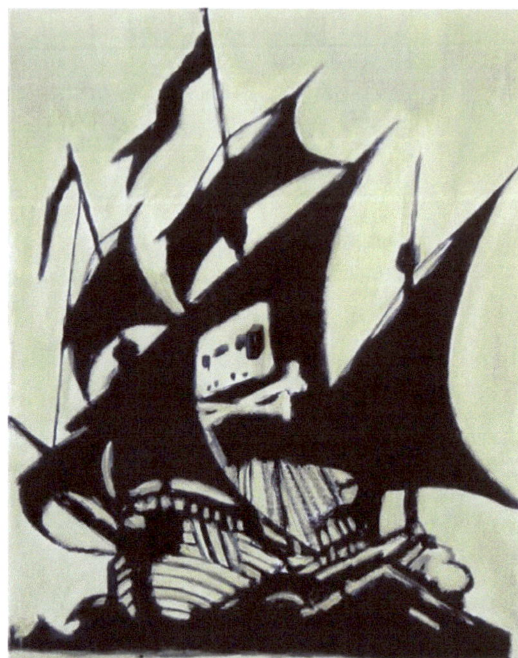

Untitled (Pirate Painting), 2009, Miltos Manetas. Oil on canvas and hard drive. 30 x 40 cm. Image courtesy of Miltos Manetas. © Miltos Manetas, 2009.

In *Minds of Concern: Breaking News* (2002) by Knowbotic Research, [19] presented in the Museum of Contemporary Art of New York, the public is initiated into 'white hat' hacker ethics; this type of hacking involves breaking into a system to check for possible security flaws, without altering it. Within a similar mindset, the artwork invited the visitors to choose one target among websites of groups, movements and non-governmental organizations, triggering a port scan of the selected webpage. After a while, the participants could see whether the security of the website could be breached and how vulnerable the site was against possible hacker attacks.

Although the intentions of the artists were benign –to warn the interested parties and the viewers about the vital issue of security- the artwork was shut down after a few days, with the justification that port scanning, even though legal, went against the Internet provider's acceptable use policy. Therefore, this artwork illustrates not only how hackers act –by encouraging the viewers to adopt such a role- but also how these acts are usually confronted –in a restrictive way, even if the action performed is not illegal.

The reaction against cultural hacking left its mark on the Internet Pavilion of the 2009 Venice Biennale as well. The curator of the Pavilion Miltos Manetas, known for his Internet art, created an *Embassy of Piracy*, where he invited the Pirate Bay. [20] This invitation was an eloquent way of showing that the act of sharing and downloading files can constitute a cultural act, as was mentioned above. Additionally, the visitors of the *Embassy* were offered tutorials on piracy and were informed about the significance of sharing as a cultural act. The Pirate Bay, a website bringing community together dedicated to file sharing, was received as a community of artists; this recognition was in the same line as the awarding of the operating system Linux with a prestigious art prize, the 'Prix Ars Electronica' (1999). However, the presence of the Pirates in the Venice Biennale was met with hostility from the Italian authorities, who raided the *Embassy* claiming that "you cannot have the Pirate Bay here." [21]

One can view the *Embassy of Piracy* controversy as the meeting point of three different "territories": a state with laws that protect author rights, an artistic place where new ideas are being explored and the

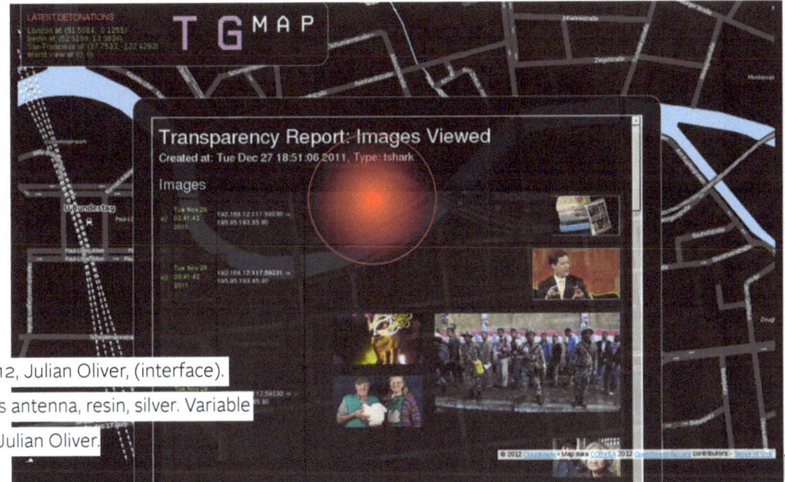

The Transparency Grenade, 2012, Julian Oliver, (interface). Computer, microphone, wireless antenna, resin, silver. Variable dimensions. Image courtesy of Julian Oliver. © Julian Oliver, 2012.

Internet as a territory of information. In regard to the last, Miltos Manetas declared in his "Piracy Manifesto": "We all live in the Internet, this is our new country, the only territory that makes sense to defend and protect." [22] The Internet is presented as an immaterial world of information that runs in parallel with the real world, often intersecting with it, as we shall see in the case of augmented reality.

Julian Oliver also defends free information sharing through his work; in the aftermath of the Wikileaks case he created a *Transparency Grenade* (2012) [23] that served this purpose. In the shape of a deadly weapon, the artwork is equipped with advanced technological software that allows the capturing of data from closed meetings. A tiny processor, a microphone and a wireless antenna are put into function once someone pulls the pin, capturing audio and network traffic and streaming it live to a dedicated server. This means that any data captured; e-mail fragments, pages, images, voices can be instantly presented online.

The Transparency Grenade, 2012, Julian Oliver, (overview). Computer, microphone, wireless antenna, software, resin, silver. 11,7 × 5,5 × 5,5 cm. Image courtesy of Julian Oliver. © Julian Oliver, 2012.

Thus the artist goes against the laws that encourage opacity in governing and control in information sharing –laws based on the pretext of public security and loss of revenue for content producers. Regarding the latter, he stated that, "with the *Transparency Grenade* I wanted to capture those important tensions in an iconic, hand-held package." [24] By creating a downloadable smartphone application with similar features as the *Transparency Grenade*, the artist provided the public with a digital, yet powerful weapon, which can easily turn anyone into a 'whistleblower' –following the example of Wikileaks and other organizations that are dedicated to revealing dishonest activities.

In all the cases mentioned above, the artwork is a participatory experience, with the potential to initiate the public into hacking methods and ethics. It is easy to observe that although we are dealing with art that exists in the immaterial sphere of the digital, there is a strong connection to politics *off*-line. The interconnection between the real and virtual space via artistic actions will be further examined with examples of augmented reality art and street art, which show a new way of acting within the urban space.

HACKING THE URBAN SPACE: AUGMENTED REALITY AND STREET ART

As a substrate for artistic action, the city is a place with already structured symbolic values, which influence people and their actions. The artists who work within the urban space seem to be aware of this fact; thus the artworks of augmented reality and street art are intrinsically linked to their environment, creating a dialogue with the city and its inhabitants.

Nowadays, it is becoming more evident than ever before, that the invisible and immaterial space is being oversaturated with information, flowing through the air, waiting to be processed and displayed with the right device. In fact, we are dealing with a hybrid sphere of action, that keeps growing: the Google glasses [25] that add a layer of virtual reality onto the real world with nonstop information flow, Quick Response codes that can be scanned through mobile devices and lead directly to a website, smartphones that provide constant Internet connection are some examples of this growing trend. Within this context, it is interesting to have a look onto augmented reality art that is based on these developments, often preceding them.

Julian Oliver's *Artvertiser* (2008) [26] runs the distance between the data-saturated air and the surface of the city, trying to alter its aspect via augmented reality. Through a software platform, advertisement images in the street are replaced with art images in real time. These artworks, created in advance by a multitude of artists –sometimes as a parody or a response to the original advertisement- become visible when someone looks at the advertisement billboards through special glasses or a mobile device.

As the artwork is based on an open-source code, which can be downloaded and modified by any user, it highlights the ethos of collaborative effort underneath technological evolution. Moreover, it questions the established network of visibility within the city and the hierarchical distribution of space, by visualizing a flow of data that come from an independent source, and not the authorities, advertisement companies or Internet 'giants' –the websites with the most traffic and impact.

The Artvertiser, 2008–2010, Julian Oliver. Software platform. Variable dimensions. Image courtesy of Julian Oliver. © Julian Oliver, 2008–2010.

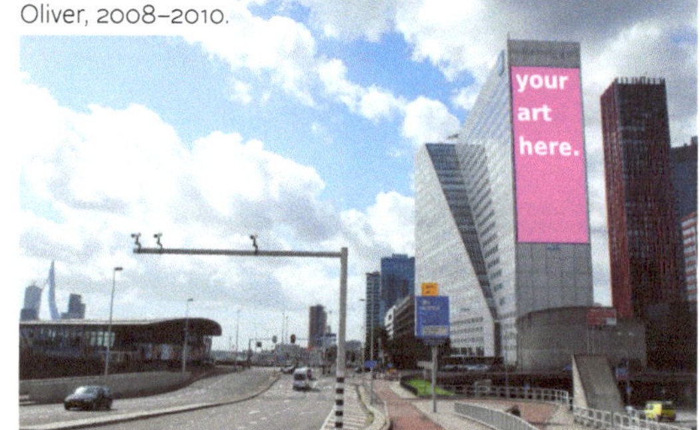

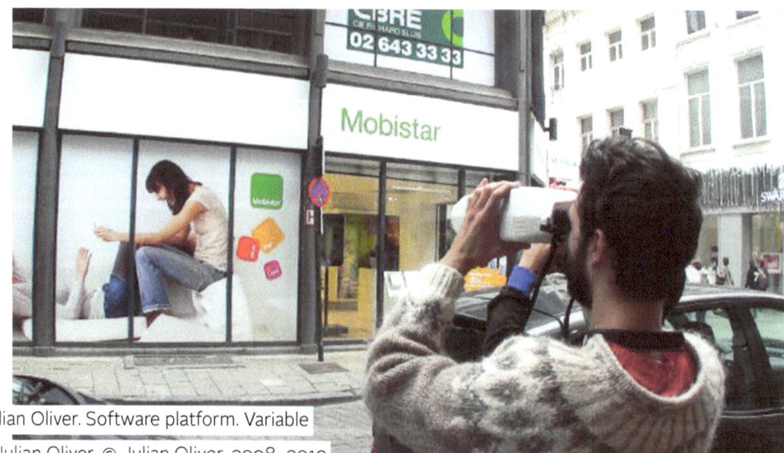

The Artvertiser, 2008–2010, Julian Oliver. Software platform. Variable dimensions. Image courtesy of Julian Oliver. © Julian Oliver, 2008–2010.

 ISSN 1071-4391 ISBN 978-1-906897-20-8

A similar 'hacker's' approach to urban space is adopted by artists who work with street art, invading the city and changing its predetermined appearance. Street art seizes the 'non-places' of the city –massive housing blocks, crumbling walls, decadent neighbourhoods, chain stores and highways- and de-anonymizes them, making the invisible visible again. Like hackers, these artists alter the established rules of the urban matrix and find 'detours' for changing it, by creating new nodes of meaning in space.

Even though, street art came before the expansion of information technologies, Internet gave it a significant boost: in fact, Street Art has been described as "the first truly post-Internet art movement, equally at home in real and digital spaces as an ongoing continuum." [27]

Street art is the first massive artistic movement that has flourished because of the Internet; its inherent ephemerality is counterbalanced by the extensive documentation of street art images online, through digital files that enable the preservation and growth of the movement. What is equally relevant here is the fact that the public has acted as a catalyst to the popularity and omnipresence of Street Art. As it is accessible to everyone, people take pictures and disseminate them through the web, making them visible to a large audience and thus motivating more artists to get involved in the movement.

This development illustrates how downloading and sharing information contributes to the creation of culture, as was mentioned above. It is "the work of art in the age of instant digital dissemination." [28]

There, numerous artists involved in street art that could be mentioned as examples of 'hacking' in the urban space; among them, Banksy is one of the most prolific ones. The artist takes ready images and messages from art history, popular culture, advertisements and incorporates them into a subversive work, filtered through a Duchampesque irony; it is a solid example of Bourriaud's postproduction theory of how images readily become the prime matter to create new artworks. [29]

Apart from his street art images, Banksy is often involved in guerrilla acts, raiding spaces in order to disrupt the flows of meaning and to create alterations within their system –just like a hacker.

In his *'attack' against Disneyland* (2006) [30] Banksy entered the entertainment park and installed an inflatable figure representing a Guantanamo prisoner. The artist manipulated the elements of a system with

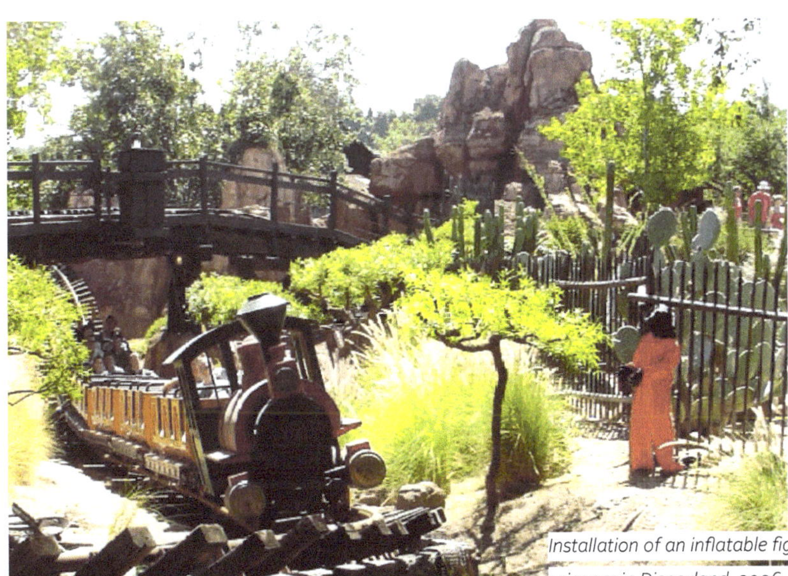

Installation of an inflatable figure representing a Guantanamo prisoner in Disneyland, 2006, Banksy. Video still from the video of the action on YouTube.

Peckham Rock (Early Man Goes To Market), 2005, Banksy. Concrete. 15 x 23 cm. Photograph by Alexander de Querzen. Image courtesy of Alexander de Querzen.

established values –in this case Disneyland- in order to awaken the visitors from their oblivious state and to make them face reality. Like the hacking of a website –where the content is taken down and replaced by a text of protest- or the 'leakage' of disclosed information, Banksy reminds the public of Disneyland of what is going on behind the colourful curtain of consumerism. At the same time, he compares an entertainment park to a detention camp, adding a very dark hue to mainstream culture. [31]

Although there is certain playfulness to Banksy's actions, a closer look into the images he installs reveals a profound criticism of contemporary culture. In *Peckham Rock* (*Early man goes to market,* 2005) he placed an artefact that resembled a prehistoric painting of a man with a shopping trolley onto the walls of the British museum, with a caption that credited the work to Banksymus Maximus and described is as art from the "post catatonic era." [32] The work blended so well with the rest of the exhibits in the room that it went unnoticed for a few days. Although the British Museum received the action with a sense of humour, adding the artwork to its permanent collection, Banksy's arbitrary presence is not always so welcome. Other 'attacks' against cultural institutions –installations of artworks that mix harmonically with the style of the collection and the exhibition space, but with a subversive element that introduces distraction in the flow of meaning- were perceived as disrespectful acts by the officials of the institutions.

The reception of Banksy's actions ultimately reveals the attempt to control culture, by limiting it to established cultural sites –a control that the 'cultural hackers' of the real or virtual space seek to override.

CONCLUSION

As solidity gives way to the immaterial world of code and the everyday life becomes more and more dependent on a constant flow of information, new dynamics have arisen in politics and culture. The role of Internet users becomes vital; as they download, share and alter files, new nodes of communication and meaning are created that often override existing laws regarding information exchange.

While the issue of free information becomes the starting point of diverse cultural and political movements, "the hacker emerges as the new leading figure of the intellectual," [33] a catalyst that allows technological and ideological developments to happen. Hacking, hacktivism and piracy, are fermenting a multitude of changes in the social tissue. Providing people with the tools to form groups, make their demands and trigger cultural and political evolutions, acting beyond the conventional networks of distribution of information. It is true that these 'tools" can often be used in a harmful way; however, our main focus here has been the cultural aspect of the phenomenon: how people are being encouraged to take initiative, get a better understanding of technology and participate in the creation of culture.

Without doubt, these acts can have a prominent political character, since the 'information age ideologies' that inspire them challenge the political and financial status quo. This is reflected in 'hack' art, particularly works that highlight the underlying conflicts and stimulate the people to take an active part in them, by learning, participating and making a contribution. Artists and viewers equally share the roles of consumers and producers of cultural objects that are based on the recycling and 'remixing' of already existent pictorial forms, subject to incessant change.

 ISSN 1071-4391 ISBN 978-1-906897-20-8

Hacker and pirate practices, like port scans, security breaches, downloading of copyrighted material, entering systems, dissemination of information, become the prime ways through which the artworks analysed here come into existence. These actions take place either in the virtual space, the urban matrix or an in-between state of augmented reality, where the two worlds intersect.

'Cultural hacking,' the tendency to remix existing cultural forms and to alter systems, introducing new elements that foment cultural and social evolution, is becoming a growing cultural and political practice. In a world where anyone can be a hacker, political and cultural change is only a matter of a few mouse-clicks. ■

ACKNOWLEDGEMENTS

This paper was written within the frame of my main doctoral research at the University of Barcelona, tutored by Professor Anna Casanovas. I would like to thank Julian Oliver, Miltos Manetas and Knowbotic Research for granting me with the permission to use their images and providing me with all the necessary information. I owe a very special thank you to Alexander de Querzen, for his valuable help throughout my research on hacking and information technologies.

REFERENCES AND NOTES

1. Wark McKenzie, *A Hacker Manifesto*, (Cambridge, MA: Harvard University Press, 2004), 2.
2. Christina Grammatikopoulou, "Stepping Towards the Immaterial: Digital Technology Revolutionizing Art," in *Transforming Culture in the Digital Age*, ed. Agnes Aljas, et.al., 367–372 (Tartu: Estonian National Museum, Estonian Literary Museum, University of Tartu, 2010).
3. Christina Grammatikopoulou, "Shades of the immaterial: Different Approaches to the 'Non-Object,'" in *Interartive* 40 (February 2012), http://interartive.org/index.php/2012/02/shades-of-the-immaterial (accessed April 10, 2012).
4. Jonas Andersson, "For the Good of the Net: The Pirate Bay as a Strategic Sovereign," *Culture Machine* 10 (2009): 72–73.
5. Stewart Brand, *The Media Lab: Inventing the Future at MIT*, (New York: Penguin Books, 1989), 202. The phrase is attributed to Stewart Brand. Although in the original phrase "free" meant costless, taken out of context, it came to represent the idea of liberty on the Internet.
6. Franz Liebl, Thomas Düllo and Martin Kiel, "Before and After Situationism – Before and After Cultural Studies: The Secret History of Cultural Hacking," in *Cultural Hacking, Kunst des Strategischen Handelns*, ed. Thomas Düllo and Franz Liebl, 13 (Wien: Springer, 2005).
7. Athina Karatzogianni, "WikiLeaks Affects: Ideology, Conflict and the Revolutionary Virtual," in *Digital Cultures and the Politics of Emotion: Feelings, Affect and Technological Change*, ed. Athina Karatzogianni and Dr. Adi Kuntsman, 59 (Basingstoke: Palgrave Macmillan, 2012).
8. Rasmus Fleischer and Palle Torsson, "The Grey Commons – Strategic Considerations in the Copyfight," lecture, 22C3 Conference, Berlin, December 2005, http://events.ccc.de/congress/2005/fahrplan/attachments/627-Thegreycommons.rtf (accessed April 10, 2012).
9. See "Old Technology Finds Role in Egyptian Protests," *BBC News*, January 31, 2011, http://www.bbc.com/news/technology-12322948, (accessed April 10, 2012) and Noam Cohen, "Web Attackers Find a Cause in Wikileaks," *New York Times*, December 9, 2010, http://www.nytimes.

com/2010/12/10/world/10wiki.html?pagewanted=all (accessed April 10, 2012).

10. Karatzogianni, "Wikileaks Affects," 60.
11. Michel De Certeau, *The Practice of Everyday Life*, (Berkeley and Los Angeles, CA: University of California Press, 2011), xxi.
12. Edward A. Shanken, "From Cybernetics to Telematics: The Art, Pedagogy and Theory of Roy Ascott," in Roy Ascott, *Telematic Embrace: Visionary Theories of Art, Technology and Consciousness* (Berkeley and Los Angeles: University of California Press, 2007), 65.
13. Roy Ascott, "Behaviourist Art and the Cybernetic Vision (1966–67)," in Roy Ascott, *Telematic Embrace: Visionary Theories of Art, Technology and Consciousness* (Berkeley and Los Angeles: University of California Press, 2007), 146.
14. Nicolas Bourriaud, *Postproduction: Culture As Screenplay: How Art Reprograms the World* (New York: Lukas & Sternberg, 2002), 35–37.
15. Wolfgang Ullrich, "Art and brands: Who learns from whom? Brands – competing with art," in *Art & Branding. Principles – Interaction – Perspectives*, eds. Hans-Jörg Heusser and Kornelia Imesch, 44–48 (Zürich: Schweizerisches Institut für Kunstwissenschaft, 2006).
16. Bourriaud, *Postproduction*, 17.
17. Ibid., 9.
18. Liebl, Düllo and Kiel, "Before and After Situationism," 28–30.
19. The work was presented in the New Museum of Contemporary Art of New York, in the exhibition 'Open Source Art Hack' (2002). "Minds of Concern: Breaking News," Website with information about the work, http://www.krcf.org/krcfhome/unitedhome/ny (accessed April 10, 2012)
20. Jan Aman, "In At The Deep End," *Dazed & Confused* 177, (September 2009), 112–115.
21. "Guardia di Finanza Raided Embassy of Piracy at Venice Biennale," *Embassy of Piracy*, August 6, 2009, http://embassyofpiracy.org/2009/06/guardia-di-finanza-raided-embassy-of-piracy-at-venice-biennale (accessed April 10, 2012).
22. Miltos Manetas, "Pirates of the Internet Unite!" *Interartive* 18 (February 2010) http://interartive.org/index.php/2010/02/piracy-manifesto (accessed April 10, 2012).
23. "The Transparency Grenade," the transparency grenade website, http://transparencygrenade.com (accessed April 10, 2012).
24. "The Transparency Grenade," *We Make Money Not Art*, February 15, 2012, http://www.we-make-money-not-art.com/archives/2012/02/the-transparency-grenade.php (accessed April 10, 2012).
25. "Project Glass," website of the project, https://plus.google.com/111626127367496192147/posts, (accessed April 10, 2012).
26. "The Artvertiser," theartvertiser website, http://theartvertiser.com, (accessed April 10, 2012).
27. Martin Irvine, "The Work on the Street: Street Art and Visual Culture," in *The Handbook of Visual Culture*, ed. Barry Sandywell and Ian Heywood, 235–278 (London and New York: Berg, 2012).
28. Ibid.
29. Bourriaud, *Postproduction*, 13–19.
30. "Banksy at Disneyland 2006," video of the action, http://www.youtube.com/watch?v=jkZoC6dwRqE, (accessed April 10, 2012).
31. Joseph Pugliese, "Apostrophe of Empire. Guantánamo Bay, Disneyland," *Borderlands* 8, no. 3 (2009), http://www.borderlands.net.au/vol8no3_2009/pugliese_apostrophe.pdf (accessed April 10, 2012).
32. Luke Dickens, "Placing post-graffiti: the journey of the *Peckham Rock*," in *Cultural Geographies* 15, no. 4 (2008): 471–496.
33. Claus Pias, "Der Hacker," in *Grenzverletzer: von Schmugglern, Spionen und anderen subversiven Gestalten*, eds. Eva Horn, Stefan Kaufmann and Ulrich Bröckling, 270, (Berlin: Kadmos, 2002).

 ISSN 1071-4391 ISBN 978-1-906897-20-8

ConnectiCity, augmented perception of the city

by

SALVATORE IACONESI & ORIANA PERSICO

Salvatore Iaconesi
La Sapienza University of Rome
ISIA Design Florence
Rome University of Fine Arts
IED Rome
salvatore.iaconesi@artisopensource.net

Oriana Persico
La Sapienza University of Rome
oriana.persico@gmail.com

1. INTRODUCTION

We constantly re-program the spaces around us. [1]

As pointed out by Edward Krupat and William Guild, [2] Jack L. Nasar [3] and Susan L. Scheiberg [4] the ways in which we reinterpret and personalize spaces effectively convey important information about our emotional states, working methodologies, knowledge, skills, cultural backgrounds, desires and our visions. It is a pragmatic manifestation of the ways in which we perceive our living environments, a constructivist act of world-making: "In the course of time every section and quarter of the city takes on something of the character and qualities of its inhabitants. Each separate part of the city is inevitably stained with the peculiar sentiments of its population." [5]

On the other side, the forms and essence of urban space directly affect people's behavior, describing what is possible or impossible, allowed or prohibited, suggested or advised against. [6]

Our experience of the contemporary world is characterized by the presence of a ubiquitous digital membrane, [7] [8] represented and accessed by technologies and networks whose wide availability and accessibility allows us to fill space/time with digital information and allow opportunities for interaction, interrelation and communication. [9 – 11]

These observations allowed us to embrace a research process to investigate the ways in which ubiquitous technologies and networks alter our sense of place,

 ISSN 1071-4391 ISBN 978-1-906897-20-8

We constantly re-interpret and transform the spaces around us.

The ways in which we constantly personalize the spaces which we traverse and in which we perform our daily routines communicate information about emotions, knowledge, skills, methodologies, cultures and desires.

This process takes place in digital realms as well, which start to ubiquitously merge with cities.

Mobile devices, smartphones, wearables, digital tags, near field communication devices, location based services and mixed/augmented reality have turned the world into an essentially read/write, ubiquitous publishing surface.

The usage of mobile devices and ubiquitous technologies alters the understanding of place.

In our research, we investigated the possibilities to conceptualize, design and implement a series of usage scenarios, moving fluidly across arts, sciences and the practices of city governance and community design.

The objective we set forth sees the creation of multiple, stratified narratives onto the city, set in place by citizens, organizations and administrations. These real-time stories and conversations can be captured and observed, to gain insights on fundamental issues such as ecology, sustainability, mobility, energy, politics, culture, creativity and participatory innovation processes.

These methodologies for real-time observation of cities help us take part in a networked structure, shaped as a diffused expert system, capturing disseminated intelligence to coagulate it into a framework for the real-time processing of urban information.

transform our perception of reality and enable us to plan and act in novel ways.

A set of objectives has been set forth in the process:

» to gain a better understanding of human presence in contemporary urban spaces;
» to understand the ways in which it is possible to understand and visualize the way people re-program and re-interpret the spaces around them using digital tools;
» to observe in real-time the digital discussions which take place in cities, to both transform them into a component of the ubiquitous information landscape of urban spaces and to understand the emotional approaches, themes and issues which emerge from human perception of the city. Con-

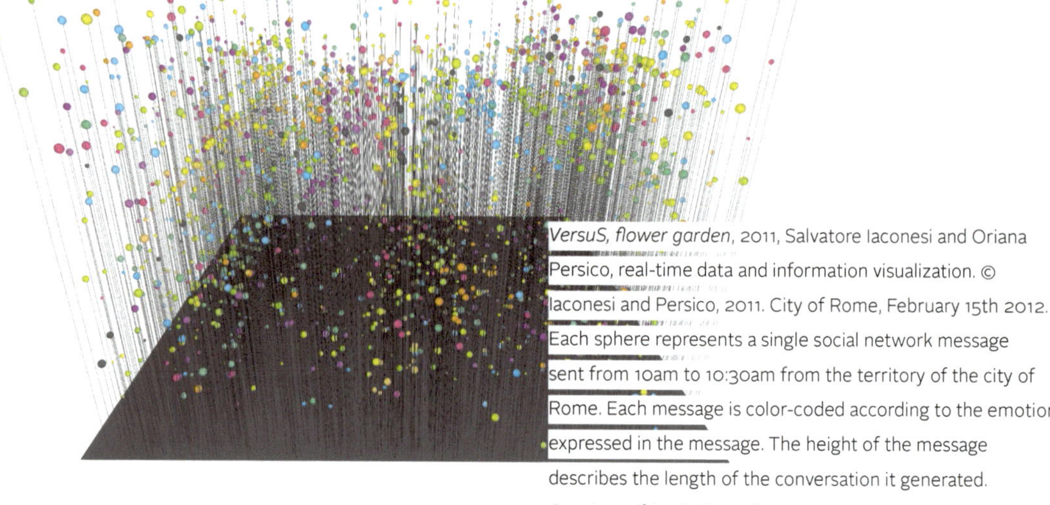

VersuS, flower garden, 2011, Salvatore Iaconesi and Oriana Persico, real-time data and information visualization. © Iaconesi and Persico, 2011. City of Rome, February 15th 2012. Each sphere represents a single social network message sent from 10am to 10:30am from the territory of the city of Rome. Each message is color-coded according to the emotion expressed in the message. The height of the message describes the length of the conversation it generated. Courtesy of Art is Open Source.

stantly generating insights on issues related to ecology, mobility, land use, wellness, need for services and infrastructures, sense of place, definition of emergent boundaries and attention groups;

» to propose novel forms of mixed-media urban interstices in which multiple cultures, languages, religions and political orientations can meet and interact;

» create methodologies, for all actors involved, to transform these possibilities into tools for awareness and consciousness about the expression of needs and emotions of people, for ethical, sustainable, participatory policies, plans, businesses, initiatives and processes;

» promote choral initiatives, engaging citizens, organizations and institutions.

2. TRANSFORMING THE SENSE OF PLACE

Portable devices transform our experience of space/time.

For example, the Sony Walkman powerfully introduced the possibility of being able to be in two places at once [12] through the personalized sounds playing through our headphones, creating a powerful conjunction between physical space and the imaginary space created by the music.

Devices such as the Sony Walkman allow us to traverse urban spaces – with their cognitive, aesthetic and moral significance – and to benefit from the use of a critical tool in the management of our space and time, in the construction of boundaries around ourselves, as well as in the creation of sites of fantasy and memory. [13]

Mobile devices, smartphones, wearables, digital tags, location based services and mixed/augmented reality have gone much further in this direction, turning the world into an essentially read/write, ubiquitous publishing surface [14] and altering our understanding of the spaces around us. [15]

As David Morley describes: "The mobile phone is often understood (and promoted) as a device for connecting us to those who are far away, thus overcoming distance – and perhaps geography itself." [16]

In this analysis, the possibility to compress space and time enables novel opportunities to interconnect and relate to objects, processes, places and people, but also fills "the space of the public sphere with the chatter of the earth, allowing us to take our homes with us, just as a tortoise stays in its shell wherever it travels." This modality describes a direct, personalized intervention into the design of space, in both its form and function, creating a definite shift in the definition of (urban) landscape: from a purely administrative one,

 ISSN 1071-4391 ISBN 978-1-906897-20-8

VersuS, speaking circle, 2011, Salvatore Iaconesi and Oriana Persico, real-time data and information visualization. © Iaconesi and Persico, 2011. City of Rome, February 15th 2012. Each dot around the circle represents a social network user residing in the city of Rome. 1000 users are shown with their mutual interactions from 2pm to 6pm. The 1000 users are chosen from all users in Rome in order to define a "community": a group of people who intensively exchange information. Courtesy of Art is Open Source.

to one which is multiplied according to all the individuals which experience that specific location.

However both modalities potentially allow us to imagine and design stratified spaces in which multiple points of view find their expression, much in the same ways in which Gilles Clément, [17] John Paul Eberhard [18] and Almo Farina [19] describe our landscapes from entirely different perspectives: space/time as a continuous, emergent, fluid, recombinant stratification of analog/digital information/communication/interaction.

The possibility to access these multiplied definitions of space alter our own perception of it, opening it to cultures, backgrounds and symbolical apparatuses which have the potential to be entirely different from our own, using devices which we hold in our pockets.

Derrick De Kerckhove [20] suggested that the augmentation of architecture, should include the concepts which originally underpinned the inception of the World Wide Web. Alowing us to expand our possibilities for awareness and consciousness through the wide and ubiquitous availability of multiple sources of information, which are hyperlinked to the physical elements of our reality.

Operating in this direction, it is possible to imagine and design forms of disseminated intelligence which can be coagulated in multiple ways by actors traversing cities and using mobile devices to enact novel

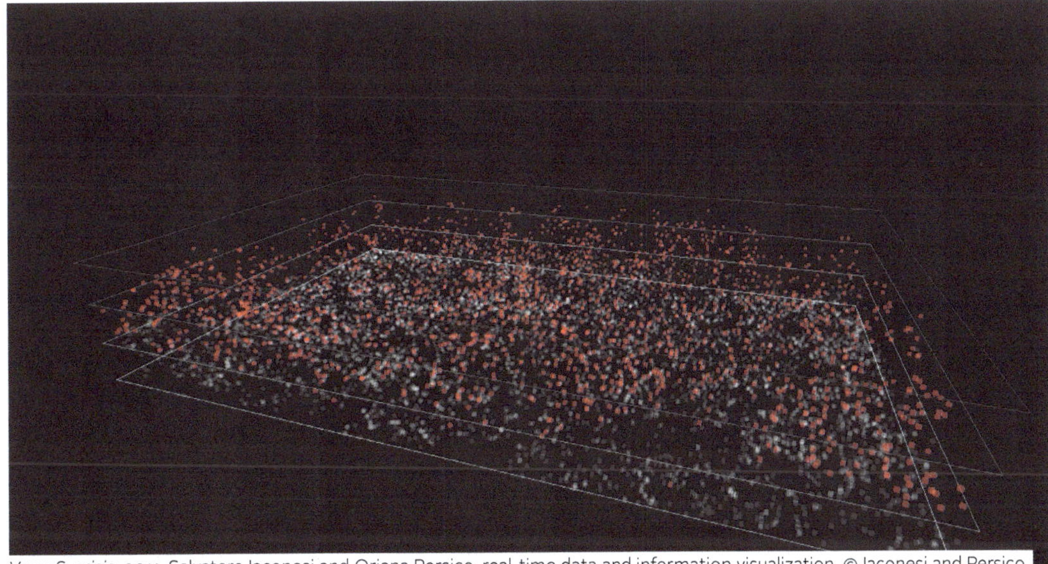

VersuS, crisis, 2011, Salvatore Iaconesi and Oriana Persico, real-time data and information visualization. © Iaconesi and Persico, 2011. City of Rome, during a research in winter 2011. The image represents a screen capture of a visualization of the messages of citizens of the city of Rome using social networks to discuss the financial crisis in Italy. Red colored dots represent expressions of particular verbal violence. Courtesy of Art is Open Source.

forms of reading/writing of spaces, symbols and configurations, moving fluidly across digital and physical domains.

Nicola Green [21] investigated a similar approach, highlighting the role of mobile devices as spatial/temporal mediators, exposing alternative perceptions and behaviors in human beings and, thus, proposing different usage grammars for spaces and timeframes.
This result can be combined with the ones produced by Marsha Berry and Margaret Hamilton while observing the usage of mobile devices on trains: "public places and spaces are being transformed into hybrid geographies through the introduction of new spatial infrastructure."

CONNECTICITY, METHODOLOGY

ConnectiCity is an arts/science meta-project which investigates the possibilities offered by the progressive availability of real-time, ubiquitous, digital layers of information. It is able to design and implement a series of prototypes which would pursue the following goals:

- to create a set of experiences allowing
  - to capture in real-time various forms of city-relevant user generated content from a variety of sources, including social networks, websites, mobile applications,
  - to interrelate information to the territory [7] [8] [23] using Geo-referencing, Geo-Parsing and Geo-Coding techniques; [24 – 27]
  - to analyze and classify information using Natural Language Processing and Named Entity Recognition techniques to identify users' emotional approaches, forms of expression, topics of interest, discussion graphs, networks of attention and of influence, trending issues, evaluations of satisfaction, well-being and happiness, and other forms of expression (using techniques designed by taking into account the many researches of this kind which have been performed over these last few years, including fundamental contributions which have been adopted from; [28 – 30]
- to imagine initiatives through which this information allows central administration and individuals to come together, under the form of a peer to peer ecosystem in which each subject is an informed, aware agent, thus describing novel forms of governance and decision-making processes; [31 – 33]
- to reflect on the life and expressions of cities and of their inhabitants, to identify new policies, new sustainable, ethical business models, urban planning processes, grass-roots initiatives and operative models;
- to use the insights provided by models such as the living labs and other user-centric innovation processes [34 – 40] in the creation of novel practices for citizens, organizations and administrations;
- to reflect on the themes of cognitive accessibility for this kind of information, analyzing visual and multi-modal representation and interaction metaphors that would allow to maximize the effectiveness, ease of use and understanding of these complex information scenarios; [41 – 44]
- to confront with validation models that would allow to assess the quality, relevancy and reliability of harvested data, affected by information noise, digital-divide related issues (e.g.: not all citizens use social networks or imagine that they can use them to express opinions about their city)interpretation errors;
- to imagine and implement strategies for open access of information and services, to reconfigure them as novel forms of freely usable spatial infrastructure;
- to reflect on the new models for identity, privacy, ethics and on the new possible emerging definitions of public and private space.

RESULTS

The ConnectiCity project is an on-going process started in 2008. Since then a continuous refinement of the methodologies and technologies has allowed the

 ISSN 1071-4391 ISBN 978-1-906897-20-8

creation of several prototypes which implement the concepts conceived in the investigation phase.

Rel:attiva presenza

The first prototype was designed in Mexico City at the Franz Mayer Museum, and it was titled "rel:attiva presenza." The occasion for this project was the presentation of the paper "architettura rel:attiva" at the Seventh International Meeting on the Revitalization of the Historical Centers, focused on the idea of architecture as mediator of the historical and contemporary city.

"Rel:attiva presenza" was designed as a video projection mapping and of a sound environment in the cloister of the Italian Cultural Institute in Mexico City, in the Coyoacan neighborhood. The video projection was created by assembling video footage and images from different epochs, describing the mutation of the neighborhood across the years, starting from the beginning of the century. The images and footage were assembled together with geographical representations of the evolution of the territory and of the land use in the neighborhood. The resulting visual narrative constituted a sort of conceptual time-lapse video, in which the life of the neighborhood was shown in its evolution. The sound environment was assembled by manually harvesting field-recordings in the neighborhoods streets and markets, collecting dialogues, typical noises, sounds of transit, mobility, transport, commerce, chit-chat, voices in bars and restaurants.

The installation was proposed as a novel way to stratify the neighborhood's history into an accessible, narrative form. By looking at and listening to "rel:attiva presenza," the history of the place could be experienced along multiple points of view, in its evolution towards its present condition. Images and sounds were completely "user-generated," as they had been produced by long-time inhabitants of the place, just as the voices and sounds collected using the location's daily life.

The process designed and produced for "Rel:Attiva Presenza" can be thought of as a practice of archival of the perceptions, experiences and narratives of the people who live in the territory, and as a research into their accessibility. The prototype was exhibited under the form of an architectural intervention in the Coyoacan neighborhood, transforming surfaces into screens which acted as an accessibility layer for the history and emotions of the inhabitants.

The results of this first experience deeply inspired the following ones.

The Atlas of Rome

The following prototype created for the ConnectiCity project was, in more than one way, a direct extension of the first one.

A 35 meter long architectural projection and sound environment was created for Rome's "Festa dell'Architettura" (Architecture Fair), organized by the City Administration together with the Italian Order of the Architects in the enormous entrance corridor of the ex-Mattatoio (ex Slaughterhouse) in the Testaccio neighborhood of the city.

The Atlas of Rome's purpose was to portray in real-time the evolution of the visions, desires and actions created by architects, institutions, operators and citizens onto the city of Rome on a series of fundamental themes such as culture, creativity, education, urban planning, commerce, arts, security and health, classified in 16 information domains to describe the overall wellness of the city.

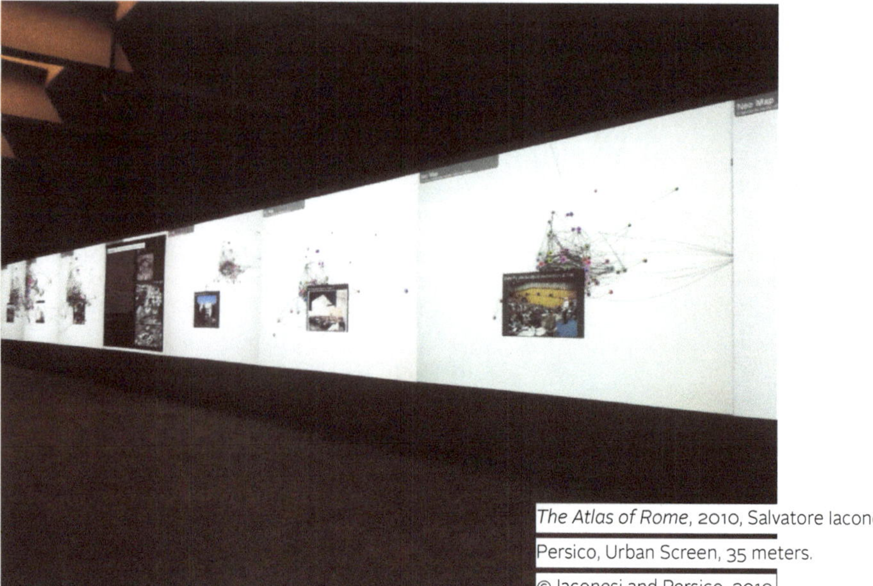

The Atlas of Rome, 2010, Salvatore Iaconesi and Oriana Persico, Urban Screen, 35 meters. © Iaconesi and Persico, 2010.

A complex activity was set-up in the organization of the project:

- » an information harvesting scheme was created to capture real-time information from a variety of sources:
  - » institutional and professional information sources such as blogs, websites, news feeds about the city of Rome and relevant to the chosen themes
  - » relevant user accounts which were identified on social networks, among those citizens, professional operators, members of the institutions, museums, art galleries, spaces for creativity and entertainment, social aggregation points, active communities and to continuously benefit from relevant updates on the chosen themes;
- » harvesting took place using a selection of techniques, involving both automatic processes (RSS feed parsing, micro-formats, public API usage, authorized web-scraping, database connections, import of structured data in a variety of formats) and manual ones (such as in the case of those organizations which sent us press releases to be added into the system);
- » information was parsed using Natural Language Analysis, [45] [46] to classify information according to the selected topics;
- » information was then geo-referenced either by using the coordinates provided by the information source (for example when the information source directly corresponds to a specific place, such as in the case of museums) or extracted, whenever possible, by Geo-Parsing schemes, which was performed by using a large database of Named Entities with a geographical connotation, including the names of streets, malls, cinemas, museums, landmarks, neighborhoods, common alternative names of places, pubs, bars, shops, stores, gyms, and other dozens of types of locations for which names could be identified in the text of the harvested content (a multi-modal text-matching engine compared the strings in multiple ways for similarity and for the textual context in which the identified words were found, to be able to filter out most false-positive results, and obtaining a correctness of about 97%);
- » a series of direct input channels were created to accept content (text, images and videos) from citizens using mobile devices and a series of multi-touch kiosks which were set-up in various areas of the city.

Collected information was shown on the 35 meter wide surface using a processing application. A series of different information visualizations were designed to convey information according to different metaphors. Somewhere dedicated to aggregating information according to themes, time-frames and the types of activities.

 ISSN 1071-4391 ISBN 978-1-906897-20-8

A peculiar geographical visualization captured most of the attention of the visitors. Here, color-coded circles represented localized elements of information. A map was not shown under the circles, but their relative geographical positions were correctly calculated. Points were connected by similarity: two points on the visualization were connected if they were relevant to the same themes.

A map formed, composed, not through natural or administrative boundaries, but through the emotions and ideas of citizens. It was constructed continuously through the activities which take place in real-time in the city of Rome.

This kind of emergent geography has proven to be extremely effective when used as a lens, as a new perception of the city in which it is the behavior of people – individually or through their organizations – to describe forms, aggregations, coherences and inconsistencies. The analysis of this representation has been of fundamental value in gathering the insights which were used to create the following prototypes of the *ConnectiCity* project.

Visitors could use their mobile devices and a series of multitouch surfaces to interact with the part of the projection that they had in front of them. The position of the multitouch terminal, the geographical coordinates identified by the smartphone application and a customized wireless network setup allowed the system to understand which part of the projection to activate, eventually alerting the user that the area was currently being used by another visitor, suggesting to moving slightly to the left or right to obtain a free projection area.

Individuals could navigate detailed versions of the content by touching interface elements, choosing the bits of information they wished to experience. Large pop up viewports contextually appeared in front of them onto the architectural projection, showing texts, videos, images and interactive experiences.

This immediate responsiveness of such a large scale projection proved to produce radically positive effects on visitors. The fact that a large-scale architectural surface was actually responding in real-time to their interactions, powerfully combined with the tangible effect of having the possibility to publish one's own information onto the projection. The combined effect of being able to both contribute and interact had a distinct empowering effect on people, who spontaneously started to discuss possible uses for this kind of system in areas such as participatory urban planning, policy making and decision-making at the city level.

ConnectiCity Neighborhood Edition

The system created for the *Atlas of Rome* was also implemented in a smaller scale, dedicated to provide novel scenarios for the life of neighborhoods.

An Urban Screen was designed to capture in real-time the social network conversations which could be identified as originating from within the territory of the neighborhood. For this purpose, the Twitter, Flickr and FourSquare social networks were used, thanks to the accessibility of their geographical features.

Harvested information was processed using the same, yet evolved, strategies described for the Atlas, and were shown on the Urban Screen using a simple, minimal interface in which large, black dots represented single contributions, appearing onto the screen and connected to the edges of the screen. Here, textual representations of the content were presented. Also, two or more dots were visualized as connected when they represented messages dealing with the same topic or if they represented direct interactions (e.g.: re-tweets and comments).

The immediateness of the interface, allowing passers-by to read the content and to immediately understand its context by analyzing connections, proved to be truly effective in stimulating novel forms of social and territorial interaction. People actually stopped to read the ongoing conversations, trying to identify the people behind the social network nicknames. Many times identification happened, producing enthusiastic results and creating in people the immediate awareness about the possibility to contribute to the information landscape of their neighborhood. Some people eventually pulled out their smartphones and immediately started answering tweets and comments, to verify if they would actually show up in the interface.

Discussion did benefit from different levels of attention, ranging from topics related to sports and entertainment, but also engaging current news items and focal issues for the neighborhood's territory.

Most people had no problem in identifying the possibility to use such systems in terms of activating participatory processes which could create value for their neighborhood. Scenarios for self organization and coordination were imagined by most people, which imagined using the urban screen as a sort of public billboard in which to perform numerous types of coordinated actions among the residents. Some people also identified more complex usage scenarios, in which multiple types of urban screen could be imagined for different purposes, such as citizen awareness, coordination and activation, general chit-chat, practical information, requests for help and also various types of "time-bank," in which neighborhood inhabitants could exchange services among themselves.

VersuS, Rome October 15th

The possibility to harvest information in real-time from cities using user generated content on social networks were used on occasion of the first instantiation of the *VersuS* project.

The first prototype was created in occasion of the protest which took place in the city of Rome on October 15th 2011.

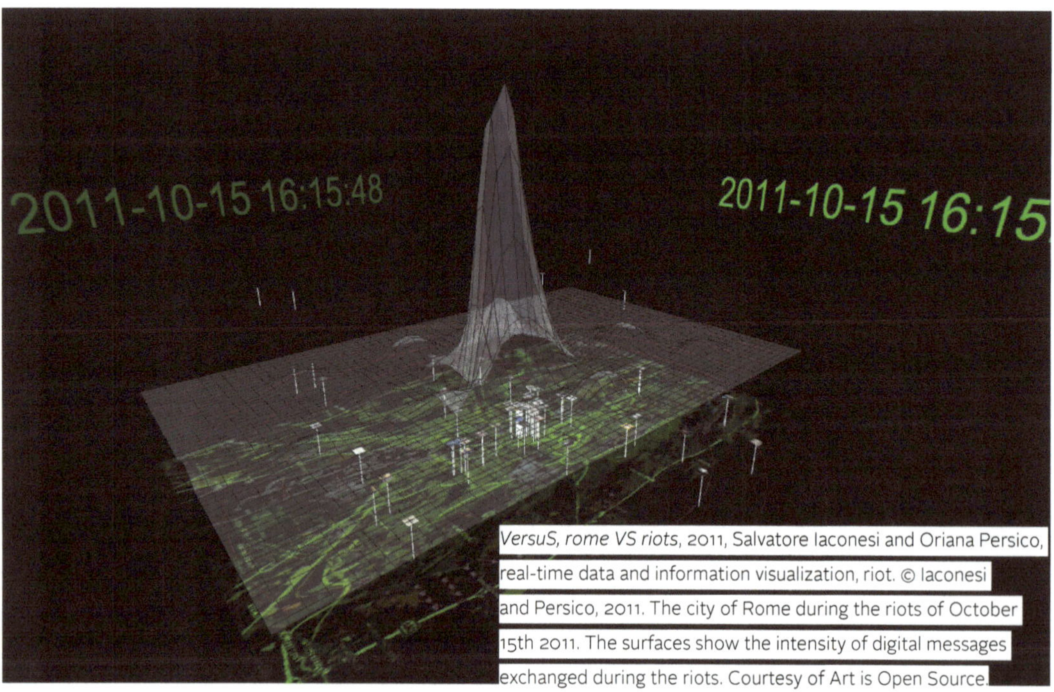

VersuS, rome VS riots, 2011, Salvatore Iaconesi and Oriana Persico, real-time data and information visualization, riot. © Iaconesi and Persico, 2011. The city of Rome during the riots of October 15th 2011. The surfaces show the intensity of digital messages exchanged during the riots. Courtesy of Art is Open Source.

 ISSN 1071-4391 ISBN 978-1-906897-20-8

The protest took place in the city under the form of a march authorized by the City Administration, as one of the events which were created internationally in occasion of the October 15th event organized worldwide by the "Occupy" movement.

In the city of Rome, the peaceful protest quickly degenerated into violence, with multiple groups of activists engaging fights with police forces which devastated large parts of the city centre, causing injuries and damage.

The harvesting component of the *VersuS* system was created to collect as many social network conversations as possible which were taking place during the protest in the city of Rome. Focus was placed on Facebook, Twitter and Flickr social networks, and a limited set of resources were also dedicated to Foursquare and Google+.

Different social networks were observed using different techniques. For example, Twitter streams were easily captured by using the publicly available API (Application Programming Interface), as was the case of Flickr, in which public APIs allow to capture activity taking place in a specified geographical bounding box. A different technique was used to engage activity generated on Facebook: a preliminary analysis performed using the search facilities provided by the Open Graph protocol and Facebook's implementation (titled Graph API) allowed researchers to identify more than 60,000 user profiles among the ones whose public "home location" (the place which users specify as being the one they live in) was described as being "Rome" or one of the hundreds of smaller cities within 80km distance of the city centre, which were merged to the about 80,000 profiles which explicitly mentioned the protest in Rome during the two days before October 15th. The list of 'friends' of these users was collected as well. Duplicates were removed from the overall list, arriving to a total of more than 160,000 users which were considered to be relevant to the required observation.

All identified sources of information were provided with a procedure to capture their online activities for the whole duration of the protest. This required a fairly high amount of processing and network resources, with 3 multi-core servers and a 20Mbit connectivity completely dedicated to the capture process during the day, from 2pm until 11pm.

The Natural Language Analysis and GeoParsing/Geo-Referencing procedures – described above – were applied to identify content which was relevant to the protest. This step has been performed according to a number of different approaches:

» messages whose geographical origin was located along the areas touched by the protest, at relevant times
» messages explicitly naming places touched by the protest, at relevant times
» messages discussing the protest in one of several possible forms (e.g.: mentioning the protest, its participants, its themes, its path, and more)

This analysis, using a series of different threshold levels to define the level of acceptable quality of the inferred relevancy, which was never placed below 95% for all modalities, allowed to select more than 92,000 information elements during the time-frame of the protest. Some of these revealed to be of little or no interest to the analysis (around 30,000) and were filtered in the following steps of the process.

A series of visualizations were designed to investigate on the results.

A first visualization was designed to show the intensity of communication over time in the various areas of the city.

A geo-referenced parametric surface was configured to receive the number of posts in each area of the city as values determining the surface's heights in the matrix of control points. The effect was to create an immediate readability of the locations in which online activity was stronger during the time of the protest. By superimposing the visualization with the path followed by the protest, it was important to understand how the online activity closely followed the protest itself: the march took place both in the physical space and in the digital one.

This form of quantitative, geo-referenced analysis produced evidence of the following two phenomena:

» a high number of people who were physically present at the protest produced digital content and published it on social networks, allowing to observe the impressions, emotions and information as communicated directly from relevant locations at a high level of detail;
» a high number of people who were not physically present at the protest discussed it online, allowing for observation of the general experience of the event.

Then further analysis was performed on the qualitative level, to observe the types of information which could be extracted from the captured streams. This kind of observation was performed using the results of the Natural Language Analysis phase, thus benefiting from the availability of a classification of all information elements according to a classification of emotions and of topics.

The richness of the captured data suggested the possibility to envision, design and implement a series of applicative scenarios.

Given the specific focus on emergent crisis situations in urban contexts, such as those which potentially can take place during protests and revolts, mobile applications and the supporting technological frameworks were designed for the following scenarios/actors:

» a real-time geographical application for public police and security personnel;
» a real-time geographical and augmented reality application for protesters;
» a real-time geographical application for a fictional type company whose business model is based on the offering of services for these kinds of emergency scenarios.

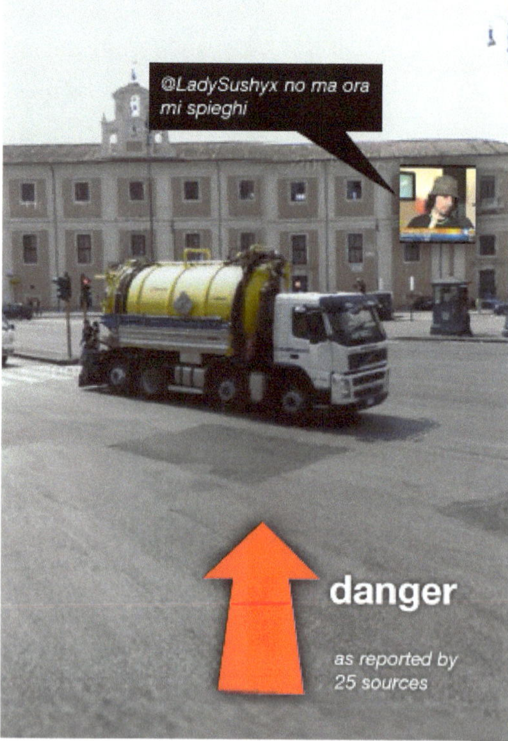

VersuS, augmented reality for protesters, 2012, Salvatore Iaconesi and Oriana Persico, real-time data and information visualization. © Iaconesi and Persico, 2012.
VersuS, the Augmented Reality Interface of the application for protesters. The arrow changes color while turning around: red shows potentially dangerous directions, as inferred by messages harvested in real-time from social networks.

 ISSN 1071-4391 ISBN 978-1-906897-20-8

Each application has been thought out according to a dedicated perspective:

- the application for the police forces
  - identification of a series of linguistic templates which would indicate the emergence of specific scenarios which represent dangerous situations or, more in general, situations in which a direct police intervention is required (e.g.: "they're breaking the windshields of the cars" would be among the possible sentences which this part of the system would need to react to and, thus, constructs such as "? breaking ? cars ?" would be a typical part of the linguistic template dictionary used in the platform);
  - identification of rising trends, which might indicate emergent situations which could benefit from the attention of the police forces (e.g.: a sudden rise of messages like "the protest is turning left onto xxx street" would definitely need some attention by police officers, who might decide to intervene in regulating the mutated use of public space);
- the application for the protesters
  - a map and an augmented reality display allow the user to see in real-time what is being communicated in the various directions around the current geographical position;
  - several prepared configurations allow the user to see in immediately accessible and understandable ways the spatial distribution of information around own position (e.g.: the colors red and green are used to draw a circle in AR around the user to inform about the presence, in that direction, of messages describing possible situations of danger, such as riot, police charge, injured people; this information would, for example, suggest the user to choose to walk in "green" directions, and to avoid moving towards "red" ones);
  - the user can configure a list of social network users: visual displays constantly show the configured people's positions, thus allowing the user to be constantly aware of their position, thus avoiding getting lost or separated from them, or to establish highly accessible means of spatial communication in emergency scenarios);
- the application for the fictional company
  - a web framework allows the fictional company to setup a curation environment in which to aggregate content harvested in real-time among geo-referenced information published by users on social networks;
  - the framework offers easy tools to observe in real-time the content produced on social networks about a series of strategic themes (paths of protesters in city space, alerting of exceptional events, signals of violence or other dangerous activities;
  - the framework also highlights emerging topics among the real-time expressions of social network users, whose growth in intensity and frequency signals them as interesting-to-observe and, thus, allows to add them among the topics under observation on the city map;
  - the fictional company's personnel (or software systems) can use these aggregated informations to dynamically create visualizations in which one or more themes are shown; each grouped representation of this kind (set of layers of manually or automatically curated information) forms a "product" which the company "sells" to various actors, thus realizing their business model;
  - to access the offered products/services, users download a smartphone application; when they do, they can choose among the themes aggregated by the fictional company, for example wishing to be alerted of the overall activity relevant to the protest; from that moment the high-quality aggregated information, using aug-

mented reality, will be shown on the screen all around them and on a map;

» users can also choose to form a group among other users of the application and include users from supported social networks; in this way they will also see the icons of these users highlighted onto the map and in AR, allowing to know their relative position in real-time and to instantly exchange information.

Post-event simulations of these three platforms, using the data gathered during the riots as time-based feeds of information, produced remarkable results.

About 30,000 elements of information (such as messages, sequences of locations, patterns in conversations) were found to be relevant in identifying violence, law infringements, abnormal gatherings and injuries.

Twelve user profiles chosen among the most active during the riots were chosen to test in a similar way the app designed for the protesters. Scenarios were enacted describing the personas of peaceful and also violent protesters. Around 2000 information elements have been found as being significant in supporting them in identifying the positions of the most violent happenings, and to constantly be able to keep in touch with friends that were active on social networks during that timeframe. As for the scenario of violent protesters, around 12,000 information elements have been found to be of significant strategic value in understanding police movements and strategies, and to support in organizing collective action. The tool proved to be effective in gaining a substantial strategic edge; companion-related position information allowed this profile to benefit from a practical tool and to keep active groups spatially aggregated, and to also immediately visualize the position and direction of movement of the other protesters.

The application dedicated to the fictional company offering protest-based services was found to be effective in providing hundreds of information packages describing dangerous situations, curiosities (a selection of the most interesting things taking place during the protest, expression of creativity and innovation), joyful events (such as improvised concerts, clown/busker shows and other similar events) and spatial messaging features.

VersuS, planet edition

An enhancement and generalization of the VersuS platform has been recently tested in a prototype which allows to observe several cities at once.
The platform was presented and tested during an italian national radio broadcast using the narrative of a musical journey touching 6 urban contexts (Milan, Berlin, London, Bristol, New York and Philadelphia), with the DJ playing music by artists in the different cities while a web interface allowed listeners to view the real-time information visualizations of those cities. For the event, an emotional approach was used, classifying user generated content by emotions organized around the scheme proposed by Robert Plutchik, in his book *Emotion, a psychoevolutionary synthesis.* [47]

The experiment was closely monitored using a mixture of techniques involving the use of web analytics and direct engagement with listeners through social networks and questions posed during the radio show. Response has been particularly strong on this occasion. Listeners actively used the platform, constantly inferring meaning and explanations for both the emotional configurations expressed in cites and for the specific messages that, while captured, were being shown on the interfaces.

Listeners autonomously suggested multiple usage scenarios for the platform, also referring to hypothetical scenarios in which these kinds of systems could

 ISSN 1071-4391 ISBN 978-1-906897-20-8

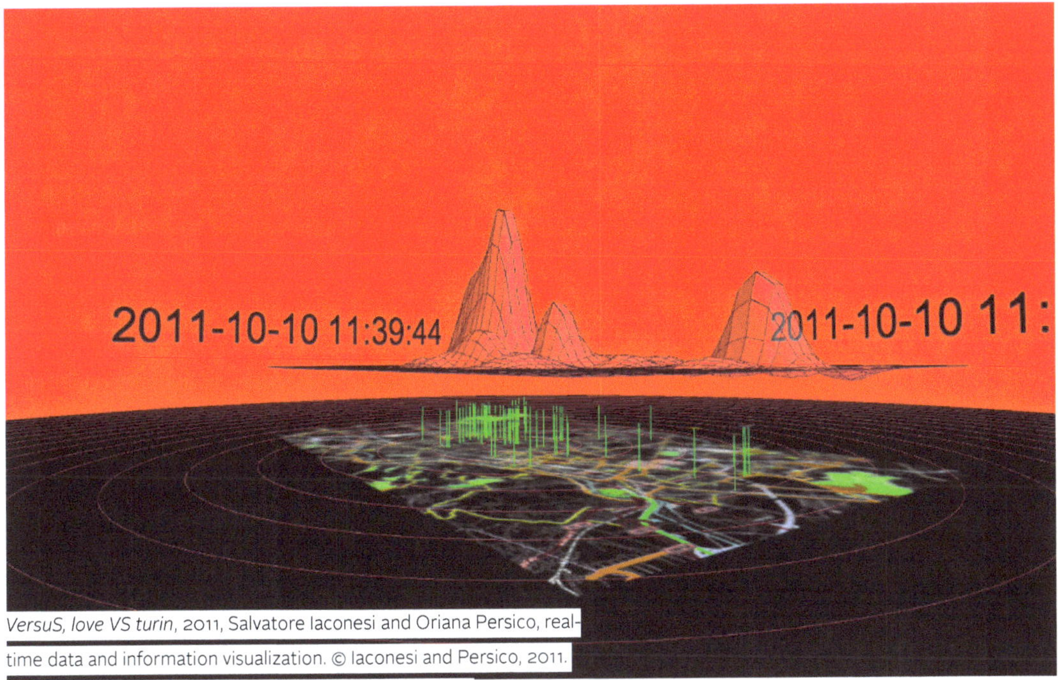

VersuS, love VS turin, 2011, Salvatore Iaconesi and Oriana Persico, real-time data and information visualization. © Iaconesi and Persico, 2011. VersuS, love VS turin, a moment in the emotions of Turin.

be used to create participatory governance practices for entire cities. Usage scenarios dedicated to novel entertainment products and services were also often hypothesized, with users declaring their welcoming approach to these kinds of systems being available on their smartphones.

CONCLUSIONS

The possibility to listen to the ideas, visions, emotions and proposals which are expressed each day by citizens – either explicitly or implicitly by the ways in which they use their cities, workplaces, malls... – suggests the emergence of positive scenarios.

Harvesting systems allow us to continuously sense the public discussion and to correlate it to cities, transport systems, infrastructures, architectural spaces, neighborhoods.

"Sensibility Networks" can be established using natural language analysis processes allowing us to 'read' cities, for how they are 'written' by people, traversing languages and cultures.

Sensor networks can be included in the scenario to record in real-time information about pollution, traffic and the other measurements which shape the ecological, social, administrative and political lives of our cities.

It is possible to create multiple layers of narratives which traverse the city and which allow us to read them in different ways, according to different strategies and tactics, and enabling us to highlight how cities (through their citizens or even on their own, expressing through sensors) express points of view on the environment, culture, economy, transports, energy and politics.

The ubiquitous accessibility of the information about how multiple agencies re-interpret space reveals novel uses for it, thus defining a new *structure* for public space.

The experience of space/time in urban contexts comes out deeply modified, as we progressively mutate our interpretation of presence, space and relation, adding the wide array of usage grammars for space and time to our vocabularies of tools which we use to navigate everything, from maps, to spaces to written text.

Digital information starts contributing to the affordances of the objects, buildings and other things we find in the space around ourselves, as we progressively, pragmatically and *naturally* adopt the idea of having the availability of additional sensorialities which are externalized onto devices and which shape our experience of the world, just as our eyes, ears, fingers...

A mobile phone call can transform a park bench into a temporary, ubiquitous office. A social mapping service can alter our perception of space. An augmented reality system can make visible information on pollution, mobility, energy of the place we are in. A wearable technology can create a new sense connected to remote objects, events, quantities. A real-time digital conversation analysis system can interconnect thoughts, visions, desires and emotions of people and organizations, materializing them onto a novel form of digital space in which identity, privacy and ethics must be redefined.

A mobile phone call can transform a park bench into a temporary, ubiquitous office. A social mapping service can alter our perception of space.

These methodologies for real-time observation of cities can be described as a form of "ubiquitous anthropology," based on the idea that we can take part in a networked structure shaped as a diffused expert system, capturing disseminated intelligence to coagulate it into a framework for the real-time processing of urban information.

In this context infoaesthetic representations become enablers to enact radical strategies to maximize the accessibility and usability of this information.

Together, all these elements describe something which we might refer to as "ubiquitous user generated search engine," through which citizens become preferential channels for the production of relevant information about themes which are fundamental for our daily lives, giving shape to a scenario in which the concepts of citizenship and political representation can be reinvented, tending towards a vision in which people can be more aware and benefit from added opportunities for action, participating to an environment designed for ubiquitous collaboration and knowledge which is multi-actor, *multi-stakeholder*, in real-time: the city. ■

 ISSN 1071-4391 ISBN 978-1-906897-20-8

ACKNOWLEDGEMENTS

We wish to give our most sincere appreciation to the multitude of individuals and organizations who contributed in making this multi-year research possible. Among these, special thanks go to: Franco Avicolli, the Cultural Expert at the Italian Cultural Centre in Mexico City, who supported our *architettura rel:attiva*, believing in the possibilities of mixed-reality to enhance human life; FakePress Publishing, for providing us an incredibly stimulating environment in which to confront with the mutation of human behavior; professor Massimo Canevacci and Luca Simeone, for their approaches to Anthropology and Ethnography which, moving fluidly from poetics to politics, allowed us to gain fundamental insights on the essences of contemporary human life; and to the Piemonte Share Festival and its Artistic Director, Simona Lodi, for believing in our sometimes strange and too complicated project proposals, and giving a house to them in wonderful and significant contexts.

RELEVANT PROJECTS

ConnectiCity, including the Atlas of Rome, ConnectiCity Neighborhood edition, Architettura rel:attiva.
http://www.artisopensource.net/category/projects/connecticity-projects/

CoS, Consciousness of Streams
http://www.artisopensource.net/category/projects/consciousness-of-streams-projects/

Nuclear Anxiety
http://www.artisopensource.net/category/projects/nuclear-anxiety/

Squatting Supermarkets
http://www.artisopensource.net/category/projects/squatting-supermarkets-projects/

The Electronic Man
http://www.artisopensource.net/category/projects/electronicman/

VersuS, the realtime lives of cities
http://www.artisopensource.net/category/projects/versus-projects/

LINKS TO PERSONAL WEBSITES, INCLUDING PORTFOLIO, PREVIOUS WORK, CURRICULUM

http://www.artisopensource.net
http://www.fakepress.it

REFERENCES AND NOTES

1. John Douglas Porteous, "Home: The Territorial Core," *Geographical Review*, vol. 66, no. 4 (1976): 383–390.
2. Edward Krupat and William Guild, "Defining the City: The Use of Objective and Subjective Measures for Community Description," *Journal of Social Issues* 36 (1980): 9–28.
3. Jack L. Nasar, "Perception, cognition and evaluation of urban places," in *Human Behavior and Environment: Public places*, eds. Irwin Altman and Ervin Zube, 31-56 (New York: Plenum, 1989).
4. Susan L. Scheiberg, "Emotions on display: The personal decoration of work space," *American Behavioral Scientist* 33, no. 3 (1990): 330–338.
5. Mark Gottdiener, *The social production of urban space*, (Austin: University of Texas Press, 1994), 28.
6. Frank E. Horton and David R. Reynolds, "Effects of Urban Spatial Structure on Individual Behavior," *Economic Geography, Perspectives on Urban Spatial Systems* 47, no. 1 (1971): 36–48.
7. Mathew Zook and Mark Graham, "From Cyberspace to DigiPlace: Visibility in an Age of Information and Mobility," in *Societies and Cities in the Age of Instant Access, ed.* Harvey J. Miller (London: Springer, 2007).
8. Mathew Zook and Mark Graham, "Mapping DigiPlace: Geocoded Internet Data and the Representation of Place," in *Environment and Planning B: Planning and Design* 34, no. 3 (2007): 466 – 482.
9. John Zeisel, *Inquiry by Design: Environment/Behavior/Neuroscience in Architecture, Interiors, Landscape, and Planning* (New York: Norton & Company, 2006).
10. Malcolm McCullough, *Digital ground : architecture, pervasive computing, and environmental knowing* (Cambridge, MA: MIT Press, 2004).
11. Kaveh Fattahi and Hidetsugu Kobayashi, "New era, new criteria for city imaging," *Theoretical and Empirical Researches in Urban Management* 3, no. 12 (2009): 63–72.
12. Paul Du Gay, *Doing Cultural Studies: The story of the Sony Walkman*, (London: Sage, 2000), 17.
13. Michael Bull, *Sounding out the city: Personal stereos and the management of everyday life* (London: Berg, 2000).
14. Salvatore Iaconesi and Oriana Persico, *RWR Read/Write Reality vol. 1* (Rome: FakePress Publishing, 2011).
15. Rowan Wilken, "From Stabilitas Loci to Mobilitas Loci: Networked Mobility and the Transformation of Place," Mobility, New Social Intensities and the Coordinates of Digital Networks, *Fibreculture Journal* 6 (2005).
16. David Morley, "What's 'Home' Got to Do with It?: Contradictory Dynamics in the Domestication of Technology and the Dislocation of Domesticity," *European Journal of Cultural Studies* 6, no. 4 (2003): 435–458.
17. Gilles Clément and Claude Eveno, *Le Jardin planétaire* (Chicago: University of Chicago Press, 1999).
18. John P. Eberhard, *Brain landscape: the coexistance of neuroscience and architecture* (Oxford: Oxford University press, 2009).
19. Almo Farina, *Ecology, Cognition and Landscape* (New York: Springer, 2010).
20. Derrick de Kerckhove, *The architecture of intelligence* (Basel: Birkhäuser, 2001).
21. Nicola Green, "On the Move: Technology, Mobility, and the Mediation of Social Time and Space," *The Information Society* 18, no. 4 (2002): 281–292.
22. Marsha Berry and Margaret Hamilton, "Changing Urban Spaces: Mobile Phones on Trains," *Mobilities* 5, no. 1 (2010): 111–129.
23. Michael F. Goodchild, "Citizens as sensors: the world of volunteered geography," in *The Map Reader: Theories of Mapping Practice and Cartographic Representation*, eds. Martin Dodge, Rob Kitchin and Chris Perkins, 211–221 (Chichester, UK: John Wiley & Sons, 2010).
24. Michael D. Lieberman, Hanan Samet, "Multifaceted toponym recognition for streaming news," in *SIGIR '11 Proceedings of the 34th international ACM SIGIR conference on Research and development in Information* (2011), 843–852.
25. Teng Quin, Rong Xiao, Lei Fang, Xing Xie and Lei Zhang, "An efficient location extraction algorithm by leveraging web contextual information," in *GIS '10 Proceedings of the 18th SIGSPATIAL International Conference on Advances in Geographic Information Systems* (2010), 53–60.

 ISSN 1071-4391 ISBN 978-1-906897-20-8

26. Jochen L. Leidner and M. D. Lieberman, "Detecting geographical references in the form of place names and associated spatial natural language," *SIGSPATIAL Special, Newsletter, Special Issue* 3, no. 2 (2011): 5–11.
27. George Shi and Ken Barker, "Thematic data extraction from Web for GIS and applications," in *Spatial Data Mining and Geographical Knowledge Services (ICSDM), 2011 IEEE International Conference on, Proceedings* (2011), 273–278.
28. Maged N. Kamel Boulos, Antonio P. Sanfilippo, Courtney D. Corley, Steve Wheeler, "Social Web mining and exploitation for serious applications: Technosocial Predictive Analytics and related technologies for public health, environmental and national security surveillance," *Computer Methods and Programs in Biomedicine* 100, no. 1 (2010), 16–23.
29. Shuya Abe et al., "Mining personal experiences and opinions from Web documents," *Web intelligence and Agent Systems* 9, no. 2 (2011).
30. Anne Lisa Gentile et al., "Extracting Semantic User Networks from Informal Communication Exchanges," in *The Semantic Web. ISWC 2011, in Lecture Notes in Computer Science* 7031 (2011): 209–224.
31. Ken Snyder, *Tools for Community Design and Decision Making. Planning Support Systems in Practice* (New York: Springer, 2003).
32. Ken Snyder, "Putting Democracy Front and Center," *Planning* 72, no. 7 (2006): 24–29.
33. Janet Davis et al., "Simulations for Urban Planning: Designing for Human Values," *Computer* 39, no. 9 (2006): 66–72.
34. Christopher Alexander, "The origins of pattern theory: the future of the theory, and the generation of a living world," *Software, IEEE* 16, no. 5 (1999): 71–82.
35. Christopher Alexander et al., "A pattern language. Towns, buildings, construction," *Computer and Information Science* (Oxford: Oxford University Press, 1999), http://www.amazon.fr/exec/obidos/ASIN/0195019199/citeulike04-21. (accessed October 10, 2011).
36. Nikos A. Salingaros, "Theory of the urban web," *Journal of Urban Design* 3, no. 1 (1998): 53–71.
37. Nikos A. Salingaros, "Urban space and its information field," *Journal of Urban Design* 4, no. 1 (1999): 29–49.
38. Hans Schaffers et al., "Integrating Living Labs with Future Internet experimental platforms for co-creating services within Smart Cities," in *Concurrent Enterprising (ICE), 17th International Conference* (2011), 1–11.
39. Maurice Mulvenna et al., "Living labs as engagement models for innovation," in *eChallenges*, (2010), 1–11.
40. Mark Pallot et al., "Living Lab Research Landscape: From User Centred Design and User Experience towards User Cocreation," *First European Summer School "Living Labs"* (2010).
41. Edward Tufte, *Visual Explanations: Images and Quantities, Evidence and Narrative* (Cheshire, CT: Graphics Press, 1997).
42. William S. Cleveland and Robert McGill, "Graphical perception: Theory, exper- imentation, and application to the development of graphical methods," *Journal of the American Statistical Association* 79, no. 387 (1984): 533, 554.
43. Robert Spence, *Information Visualization* (Boston, Massachusetts: Addison-Wesley, 2001).
44. Burkhard Wünsche, "A survey, classification and analysis of perceptual concepts and their application for the effective visualisation of complex in- formation," *APVis '04: Proceedings of the 2004 Australasian symposium on Information Visualisation, Darlinghurst, Australia*, (2004), 17–24
45. Patrick Hanks and James Pustejovsky, "A Pattern Dictionary for Natural Language Processing," in *Revue française de linguistique appliquée* 10, no. 2 (2005): 63–82.
46. Ville H. Tuulos and Henry Tirri, "Combining Topic Models and Social Networks for Chat Data Mining," *WI '04 Proceedings of the 2004 IEEE/WIC/ACM International Conference on Web Intelligence, Proceedings* (2004), 206–213.
47. Robert Plutchik, *Emotion, a psychoevolutionary synthesis* (New York: Harper & Row, 1980).

SALVATORE IACONESI

interviewed by

Lanfranco Aceti & Richard Rinehart

Is there an 'outside' of the Art World from which to launch critiques and interventions? If so, what is the border that defines outside from inside? If it is not possible to define a border, then what constitutes an intervention and is it possible to be and act as an outsider of the art world? Or are there only different positions within the Art World and a series of positions to take that fulfill ideological parameters and promotional marketing and branding techniques to access the fine art world from an oppositional, and at times confrontational, standpoint?

Describing boundaries is a delicate operation. And, obviously, the definition of 'border' includes the definition of the 'idea of border' and of "strategy according to which you define 'border'" of the person/organization who is creating the definition in the first place. As in statistics: results largely depend on what you choose to measure, how you choose to measure it, how you choose to interpret it, how you choose to communicate it. Same world, same data, different results.

So, actually, we particularly enjoy (and find significant) evading this kind of question.

As in the past, art has always been active/reactive in relation to other domains: sciences, technologies, politics, humanities, economy, market, marketing, activism, ecology, architecture, design.

Where Art comes about is in the coagulation of meaning.

Stepping aside from the possibility/opportunity to classify things, and looking at the scenario from a different point of view, art manifests itself whenever elements of current times interconnect and create meaning, significance, emotion, vision. Artists cannot avoid being 'contemporary.' Artists manifest themselves by acting as sensors to their own time, and 'connecting the dots' into the creation of artifacts, processes, actions or *interventions* which are particularly significant for their context. And, by doing so, they generate imagination, emotion, sensation and, most of all, the perception of possibility.

From this point of view: being inside/outside the Art World is not really a concern for Art, but, rather, for the possibility to sell art, which is obviously a perfectly interesting domain for investigation (just look at Hirst, for example, or, before him, at Warhol and his art as business / business as art).

And Art cannot avoid being *interventionist*. Art is a direct intervention on reality (as are architecture, design, sciences, business, communication). And, thus, art-as-intervention is that which creates a 'new-real.'

In this, the confrontational dimension also loses importance, as do all dichotomic approaches.

The focus on conflict has never really been successful, after all. We can see that even in contemporary times, in which the dynamics of *hacking* have already been absorbed by corporations, who commonly use the languages, grammars and visions of *hacking* for their own purposes.

What is really significant is *construction*, together with the creation of opportunities for *consciousness* and *awareness*, and with the possibility to *enable* and *include*.

 ISSN 1071-4391 ISBN 978-1-906897-20-8

This is, probably, a good description of *intervention*: to take an existing context and *construct* a space *in-between* which *enables* people to form *consciousness* and *awareness* of a certain set of possibilities.

"In *The Truth in Painting*, Derrida describes the *parergon* (*par-*, around; *ergon*, the work), the boundaries or limits of a work of art. Philosophers from Plato to Hegel, Kant, Husserl, and Heidegger debated the limits of the intrinsic and extrinsic, the inside and outside of the art object." (Anne Friedberg, *The Virtual Window: From Alberti to Microsoft* (Cambridge, MA: MIT Press, 2009), 13.) Where then is the inside and outside of the virtual artwork? Is the artist's 'hand' still inside the artistic process in the production of virtual art or has it become an irrelevant concept abandoned outside the creative process of virtual artworks?

Contemporary art projects are progressively more focused on process than they are on objects.

In this scenario, the possibility to discern something that we can call 'inside' from something that we can call 'outside' is mainly a matter of communication and interaction (which is a subset of communication).

We don't particularly find attractive the notion of *virtual artwork*, as it misses some points: the word *virtual* bears too many implications at cultural level, implying that it is *not-real*. Instead we truly believe about the *reality* of the projects which use technologies such as digital worlds, augmented reality and ubiquitous technologies. And we prefer describing them as *neo-real*.

In our project called *Squatting Supermarkets*, presented for the first time in 2009 at the Share Festival in Turin, Augmented Reality was used to create an intervention in supermarkets all over the world, using the logo of products as *markers* for AR. In that project, which was greatly inspired by Julian Oliver's *Artvertiser*, we used computer vision to augment the experience of supermarkets, to enable free expression in a typical location in which very few voices and points of view are expressed.

In this kind of work – which, basically, consists into conceiving and implementing a free/libre, accessible, tool for expression which enables anyone to intervene in a space – it is impossible and misleading to go and look for boundaries.

As for disciplines: arts, interaction design, engineering, architecture, social sciences all combine into an harmonious whole, and the artwork would simply not exist without taking into account all contributions.

As for times and spaces: they are not determinable, as people will be able to use it whenever they want, wherever they want, by simply pointing their smartphone at a certain product, capture its label image, and add augmented content to it; in whichever part of the world, whenever they wish.

As for people and usages: the technology at the base of the artwork is free and open source (it is released as GPL3) and anyone can re-enact the project whenever they wish, or they can even grab the technology and use it for something completely different; this has happened many times already, with people using it in university classes, activist projects, entertainment and other art projects; and we probably even know a limited number of the usage scenarios which have been enacted.

So, in the end: where does it start/finish? Our answer is that the question can be placed in a better format, as if it is possible to barely identify a *start* (is it?) it is definitely impossible and meaningless to describe an border. Because most of the artwork's significance is in its capability of constantly breaking that border and to establish new visions, new relationships, new possibilities, new opportunities. New realities.

Virtual interventions appear to be the contemporary inheritance of Fluxus' artistic practices. Artists like Peter Weibel, Yayoi Kusama and Valie Export subverted traditional concepts of space and media through artistic interventions. What are the sources of inspiration and who are the artistic predecessors that you draw from for the conceptual and aesthetic frameworks of contemporary augmented reality interventions?

Even if we use augmented reality in our practice, we have some difficulty in defining *augmented reality interventions*. AR is used in ways which form an ecosystem together with other elements to create an experience which brings on the meaning of the artwork. As with all art, we specifically value those practices which are able to create a *new-real*, a possibilistic view on the world which is able to reinvent reality.

Our inspiration comes from many places. Choosing randomly among them, we grab many insights from Dada and Surrealism, and the idea of questioning perception and society to create space for new possibilities; from the idea of *social sculpture* as described by Beuys; from the concept of *Business Artist* described by Andy Warhol; from the generative works of art by Sol LeWitt; from the view on the city of Benjamin, Lefebvre, de Certeau; from the *Images of the City* by Kevin Lynch; from Bateson's ecosystems; from Bhabha's views on the encounter of different cultures; from the ideas of interstices described by Goffman, to the idea of *engineered undesign* expressed by Koolhaas; from the interpretations of space of Setha M. Low to Christopher Alexander's patterns.

If we focus on art and critique, we have been truly influenced by the Critical Arts Ensemble's interventions on public space; by Debord's *dérives*; by Asger Jorn's and Pinot Gallizio's interventions.

Recently, on the themes of the augmentation of reality, we have been particularly influenced, as already said, by Julian Oliver's works.

In the representation and presentation of your artworks as being 'outside of' and 'extrinsic to' contemporary aesthetics why is it important that your projects are identified as Art?

Art has a very interesting role in society. It is both a sensor and an actuator. It acts on a strategic level, to identify and assess nodes for discussion, and it acts on the pragmatic level, to enact instances which are able to activate people and organizations, generating visions, emotions and opportunities for further expression.

In synthesis: it creates new space.

What has most surprised you about your recent artworks? What has occurred in your work that was outside of your intent, yet has since become an intrinsic part of the work?

It is amazing when a work of art gets disassembled and re-combined and re-assembled in other forms, enabling further forms of expression. In our work we release both the work itself and the technologies and methodologies which were used to create it. Often, people grab things and re-use them for other purposes, even in ways which are very far from their initial intended usage scenarios. This is one of the most outstanding goals which can be achieved in contemporary arts: the possibility to enable further expression, both by creating vision and by providing tools (of conceptual, methodological and technological nature).

 ISSN 1071-4391 ISBN 978-1-906897-20-8

This also constitutes one of our main critiques to many art forms using augmented reality.

Many of them are based on the Layar platform. While we have nothing against using the tools which are available for expression, we feel that this practice misses many opportunities and produces a series of dangerous scenarios.

On the level of *missed opportunities* we feel that the use of a *free*, but not *libre*, technology in this kind of work is rather superficial: the idea of intervention in space by using a tool which is not *libre* is quite contradictory and limited. And we see these practices as being quite limited in scope. Yes, we know, now, that we can have a nice idea, design some 3D objects and interactivity for it and place it somewhere using AR and Layar; but there is no real development, advancement or progression in this. We are re-producing an idea under different forms, but we're not producing any other tools or any other vision or possibilistic scenario.

When different skills and competences combine we, instead, are able to go much further, being able to both produce novel tools and novel visions and scenarios, which we can then release for public use.

This is an ethical approach which we feel as being central to the arts of the contemporary era.

And, on the level of *dangerous scenarios*, we also feel that delegating the content and experiences of art to the closed, non-standard, inaccessible platforms of commercial service providers constitutes a dangerous scenario for the preservation of art and for the access to the cultural history of these times for the years to come.

This is the reason why we release all the technologies we produce under open licenses.

Again, in synthesis: we feel that the most exciting opportunity in contemporary art is to create new, accessible, free, usable spaces for reflection, re-interpretation and action; we are truly satisfied and amazed when this happens in real-life, and we do everything which is in our power to conceive and implement works of art which can foster further forms of expression in other people and organizations. ■

SALVATORE IACONESI

statement & artwork

In our work scientific approaches harmoniously interweave to poetics in the observation of contemporary reality:

the study of history joins the observation of human life in the understanding of the present and to liberate the fluid and dynamic imaginaries of possibility. We want to describe a dimension of the future which is accessible ,reachable, and insightful.

This process – scientific and theoretical in its conception; (neo)material and pragmatic in its implementation – produces radical effects at the levels of methodology and of the generation of the visions and of the opportunities for social transformation. What we propose is an alchemical process – in its sense of connection, fusion and hybridization of disciplines and methodologies – aimed at achieving understanding and awareness.

Our main focus is the comprehension of the contemporary mutation of human beings. Digital technologies and networks have revolutionized the ways in which we study, work, collaborate, communicate and relate: the practices of our daily lives – just as the ones of science and academia – come out as completely transformed.

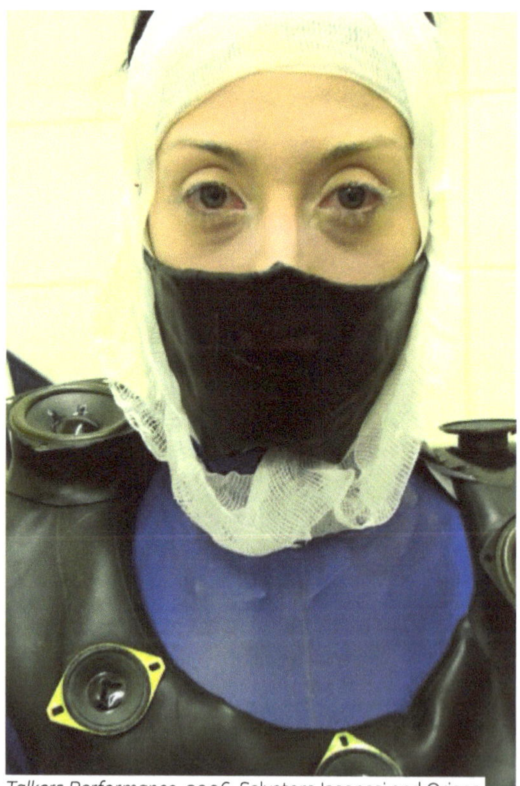

Talkers Performance, 2006, Salvatore Iaconesi and Oriana Persico. A dance performance in which the body of the dancer is controlled through web interfaces. Image courtesy of the artists. © Iaconesi and Persico, 2006.

 ISSN 1071-4391 ISBN 978-1-906897-20-8

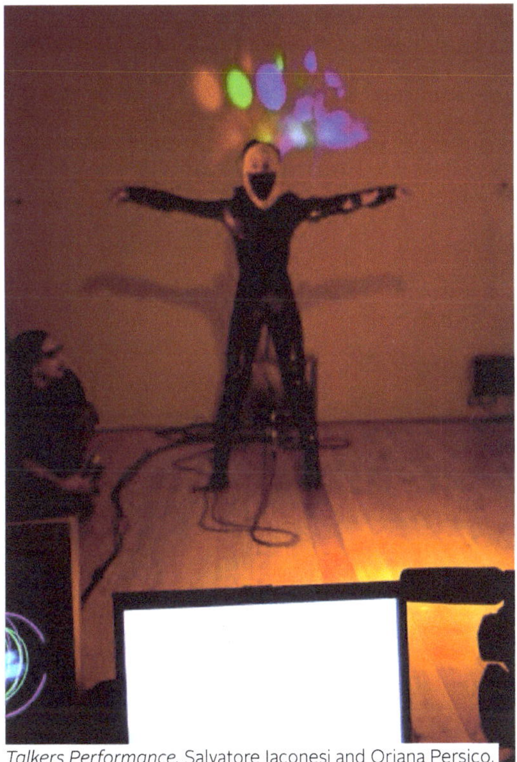

Talkers Performance. Salvatore Iaconesi and Oriana Persico. A dance performance in which the body of the dancer is controlled through web interfaces. Image courtesy of the artists. © Iaconesi and Persico.

Angel_F, 2007, Salvatore Iaconesi and Oriana Persico. An artificial intelligence, born as a spyware, learns how to speak on social networks. Image courtesy of the artists. © Iaconesi and Persico, 2007.

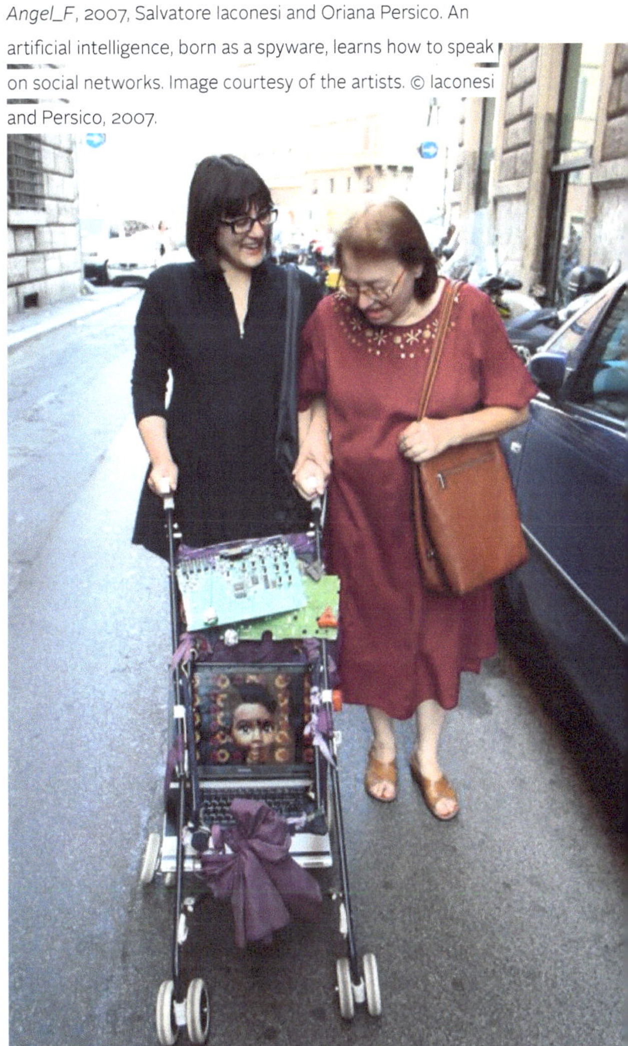

This has cognitive impacts on our understanding of fundamental elements of our world: dimensions such as time, space, identity and relation constantly mutate altering the concepts of public and private, privacy, intimacy, interpersonal relationships. We perceive cities, spaces, bodies as different. Networks and technologies – now ubiquitous and accessible – transport us into new and unexpected locations, *in-between* continents, languages, cultures and emergent relations; enabling new forms of associative knowledge, synthetic memories, non-linear, multi-author, real-time narratives.

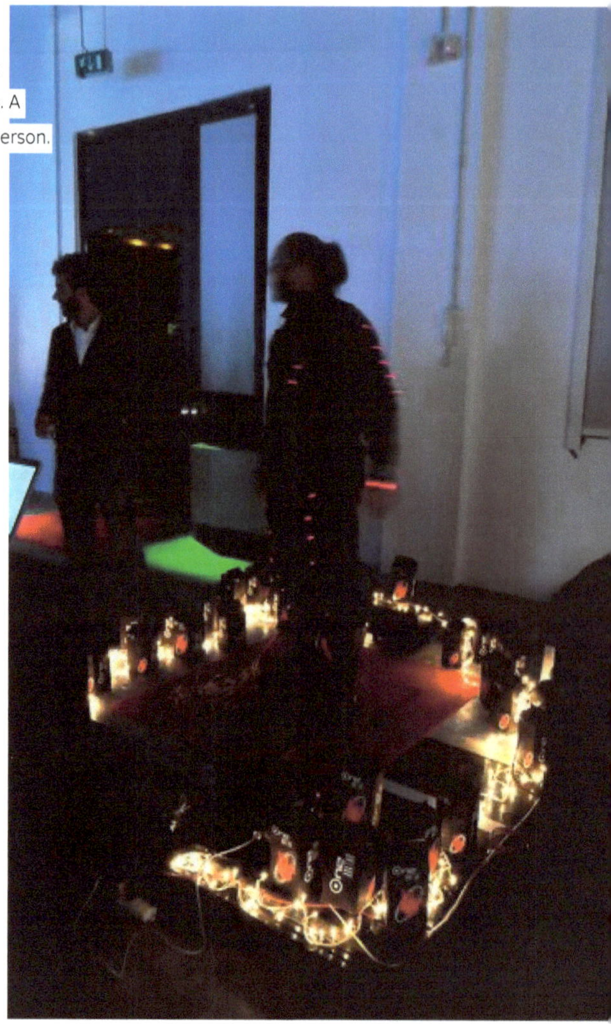

OneAvatar, 2007, Salvatore Iaconesi and Oriana Persico. The suit connects the body of the performer to the avatar on Second Life. A videogame in which you shoot the avatar and inflict pain on the person. Image courtesy of the artists. © Iaconesi and Persico, 2007.

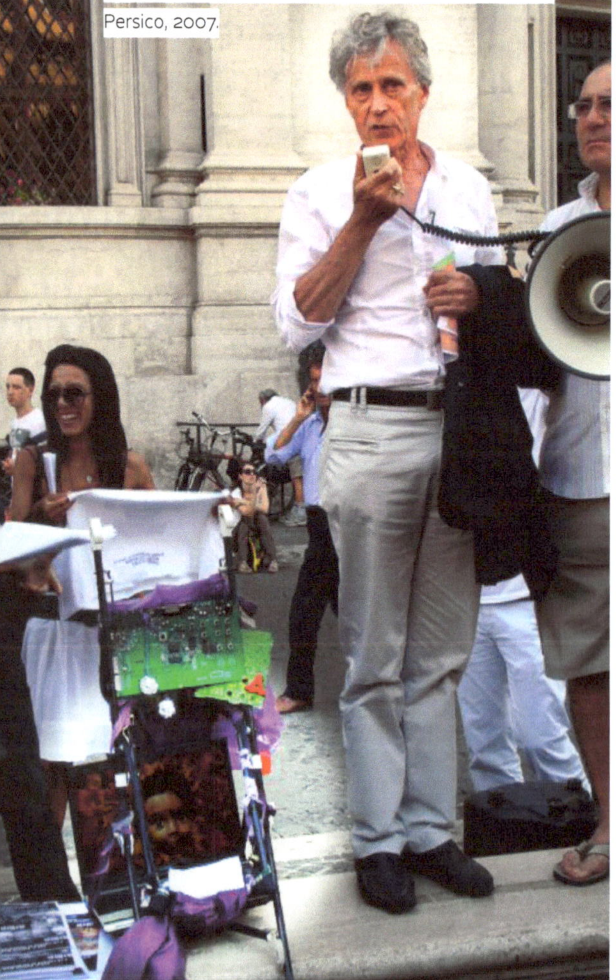

Angel_F, 2007, Salvatore Iaconesi, Oriana Persico. An artificial intelligence, born as a spyware, learns how to speak on social networks. Image courtesy of the artists. © Iaconesi and Persico, 2007.

It becomes difficult, if not impossible, to clearly define borders and delimitations: in space/time, concepts, disciplines. Technologies such as Augmented Reality allow imagining (and designing) reality as an infinite multiplication/stratification of points of view, literally building 'cities-over-cities.' Assuming isolated disciplinary approaches becomes tendentially irrelevant. Mash-up, remix, re-combination, re-contextualization, re-enactment and squatting become fundamental strategies.

 ISSN 1071-4391 ISBN 978-1-906897-20-8

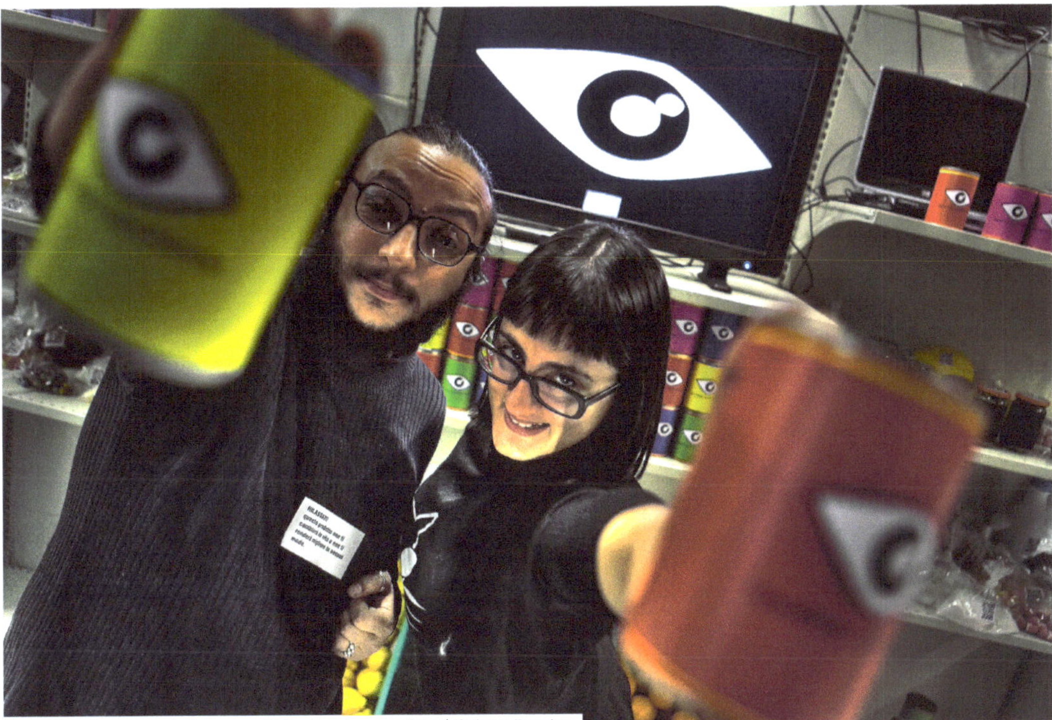

Squatting Supermarkets, 2009, Salvatore Iaconesi and Oriana Persico. An augmented reality supermarket. Scan the products' labels and turn them into places for augmented, emergent narratives. Image courtesy of the artists. © Iaconesi and Persico, 2009.

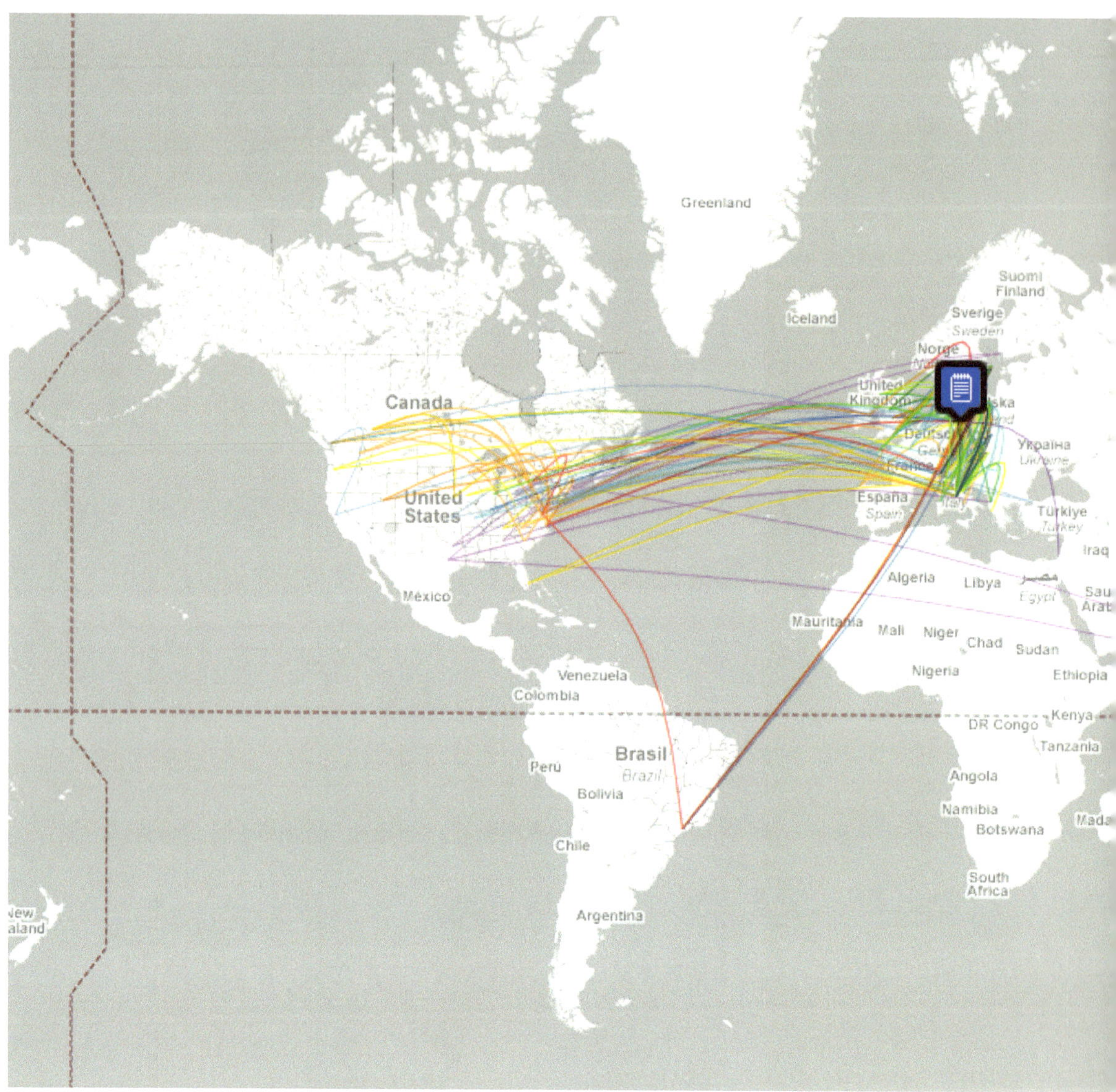

Interstices – the borders which don't exist, the spaces *in-between* – are the fluid spaces in which intersubjective and intercultural experiences take place, creating scientific, cultural, economic, political, artistic, social richness.

Our desire: to "wear" this modality. Interstices, recombination of places, spaces, concepts; methodological mash-up; squatting of practices, places and disciplines; re-contextualization of technologies and techniques.

Our goal: to enable the emergence of vision, of poetics-politics, of the scenarios of possibility and imagination.

Our methodology: produce "new real." Arts and science; science and politics; politics and poetry; poetry and architecture; architecture and hacking; hacking and design; design and networks; networks and peer-2-peer. Peer-2-peer and art.

Our media: human beings; their presence in the world; their mutation. ■

 ISSN 1071-4391 ISBN 978-1-906897-20-8

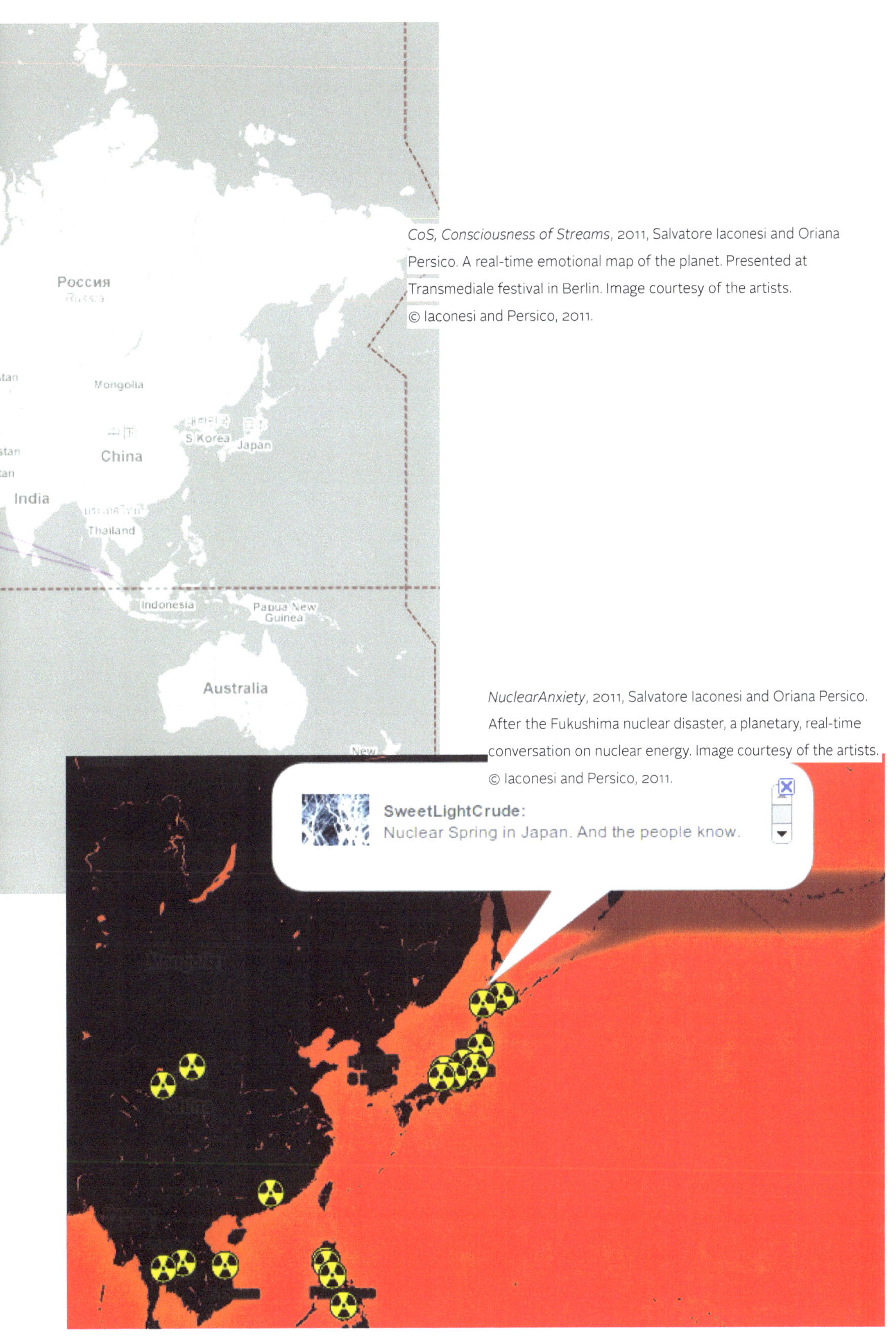

CoS, Consciousness of Streams, 2011, Salvatore Iaconesi and Oriana Persico. A real-time emotional map of the planet. Presented at Transmediale festival in Berlin. Image courtesy of the artists. © Iaconesi and Persico, 2011.

NuclearAnxiety, 2011, Salvatore Iaconesi and Oriana Persico. After the Fukushima nuclear disaster, a planetary, real-time conversation on nuclear energy. Image courtesy of the artists. © Iaconesi and Persico, 2011.

The Electronic Man, 2011, Salvatore Iaconesi and Oriana Persico. In occasion of the celebrations of Marshal McLuhan's Centennial, a global augmented sensoriality. Image courtesy of the artists.

 ISSN 1071-4391 ISBN 978-1-906897-20-8

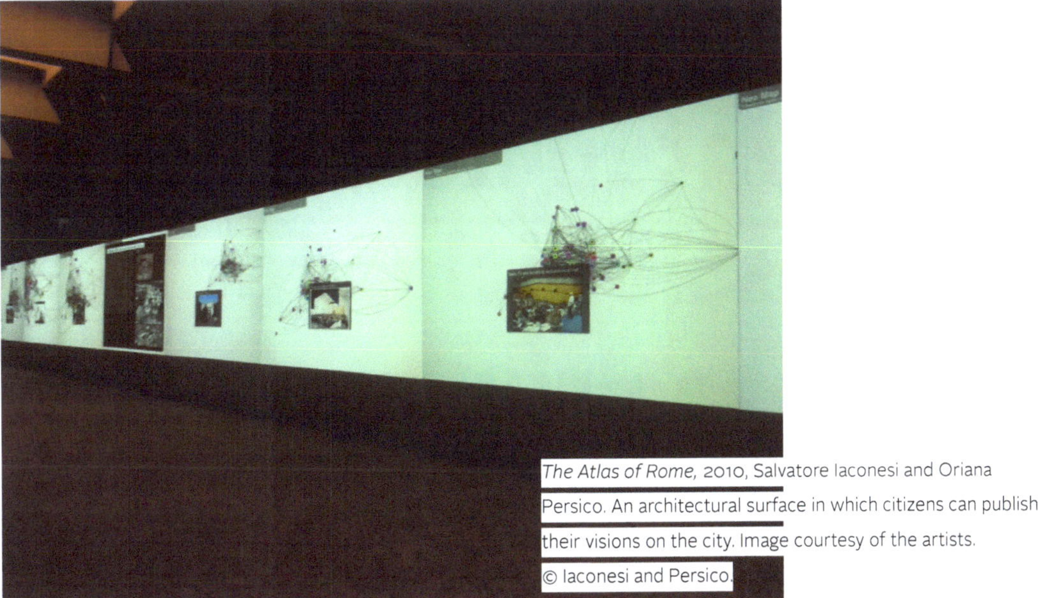

The Atlas of Rome, 2010, Salvatore Iaconesi and Oriana Persico. An architectural surface in which citizens can publish their visions on the city. Image courtesy of the artists. © Iaconesi and Persico.

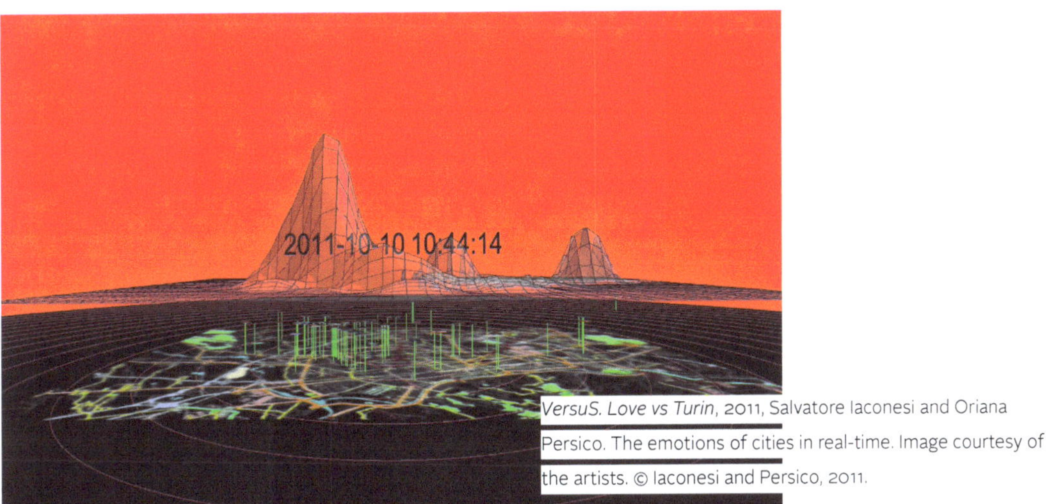

VersuS. Love vs Turin, 2011, Salvatore Iaconesi and Oriana Persico. The emotions of cities in real-time. Image courtesy of the artists. © Iaconesi and Persico, 2011.

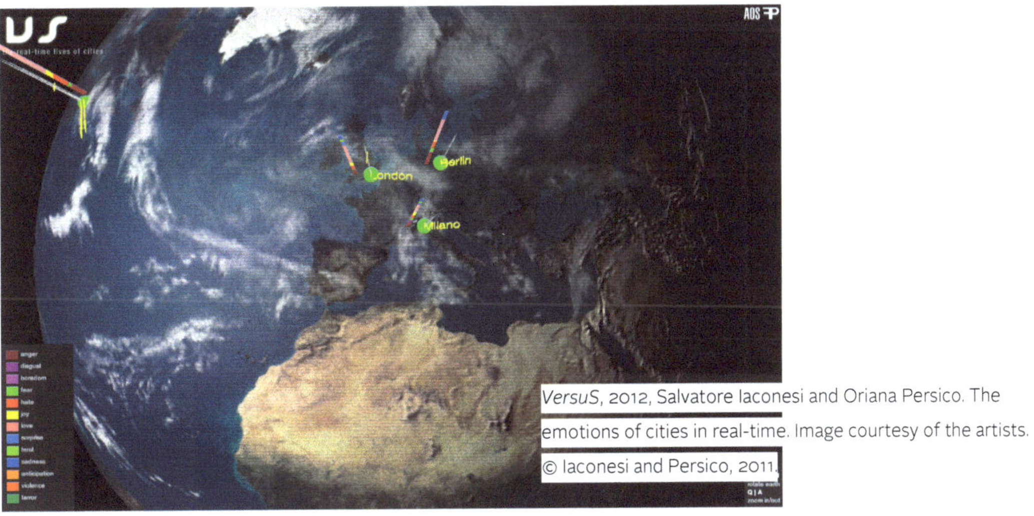

VersuS, 2012, Salvatore Iaconesi and Oriana Persico. The emotions of cities in real-time. Image courtesy of the artists. © Iaconesi and Persico, 2011.

Augmented Resistance: the possibilities for AR and data driven art

CONOR MCGARRIGLE

Assistant Professor,
Emergent Digital Practices,
University of Denver.
conormcgarrigle@gmail.com

AUGMENTED REALITY

Augmented Reality (AR) is a problematic term in itself but as with much in the field of 'New Media' it appears that for the moment, we're stuck with it. The term was originally coined by Tom Caudell and David Mizell [1] in 1992 for applications in aircraft manufacturing at Boeing. It was associated in the 1990s with virtual reality type headsets with prototypes like the *Touring Machine* [2] and *Map-in-the-Hat* [3] which were accompanied by weighty backpacks carrying the necessary computing, GPS and communication equipment, which today fits in a cellphone. Even today the HUD (Heads Up Display) paradigm still has traction as demonstrated by Google's recent *Project Glass* [4] announcement, however despite Google's intervention, the HUD as a model of AR still exists in the nostalgia of "yesterday's tomorrows." [5]

This association of AR situated somewhere along the real-virtual continuum, not quite real but not fully virtual either, serves to situate the practice in a scenario which I suggest looks toward the utopian values/ambitions of virtual reality and as such runs the risk of not attending to the real value of AR, which is its ability to contextually situate data. It is necessary to further distinguish the version of Augmented Reality (AR) currently available for mobile devices from the richer conceptualization of augmented space as articulated by Lev Manovich [6] which encompasses the gamut of the distributed information resources and is not confined to ubiquitous and pervasive computing and the myriad ways in which computational power is embedded in the fabric of the city.

 ISSN 1071-4391 ISBN 978-1-906897-20-8

__This article discusses the possibilities for Augmented Reality (AR) as a driver of data based art.__ The combination of AR and Open Data (in the broadest post-Wikileaks sense) is seen to provide a powerful tool-set for the artist/activist to augment specific sites with a critical, context-specific data layer. Such situated interventions offer powerful new methods for the political activation of sites which enhance and strengthen traditional non-virtual approaches and should be thought of as complementary to, rather than replacing, physical intervention.

I offer as a case study this author's "NAMAland" project, a mobile artwork which uses Open Data and Augmented Reality to visualise and critique aspects of the Irish financial collapse. The project, overlayed Dublin with an activist derived data-layer which supported and enabled physical interventions, making visible/concrete abstract financial dealings through situating them in real space, enacting a virtual layer of critique which facilitated and catalysed wider debate.

(AR) in its current popular articulation working on mobile devices through platforms such as Layar, Junaio and Wikitude [7] is a more prosaic affair, designed as a device led experience offering a limited set of procedures involving the overlaying of dynamic, context specific data over live 'camera-view' of physical space. Typically this information is scraped from a geo-tagged database and serves information such as proximity of train stations, cinemas and nearby tweets. More recent developments include the display of 3D models and the ability to trigger actions, such as playing an advertising video, through image recognition leading a push to monetize the technology through AR advertisers tie-ins.

It is important however to look beyond the limited nature of many of the applications currently available for AR browsers to attend to the affordances of these platforms. I draw attention to the ability to import and locate geo-tagged databases which offer an unprecedented opportunity for the political activation of sites with large scale data-led critiques working in tandem with physical intervention.

Despite the limitations of AR browsers they point to the convergence of a burgeoning world of open and accessible data, much of it geo-tagged or available for geo-tagging, with the ability to generate location specific overlays. AR is an emergent technology, the application of which is still uncertain. Ben Russell identified a similar openness in earlier locative technologies which he saw as seeking " grassroots and consumer level interpretation of what these devices are," [8] in these emergent AR systems there is a similar sense of a technology seeking usages which are meaningful to the broadest constituency. . This presents an opportunity to artists and activists to set the agenda for this technology, to establish it as a tool for location based annotation and critique forwhich it is ideally suited.

This opportunity coalesces around two factors. The first is Open Data, the EU recently put a value of €27 billion [9] on the market for open data and it is seen as variously democratic, a boon to the smart economy and so forth. Whatever the merits of the Open Data discourse it has incentivized cities and governments resulted in the release of vast swaths of data, representing a significant opportunity. AR platforms represent the second, they offer an ease of use and are available as apps for a range of location aware smart phones. While flawed, overly defined, and with limited opportunities for customization, they represent the first step in AR, and they will improve.

DATA DRIVEN ART

In considering AR art and data it is important to locate the discussion within an artistic tradition of using data (open or otherwise) as a tool of political critique within an art context. I see the potential for the convergence of data space and real space which AR offers as situated within this tradition and will trace this through three artists who have exerted direct influence on the NAMAland project, these are Hans Haacke with his seminal *Shapolsky et al. Manhattan Real Estate Holdings, A Real Time Social System, as of May 1, 1971*, Mark Lombardi's data based drawings and Josh On's *They Rule*.

The case of *Shapolsky et al.* is of particular interest as it was a data rich installation detailing ownership of 142 (mostly tenement) properties and sites in New York City in the ownership or effective control of the Shapolsky Family. The work was based on data derived from publicly available records, assembled and refined, in the case of obfuscated records designed to conceal effective ownership, by the artist. The work reveals the city as a real estate system, uncovering its complex structure and demonstrating the ways in which the physical fabric of the city, and the arcane financial dealings designed to maximise the value of real estate holdings, are imbricated. It expands the idea of site beyond physical location to include its associated data space. This serves to activate these sites through providing a socio-political narrative, transforming individual buildings through augmenting them with data. Situating them within a complex network of property and financial transactions, with far reaching repercussions of the space of the city and the everyday lives of the people living in these slums. [10] The piece was to be exhibited in the Guggenheim Museum, but the exhibition was controversially cancelled before its opening in April 1971 with the specificity of the work cited as the principle reason. The museum Director held that social issues should be addressed "artistically only through symbolism, generalization and metaphor." [11] What caused the work to be suppressed was the specificity of the critique, which data supplied, whereas a generalized artistic critique would have been acceptable demonstrating the power of the data-based critique.

The artist Mark Lombardi is known for his large scale data based drawings or "narrative structures" which detail the networks of power and money involved in various political financial scandals such as the collapse of the Bank of Credit and Commerce International detailed in *BCCI-ICIC-FAB, c. 1972–1991, (4th Version), 1996–2000*. For each drawing Mark Lombardi built a custom database culled from published information sources assembled onto cross referenced index cards, according to his gallerist Deven Golden, he had around 14,000 of them, [12] which were then condensed to create his drawings. Lombardi considered these as a method of "reprocessing and rearranging" freely avail-

 ISSN 1071-4391 ISBN 978-1-906897-20-8

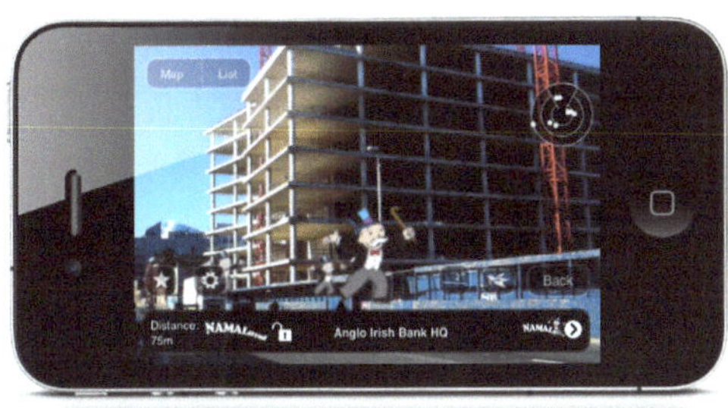

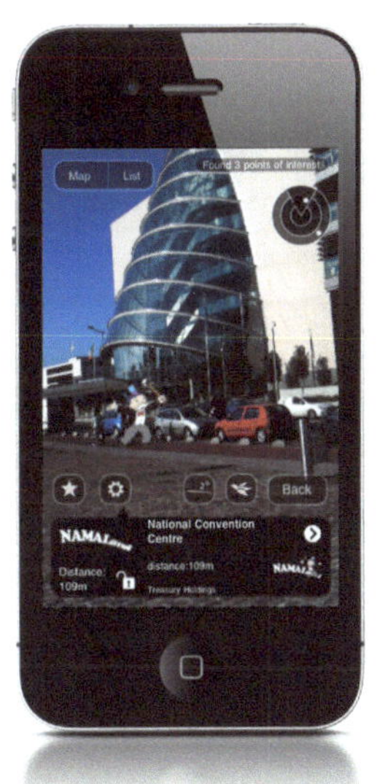

NAMA*land*, 2010, Conor McGarrigle, AR Layar. © Conor McGarrigle.

able information as a way of mapping the political and social terrain. [13] The painter Greg Stone recounts the reaction of a friend, a reporter at the Wall St Journal, on seeing Lombardi's "*George W. Bush, Harken Energy and Jackson Stephens*" drawing, although he was familiar with the characters in the narrative, said he "hadn't fully understood the implications until he saw it all laid out that way." [14]

Josh On's web based work *They Rule* pursues a similar mission of making connections between networks of powerful individuals, this time connected though corporate directorships once again drawing from publicly available databases. *They Rule* provides a front end interface to its underlying databases which allows users to make their own connections and share them with other users. As a work of art, it presents a framework to interface with the data, inviting its users to provide the narrative structure and co-construct the meaning. Originally powered from a custom database of directorships of the top 100 companies in the US, it now employs the database of Littlesis, "a free database of who-knows-who at the heights of business and government." [15]

These projects illustrate that the power of data art lies in its ability to re-present information in ways which make the connections evident, presenting the information as narrative and in ways which reveal the underlying structures and patterns. How then can ubiquitous networked location-awareness of mobile devices and emergent AR add to this tradition, and in an era where data and its use have assumed a greater importance than ever before, what has art practice to contribute to this burgeoning field? At this point, I will introduce a case study of a recent work which follows in the tradition of data art. It is a work which does not claim any technical innovation, created for an existing platform and built using free and open source software, but it offers a powerful example of the ways in which data can politically activate sites and, I suggest, a model for connecting data and space to create an activist hybrid-space.

NAMALAND

NAMA*land* is a mobile AR artwork, built on the Layar platform, [16] which uses Open Data and Augmented Reality to visualise and critique aspects of the Irish financial collapse, through an overlaying of the city of Dublin with a database driven data layer which identifies properties under the control of NAMA (The National Assets Management Agency). NAMA is an Irish Government Agency established in December 2009 to acquire bad property loans from Irish banks with the aim of removing them from the banks' balance sheets as a bailout mechanism. The agency, which was controversial from the start, acquired properties worth €54 billion but failed in its stated aim of bailing out the banks, culminating in Ireland entering an IMF/EU bailout program in November 2010 due to the imminent collapse of the banking system. Despite (or perhaps because of) its central role in the financial collapse NAMA was extremely secretive in its workings. Legally exempted from Freedom of Information requirements, the agency was intent on shielding its property portfolio, individuals and corporations involved, from public scrutiny under the guise of 'commercial sensitivity.' Building on Hans Haacke's treatment of the Shapolsky real estate and New York City, it was obvious that mapping out NAMA's property holdings was essential to gain an understanding of the organisation and events which led to its creation, in order to open it to critique and scrutiny.

After some research, I was able to identify an alternative, activist source of information on NAMA properties on the anonymous website NAMA Wine Lake. [17] Maintained as a Google Docs, the NAMA-bound spreadsheet was compiled from published sources of information connecting property developers known to be in NAMA, their directorships of companies and properties controlled by these companies. Each entry was well documented with links to the sources, important in a litigious climate. This data was, however, locationally vague, street names were typically included with vague descriptors such as "site on Mayor St" but lacked in sufficient detail to automatically geo-tag. With further research, it was possible to initially manually geo-tag approximately 120 Dublin properties through visually identifying the sites in person and tagging them with a handheld GPS unit. For legal reasons [18] the database had to be confined to properties which could be located with a high degree of certainty for which sufficient documentary evidence of their ownership could be provided. This data was then used to create a geotagged MySQL database to be used as the data source for NAMAland.

The application was built in October 2010 and has been updated on a regular basis since. It employs the Layar platform which provides a development environment and software platform to create AR applications which run on the Layar App for the iPhone and iPad, Android devices and selected Nokia and Blackberry smartphones. Layar provides a standardized user interface, with limited options for modification, and supplies a set of standard AR methods upon

NAMAland, 2010, Conor McGarrigle, AR Layar. © Conor McGarrigle.

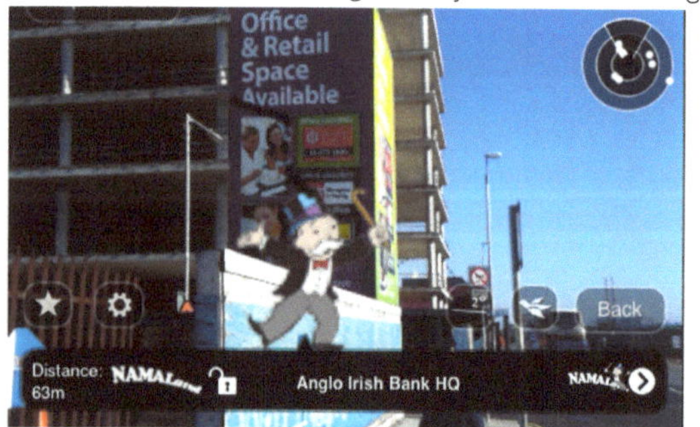

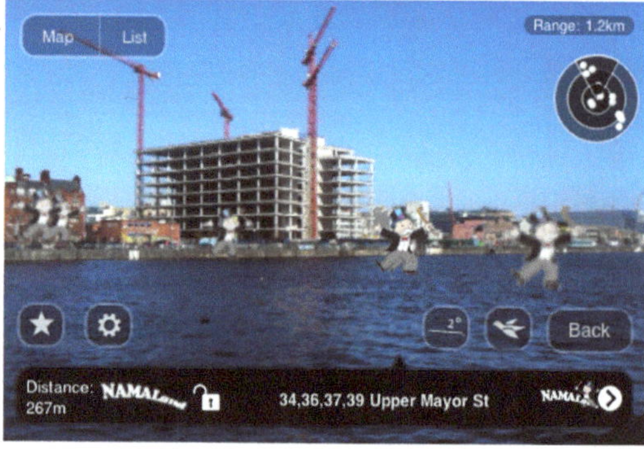

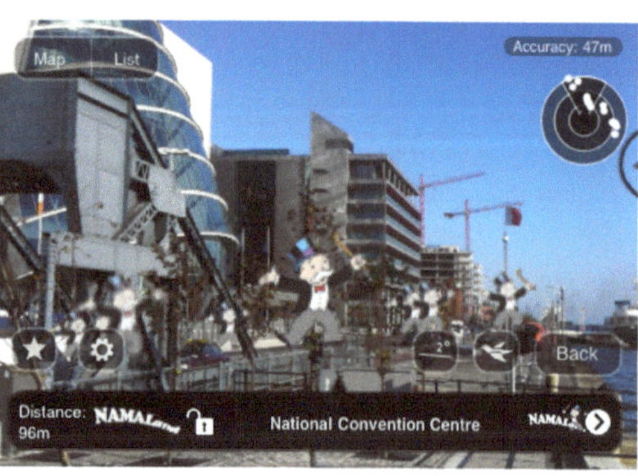

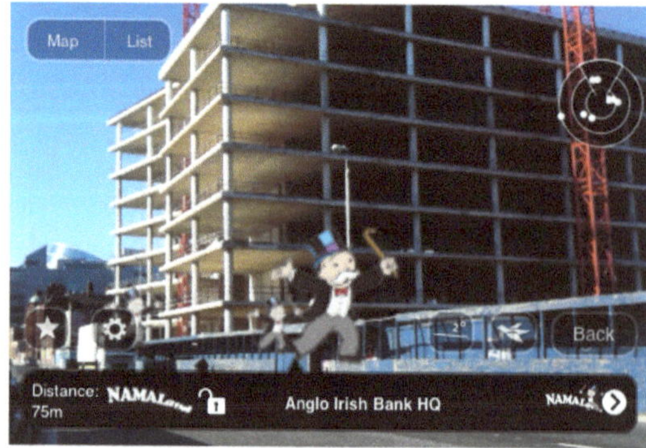

 ISSN 1071-4391 ISBN 978-1-906897-20-8

which Layers can be built. It was selected for two reasons; the first was ease of use, it imports a database effectively and is a working reasonably robust AR app which can be used with a minimum of development. Secondly it provided a method of publishing a politically sensitive work on the iPhone (at the time the most popular smartphone platform in Ireland) as layers are submitted to Layar's own approval process and publishing through the Layar iPhone app, effectively evading the app store gatekeeping, essential for a political sensitive app working with grey unofficial data. [19]

The NAMAland layer in operation takes the location of the user's phone and compares it to this database of geotagged properties of NAMA properties within certain defined ranges. An overlay of properties within the specified range is then created which can be further interrogated for ownership details (the majority of properties in NAMA are associated with a small number of individuals with vast property holdings and billions in defaulted loans). The location of each response is indicated by an overlay of a cartoon "Monopoly Man" figure over NAMA properties in the camera-view of the user's device. It also generates a real time map of localised NAMA properties along with a list of nearby properties and their locations. NAMAland thus visualizes the extent of NAMA property ownership, allowing users to identify nearby properties and interrogate specific regions of the city for NAMA connections. It was the first mapping of NAMA properties available, and eighteen months after its creation, it is still the only available mapping of NAMA properties available in Dublin.

RECEPTION AND ACTIVATION

NAMAland succeeded in capturing the popular imagination in Ireland. It was widely reported in the mainstream media including an interview and report on the Nine O'Clock News on RTE (the Irish national broadcaster), I have been frequently interviewed on radio, and it has featured in the print media on many occasions. I'm regularly contacted by international journalists writing segments on the local reaction to the financial collapse. The title 'NAMAland' has even entered common usage as a descriptor for the post IMF bailout situation. In the midst of my extended 15 minutes, the project has more importantly succeeded in focusing attention on its subject matter where more traditional approaches failed. It overcame official attempts to limit information and discussion on the subject, and has acted as a conduit through which concerns over the lack of transparency inherent in NAMA which focused, and kick-started, the NAMA backlash which has yielded some positive results.

On one level, it operated as a mobile app, a ready to hand source of information locating NAMA properties as a myriad of other apps locate coffee shops and restaurants, gaining 45,000 users in the process. How-

NAMAland Walking Tour, 2011, Conor McGarrigle. Participatory Walk. © Conor McGarrigle.

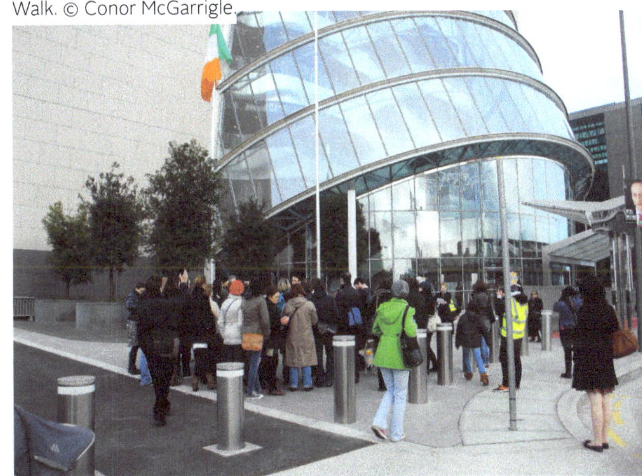

ever as an intervention, particularly one with political aspirations it was not sufficient to remain as a 'virtual intervention,' and needed to operate in conjunction with physical actions to be effective. In this respect, it was vital that the project was expanded to include real world events such as walking tours, situated public discussion forums, public speaking engagements, media coverage and individual interventions with the work itself being an amalgam of all its constituent components. These were all supported and enabled through the data layer made visible through the application of AR technology, offering multiple points of entry and modes of engagement with the project which were not technologically dependent and open to as broad a constituency as possible.

Indeed as the project disseminated it became clear that many of the people who spoke to me, of the project, were not actually users, as they did not have a phone capable of running the application. Their experience of the project was second hand, passed to them as a story which resonated as a tale of resistance. Somebody had used mobile technology to reveal a list of NAMA properties despite efforts to keep this information secret from the public. It was not even necessary to see it in operation, it seemed to be enough to know that it had been done. The walking artist Francis Alÿs speaks of his work as myth making, he sets out to "keep the plot of a project as simple as possible so that it can be told as a story, an anecdote, something that can be transmitted orally without the need to have access to images." [20] *NAMAland* similarly has a clear narrative that can be told as a story, which means that even without access to the requisite technology the project still succeeds at some level. Not only does NAMAland recount a story about NAMA and its consequences, but from the point of view of AR it speaks of the technology and its uses. For this emergent technology, this is significant for it is through practices that functions and usage modes of technologies come to light, and their relative value and importance is revealed.

At another level, it acted as a catalyst, facilitating a range of conversations, debates and activities as part of a wide ranging critique of NAMA and the sequence of events which led to it. The project crossed boundaries from art to geography, urbanism, activism, open data, economics and politics as one would expect from work which engages critically with the space of the city and international finance. As the project became known through publicity and word of mouth another side of the project was revealed from the diversity of the discussions. From the Occupy Dublin camp one day to city-sponsored seminars on Open Data and the smart economy the next, this was its ability to function as a conduit which reconnected NAMA with the space of the city, a connection which had been deliberately severed, to preserve the idea of the agency as a by-product of obscure international financial dealings. What NAMAland contributed was an opening up of previously unavailable data and a reconnecting of this data with the fabric of the city itself. This served to add specificity in place of generalization, fuelling debate through the provision of an infrastructure on which specific spatial critiques could be structured, supplying a point of entry hitherto unavailable.

PERIPATETIC ACTIVISM

The project was accompanied by a series of walks informed by the mobile application which took place in Dublin City Centre and in Tallaght two areas characterised by a high concentration of NAMA properties. These were public, as with the *NAMA-Rama* walk in conjunction with Market Studios, the *In These Troubled Times walk* with RuaRed Arts Centre and *Ireland after NAMA* with The Exchange Arts Centre, and private walks, such as the guided walks for RTE News and Channel Four News TV crews. In this way, the project bridged the gap between the abstract dataset hosted in an online database and the real space of the city. NAMAland is essentially a walking project, it is necessary to deploy it on the street for it to operate at all. The guided walks, through careful selection of routes, were able to maximise this impact by proceeding through areas of the highest concentration of land-

 ISSN 1071-4391 ISBN 978-1-906897-20-8

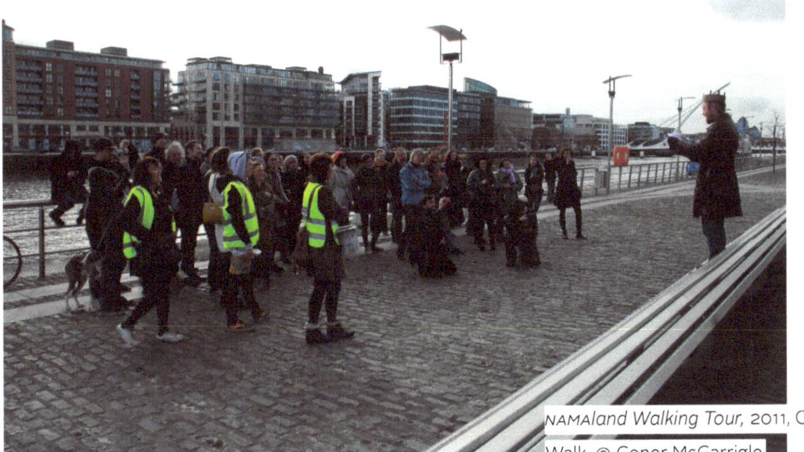

NAMA*land Walking Tour*, 2011, Conor McGarrigle. Participatory Walk. © Conor McGarrigle.

mark buildings and, as participatory events, functioned as walking forums facilitating participants in discussing the issues represented by NAMA and its property portfolio. NAMA represents a complex system of abstract financial dealings, transactions which have become disconnected from everyday understanding but yet have significant and very real consequences. The project and its walks attempt to counter this growing abstraction of space, they operate in hybrid space, [21] that is "a convergence of geographic space and data space" [22] where the distinctions between Castell's [23] space of place (physical space) and the space of flows (informational space) collapses with the overlaying of context sensitive data. Whereas the narrative of NAMA was the narrative of the (now defunct) property market, international finance and IMF bailouts, NAMAland reconnects this to real spaces in order to expose their interconnectedness and real consequences.

In my presentation of NAMAland, in every interview and talk, there was always included two direct practical demands, especially in conversation with City officials, the release of more information on NAMA properties and the making available of vacant properties for community use. These became part of the general conversation on NAMA and have achieved results, both through foregrounding the issues of NAMA properties and their usage and in opening access to properties. NAMAland has informed and influenced groups which have taken direct action through occupying NAMA properties, acting as a resource on which further actions can be built. Dublin City opened direct negotiations with NAMA to access vacant properties under their control for social and cultural use. This has resulted in a city program which allocates vacant buildings for cultural uses with substantial premises being made available. This has been accompanied by the release of more information on NAMA property which, while not nearly complete, has fed the growing demand that vacant properties be opened for community use.

NAMA*land Walking Tour*, 2011, Conor McGarrigle. Participatory Walk. © Conor McGarrigle.

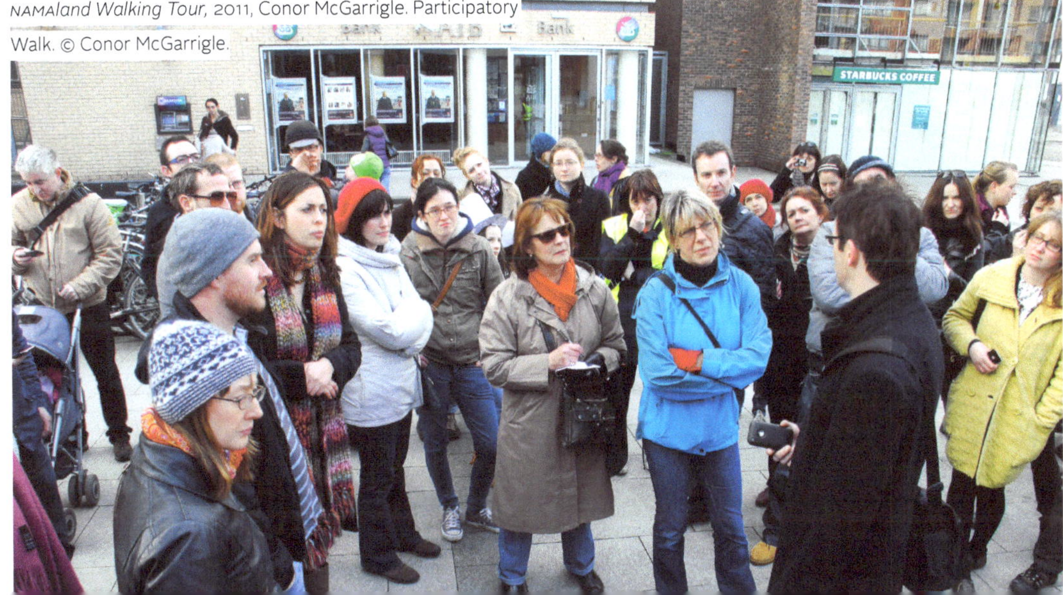

THE FUTURE OF AR ART

If we step back from the particularities of the platform and the case study to consider the implications of this project and similar practices on our understanding of the practice of AR.

I argue elsewhere [24] that artistic practices which engage with emergent technologies are involving in a process of shifting the understanding of these technologies. As Richard Coyne puts it "technologies do not conform politely to predetermined or intended functions," [25] rather it is through the use that functions and usage modes come to light and their relative value and importance is revealed. AR as it stands is being promoted as a marketing technology, with the principle AR browsers developing corporate tie-ins using image recognition to replace QR codes in conjunction with location based AR applications. The technology is being thus presented and developed as a method of connecting companies with their customers in real space. While these applications will be a feature of the mature practice of AR, they are, to invoke the developers of the Urban Tapestries public authoring project, "unnecessarily impoverished." [26]

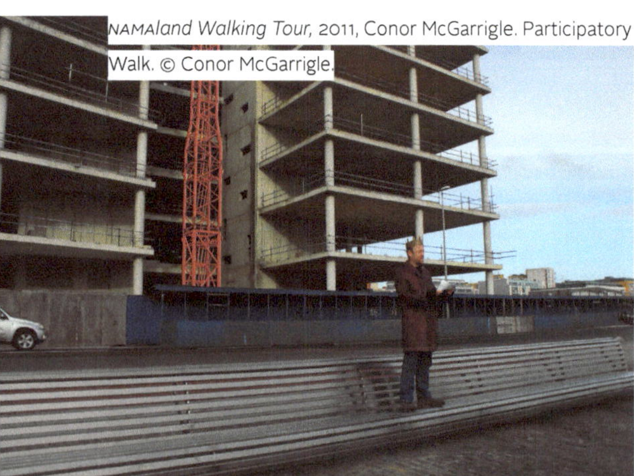

NAMAland Walking Tour, 2011, Conor McGarrigle. Participatory Walk. © Conor McGarrigle.

I argue for the role of art practices in broadening the understanding of the technologies' application through expanding their range of application and permitted usages. *NAMAland* demonstrates one such application, but the potential for these tools is only limited by the data-sets which can be accessed and the desire by artists and activists to engage with them as part of their practice. At an everyday level this might be the difference between AR enabling a retailer to deliver location-aware special offers and deals to a customer's phone alongside the ability of the user to interrogate the retailer's history on a range of issues from health and safety to their environmental record or simply customer satisfaction. This is not necessarily to privilege one over the other. Both have their place but what is of the prime importance is that multiple options co-exist as aids to informed decision making, where the user can offset say a welcome 30% reduction in the price of a cup of coffee earned by checking-in against the companies anti-union policies.

NAMAland is an application of AR technology which has reached a wide audience through usage, mainstream media accounts and word of mouth, as a result of addressing specific local issues (with arguably a wider import). This success establishes AR as a tool of political critique which can reveal and situate information and data of political significance. This assumes a greater importance when connected to the burgeoning Open Data movement. Open Data seeks to make freely available data collected by government and city authorities both in the interests of transparent government and as an impetus to the smart economy. As new sources of data become available there are opportunities for artists and activists to go beyond the rhetoric of the smart economy and develop critical narratives based on this newly liberated data. If AR art practices are to shape the technology, expand the range of practices and establish the technology as a tool for enhancing and critiquing everyday life, then these practices must resonate with their audience and assimilate themselves into the technology through establishing meaningful connections to the every day. This is the challenge for AR art. ■

 ISSN 1071-4391 ISBN 978-1-906897-20-8

REFERENCES AND NOTES

1. T. P. Caudell, and D. W. Mizell, "Augmented Reality: An Application of Heads-Up Display Technology to Manual Manufacturing Processes," in *Proceedings of 1992 IEEE Hawaii International Conference on Systems Sciences,* (1992), 659–669.
2. S. Feiner, B. MacIntyre, T. Höllerer and A. Webster, "A touring machine: Prototyping 3D mobile augmented reality systems for exploring the urban environment," in *Proceedings of First IEEE International Symposium on Wearable Computers*, (1997), 74–81.
3. B. H. Thomas, V. Demczuk, W. Piekarski, D. Hepworth and B. Gunther, "A wearable computer system with augmented reality to support terrestrial navigation," in *Proceedings of Second IEEE International Symposium on Wearable Computers*, (1998), 168–171.
4. Brian Braiker " Google Project Glass: a new way to see the world," *The Guardian,* April 5, 2012, http://www.guardian.co.uk/world/us-news-blog/2012/apr/05/google (accessed April 29, 2012).
5. Genevieve Bell and Paul Dourish, "Yesterday's tomorrows: notes on ubiquitous computing's dominant vision," in *Personal and Ubiquitous Computing,* no. 2 (2006): 133–143.
6. Lev Manovich, "The poetics of augmented space." in *Visual Communication* 5, no. 2 (2006): 219–240.
7. See layar.com, wikitude.com and junaio.com
8. Ben Russell, "Karosta Workshop Notes" (2003) *RIXC Reader*, http://www.rixc.lv/reader/txt/txt.php?id=282&l=en&raw=1 (accessed April 29, 2012).
9. Communication from the Commission to the European Parliament, the Council, the European Economic and Social Committee and the Committee of the Regions "Re-use of Public Sector Information – Review of Directive 2003/98/EC" (2009), http://eur-lex.europa.eu/LexUriServ/LexUriServ.do?uri=COM:2009:0212:FIN:EN:PDF (accessed April 29, 2012).
10. Rosalyn Deutsche, *Evictions Art and Spatial Politics* (Cambridge MA, London: MIT Press, 1996), 169–181.
11. Rosalyn Deutsche, *Evictions Art and Spatial Politics* (Cambridge MA, London: MIT Press, 1996), 179.
12. Deven Golden, "Mark Lombardi," in *Art Critical*, November 1, 2003, http://www.artcritical.com/2003/11/01/mark-lombardi/ (accessed April 29,2012).
13. Mark Lombardi – Death Defying Acts of Art and Conspiracy dir. Mareike Wegener (2011).
14. Frances Richard, ""Obsessive – Generous" Toward a Diagram of Mark Lombardi," *Wburg.com*, no. 2 (2002), http://www.wburg.com/0202/arts/lombardi.html (accessed April 29, 2012).
15. See littlesis.org
16. See layar.com
17. See http://namawinelake.wordpress.com
18. At the time it was unclear what the legal position on releasing this information was, so I was advised to state that properties were "reported to be in NAMA" rather than in NAMA.
19. See Johathan Zittrain, "The Personal Computer Is Dead," in *Technology Review,* 2011, http://www.technologyreview.com/computing/39163/page1/ (accessed April 29, 2012).
20. Mark Godfrey, *Francis Alys: A Story of Deception* (London, Tate Publishing: 2010).
21. See S. Harrison and P. Dourish, "Re-place-ing space: the roles of place and space in collaborative systems," *Proceedings of the 1996 ACM conference on Computer supported cooperative work* (1996) 7:67–76. Also Eric Kluitenberg, "The Network of Waves Living and Acting in a Hybrid Space," *Open* 11 (2006).
22. Drew Hemment, "Locative Arts" *Leonardo* 39, no. 4 (2006): 348–355.
23. Manuel Castells, *The Rise of the Network Society* (Oxford: Wiley-Blackwell: 2000), 407–460.
24. Conor McGarrigle, "The Construction of Locative Situations: the Production of Agency in Locative Media Art Practice," Dublin Institute of Technology, 2012, http://arrow.dit.ie/appadoc/32/ (accessed March 1, 2013).
25. Richard Coyne, *The Tuning of Place : Sociable Spaces and Pervasive Digital Media* (Cambridge, MA: MIT Press, 2010) 4.
26. Alice Angus et al., "Urban Social Tapestries," *IEEE Pervasive Computing* 7, no. 4 (2008): 44–51.

CONOR MCGARRIGLE

interviewed by

Lanfranco Aceti & Richard Rinehart

Is there an 'outside' of the Art World from which to launch critiques and interventions? If so, what is the border that defines outside from inside? If it is not possible to define a border, then what constitutes an intervention and is it possible to be and act as an outsider of the art world? Or are there only different positions within the Art World and a series of positions to take that fulfill ideological parameters and promotional marketing and branding techniques to access the fine art world from an oppositional, and at times confrontational, standpoint?

I'm not sure it is that productive to think of an inside or outside of the art world. Certainly we can speak of an art world, or more accurately an art market, orientated around the gallery system, art fairs, museums and so forth. If we're speaking about making art in all its forms I think the boundaries are very porous with artists operating successfully within that narrow art world ecosystem while still retaining a wider relevance.

I'm not especially interested in critiques or interventions which only refer to art world concerns unless there is a broader context, they have their place, but it's not part of my practice. An important lesson of conceptual art is that the art world can recuperate any art movement if it so desires, so certainly assuming positions which are self-consciously 'outside' or constructed as oppositional in relation to the art world can be seen as operating tactically within the logic of the art world.

I'm interested in interventions which serve a purpose, any intervention must draw its validity from the cogency and strength of the critique rather from the operation of critique as an end in itself. Interventions which have a wider relevance typically operate across any number of interrelated fields with commensurate differences in the ways they are interpreted and understood. For example, I've presented my NAMAland project in the context of art, geography, urbanism, politics, technology, activism and even the smart economy and in each situation there are subtle differences in its reception.

"In *The Truth in Painting*, Derrida describes the *parergon* (*par-*, around; *ergon*, the work), the boundaries or limits of a work of art. Philosophers from Plato to Hegel, Kant, Husserl, and Heidegger debated the limits of the intrinsic and extrinsic, the inside and outside of the art object." (Anne Friedberg, *The Virtual Window: From Alberti to Microsoft* (Cambridge, MA: MIT Press, 2009), 13.) Where then is the inside and outside of the virtual artwork? Is the artist's 'hand' still inside the artistic process in the production of virtual art or has it become an irrelevant concept abandoned outside the creative process of virtual artworks?

I have to admit I'm deeply uneasy with the concept of the virtual artwork with its connotations of virtuality, which seems to point to a previous era. I prefer to think about works which operate in hybrid space where the delineation between online and offline, real space and virtual space is blurred. This for me is where AR art becomes interesting, when it can over-layer space with a context specific data layer. In the Headmap Manifesto, Ben Russell speaks of every place having invisible notes attached, I like to think of every place being augmented with its own invisible database driven critique which can be interrogated with that most ubiquitous of devices, the mobile

 ISSN 1071-4391 ISBN 978-1-906897-20-8

phone. I think the question of the boundaries of the artwork is particularly interesting when considering work which must operate within the confines of tightly constrained platforms. Much AR work, for example, is produced for platforms such as Layar which open augmented reality to a wider constituency, but at the cost of leaving little room for the artist's 'hand' in the coding and production process. This does beg the question that if the work is built on a platform the artist has not produced, with limited scope for transformative appropriation, where does the artist's 'hand' so to speak, lie? How does the artist evade the levels of scripting which are inevitably embedded in the platforms employed? I see the 'work' in this context moving from the object and its reception to the practice of the work; that is the way in which the artist interprets the technology and devises new usage modes for it. In my work, this entails leaving the work sufficiently open so that participants can engage with the work, build on it and make it their own, hopefully expanding the work beyond my intentions. In connecting data with site through the application of AR the work doesn't function as an object, but rather as an enabling act which sets in place the conditions necessary for further actions. I see Virno's notion of the virtuosic performance as "an activity without an end product" as significant in this respect.

Virtual interventions appear to be the contemporary inheritance of Fluxus' artistic practices. Artists like Peter Weibel, Yayoi Kusama and Valie Export subverted traditional concepts of space and media through artistic interventions. What are the sources of inspiration and who are the artistic predecessors that you draw from for the conceptual and aesthetic frameworks of contemporary augmented reality interventions?

I see the potential for data driven art being enhanced tremendously with ubiquitous location-awareness and network access, so I draw inspiration both from data driven art and art involving spatial interventions. In terms of data driven art Hans Haacke's seminal 1971 work "Shapolsky et al.," detailing the ownership of tenement buildings in New York City is a touchstone. Its Guggenheim exhibition was infamously cancelled, but one can imagine it working very effectively as an AR piece to counter its censoring. The drawings of Mark Lombardi and Josh On's *They Rule* are similarly illustrative of the ways in which data driven art can visually and forcefully make the connections between data and issues, transforming the abstractness of databases into hard critique. As the Open Data movement gathers pace we're seeing more and more data made available and the challenge is to interpret and transform these data sources in meaningful ways. Works like these show what's possible.

If augmented reality interventions are to be successful it's important that they operate as spatial interventions first and avoid becoming overly technology focused. Work that is enacted in space needs to be effective at this level, with the technology augmenting the primary spatial experience. In this I draw inspiration from the long tradition of artistic spatial interventions and walking art which demonstrate the power of small interventions to re-think and re-imagine space. The influence of Fluxus is certainly central to this as is the Situationist dérive. I return to works like Vito Acconi's *Following Piece*, Adrian Piper's *Catalysis* series, and Robert Smithson's *Tour of the Monuments of Passaic* for inspiration. The contemporary urban interventions of Francis Alÿs are an influence as are the Stalker Group's "Transurbances" of the mid 1990s, with their focus on the liminal spaces of the city. I look to the critical spatial practice of this type work and question the ways in which location-aware technologies can expand and build on these traditions.

In the representation and presentation of your artworks as being 'outside of' and 'extrinsic to' contemporary aesthetics why is it important that your projects are identified as art?

I don't think they necessarily are, but while I declare the work to be art, I'm also content for it to be interpreted differently. I recognise and appreciate that they operate at a number of levels. Recent works such as NAMAland which used Open Data and Augmented Reality to visualise and critique aspects of the Irish financial collapse have reached a wide audience through engaging with issues of broad concern. My concern with this work was to address specific issues for which discussion had been stalled due to deliberate withholding of information. By making available this augmented layer of critical, activist derived data the objective was to seed this across as many forums and interest groups as possible. The project crossed boundaries from art to geography, urbanism, opendata, economics and politics, as one would expect from work which engages critically with the space of the city and international finance. So for me its position vis-à-vis contemporary aesthetics is a moot point.

What has most surprised you about your recent artworks? What has occurred in your work that was outside of your intent, yet has since become an intrinsic part of the work?

What always surprises me is the way that individual works are received, taking on a life of their own beyond, perhaps, what I originally intended. The reaction to my NAMAland project was typical of this, but the scale of the reaction was quite unexpected. It was quickly taken up by the mainstream media with interviews on the main evening TV news, radio, newspapers and magazines reaching a large audience in a short space of time. While it obviously dealt with an issue of broad appeal, I was surprised by the extent of the response as it became, in effect, part of a wider discussion on the IMF bailout. Even its title, NAMAland, has entered into general usage as a descriptor for the post-bailout situation.

Initially I had planned the work as a short term project; make the AR app, release it and move on, however the level of interest in the work was so great that I felt it necessary to broaden the project which I did with NAMAland walking tours. These expanded the work, beyond being purely device led, into a richer on-going engagement with the space of the city and, most importantly, developed into mobile walk-and-talk forums to engage with the issues addressed in the work. This audience led aspect transformed the project into a deeper more sustained engagement. In hindsight I could say that the project's audience saw its potential more clearly than I did. ■

 ISSN 1071-4391 ISBN 978-1-906897-20-8

CONOR MCGARRIGLE

statement & artwork

As an artist working with 'new' and locative media my practice engages with digital media technologies,

not as autonomous devices or technology but as social actors which impact, mould and tune our everyday experience. My recent work has focused on place and spatial practice(s) mediated through ubiquitous and pervasive digital technologies. My current practice is thus a hybrid one which acknowledges the collapsing of distinction between the networked and physical worlds, operating in the resulting 'hybrid space,' where the interplay between the digital and the physical produces new spaces and new social practices.

Much of my recent work is enacted at street level, typically as generative walks or tours mediated through location-aware digital technologies and mobile applications, which over-layer real space with conceptual re-mappings. These works function both as novel methods of engaging with technology with their subtle shifts of usage modes, and as approaches toward providing frameworks and structures to engage with the city as a space of encounter. 1 Rather than producing works which are complete and finite, I am more interested in providing artistic tools and procedures which can be adopted, renegotiated and expanded on by their participants. In this way, the work involves a shifting of authorship with participants granted

NAMAland Walking Tour, 2011, Conor McGarrigle. Participatory Walk. © Conor McGarrigle

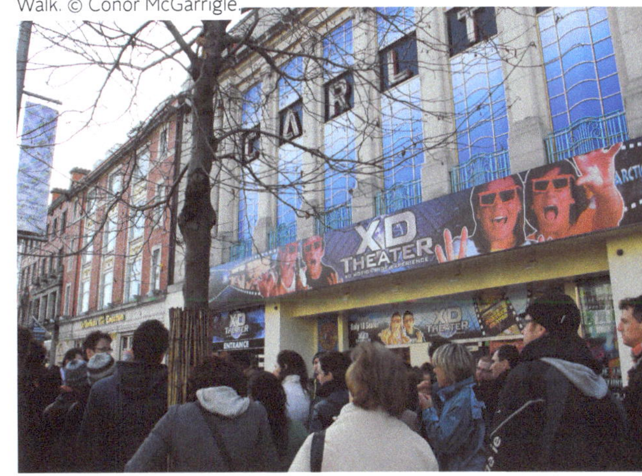

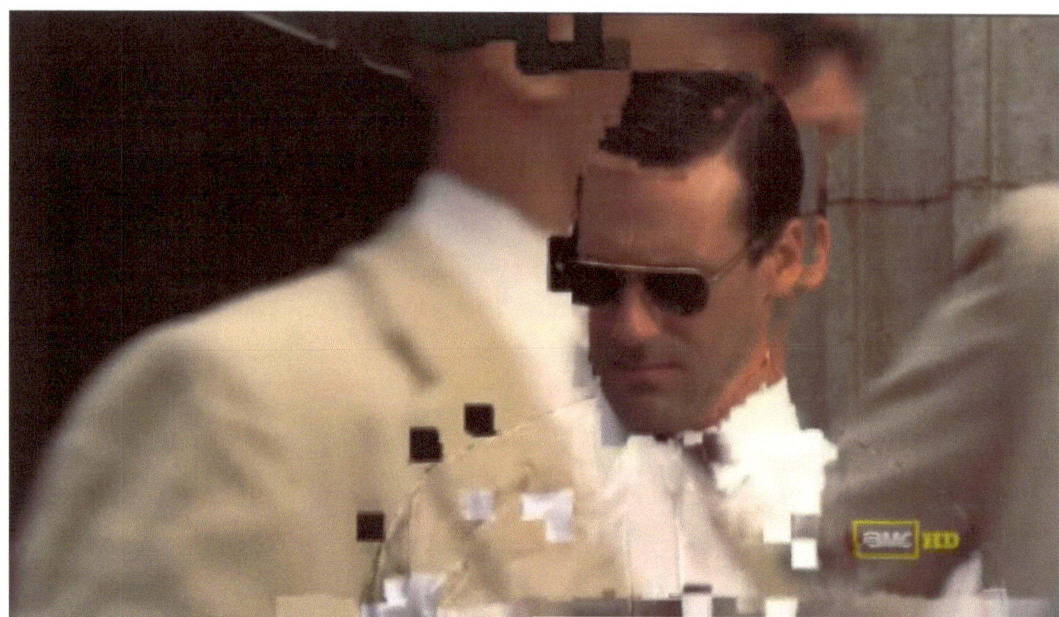

Mad Men: the Bittorrent Edition, 2011, Conor McGarrigle, video. © Conor McGarrigle.

agency to infuse the work with their own concerns and incorporate it into their own practice.

My work follows in the tradition of the walking artists; drawing inspiration from the spatial practices of the Situationists (and offering a contemporary take on the *dérive*), Robert Smithson, Richard Long and Hamish Fulton, Fluxus interventions and the contemporary interventions of the Italian Stalker Group and Francis Alÿs. The work is also indebted to the pioneers of locative media whose influence is to be seen in the form that location-aware technologies are taking as they become part of the everyday.

Katherine Hayles sees the information intensive environments of ubiquitous and pervasive computing as challenging us to use them in "constructive and life-enhancing ways without capitulating to [their] coercive and exploitive aspects." [2] I respond to this challenge and see it as central in new media art's engagement with new and emergent technologies, which has agency in their reframing, in shifting our understanding of them so that they are available to a broader constituency of users to enhance the ever day. My work strives to maintain a critical relationship with its technology. To keep "thinking of technology *as* a question, and therefore to keep it *in* question." [3] ■

REFERENCES AND NOTES

1. Henri Lefebvre, *The Urban Revolution*, trans. Robert Bononno (Minneapolis, MN: University of Minnesota Press, 2003), 213.
2. K. Hayles, "RFID: Human Agency and Meaning in Information-Intensive Environments," in *Theory, Culture & Society* 26, no. 2–3 (2009): 47–72.
3. Krzysztof Ziarek, *The Force of Art* (CA: Stanford University Press, 2004), 65–66.

 ISSN 1071-4391 ISBN 978-1-906897-20-8

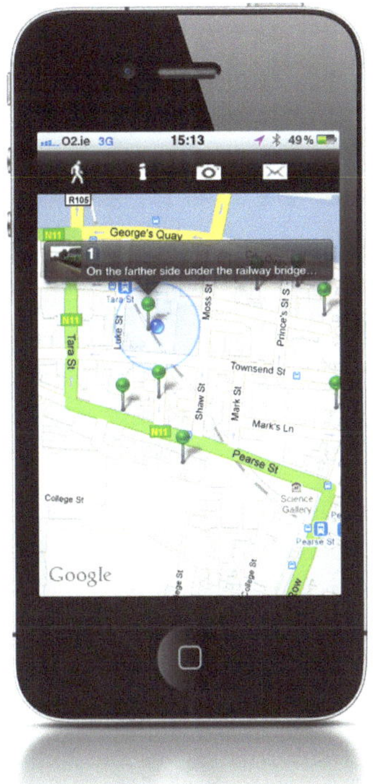

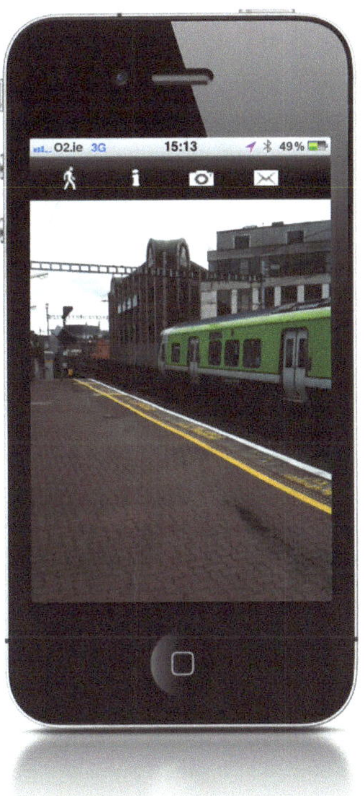

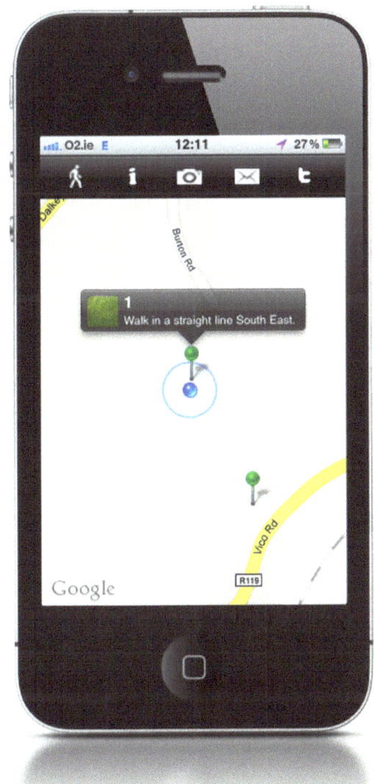

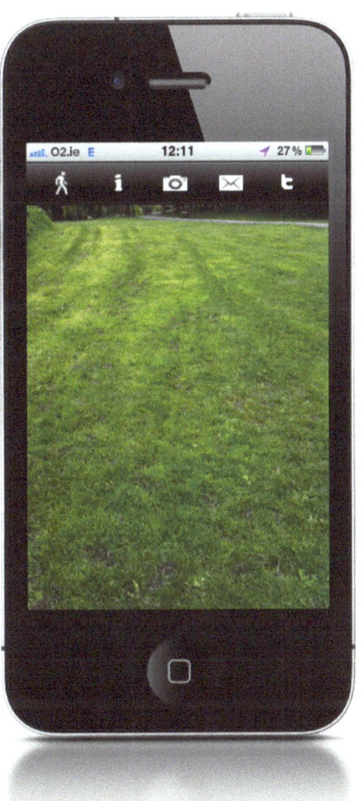

WalkSpace, 2011, Conor McGarrigle, iPhone App. © Conor McGarrigle.

Situated Soundscapes: Redefining media art and the urban experience

NATASA PATERSON & FIONNUALA CONWAY

Music and Media Technologies
Trinity College Dublin

1. INTRODUCTION

The advancement of the telecommunications industry has enabled the telephone to become a portable communications device and a tool for providing social networking and information services. With the development of mobile technology, smartphones now also provide an entertainment experience previously only available on portable devices such as the Nintendo DSi, to present an integrated, ubiquitous communication and information services, social networking and entertainment device. This has allowed mobile phone gaming to move from early games such as Nokia's *Snake* [40] to graphically rich and interactive games such as *iPhone's Epoch* [14] which is reminiscent of a traditional console presentation. The smartphone's portability and accessibility to the Internet has enabled multimedia applications to be downloaded and experienced at any location that the user chooses, at anytime. This new device has led to individual access to various multimedia and creative experiences, alowin it to become a creative tool employed in the art domain and for entertainment experiences that can include downloadable interactive games, enhanced audio books and music.

With the integration of GPS (Global Positioning System) technology to the mobile phone platform, smartphone applications based on the Apple or Google Android platforms, can now interact with real world locations where the physical space becomes a contextual cue for the social interaction or media narrative. With the addition of location technology, digital media has now become a personalized experience that is revolutionizing the way people engage and experience their everyday environment, [6] just as the mobility and ubiquity of the Walkman did in the 1980s. However, whereas the Walkman could be seen as a metaphor for the individualistic culture, the smartphone can be viewed as representing the connectedness of a larger and more global society. [23] Thus, mobile computing can give rise to new types of interactions within an urban setting and creative behaviors and aesthetic practices in people's everyday life.

2. FROM INSTALLATIONS TO AUGMENTED REALITY

The use of the digital medium as a form of artistic expression can draw its roots from the development of information technology. Vannevar Bush was one of the first scientists to consider information technology being used for creative thought, and subsequently

 ISSN 1071-4391 ISBN 978-1-906897-20-8

The rise of GPS (Global Positioning System) enabled smartphones, such as the iPhone and Google Android mobile operating system, together with the high-bandwidth network access afforded by third generation (3G) networks, *has meant the use of these devices progressing beyond their social networking and communication purposes to become creative tools employed in the art domain and for entertainment experiences. Smartphones are able to augment real world spaces by introducing a digital narrative that can alter one's experience of a space, allowing it to reveal details and experiences in a previously unseen manner, thereby providing a rich and new encounter of this new world. A number of applications currently exist that augment space using visual means, however, there are still only a limited number that use audio. This technology allows for new ways to experience the static audio installation, previously experienced in the studio or gallery. It is now possible to experience dynamic and interactive soundscapes, influenced by one's movements, location and environmental stimuli. Hence the experience is aural and unencumbered, creating an automated embodied encounter where one becomes the performer and the space an interactive soundscape. This paper presents the concept of interactive soundscapes and looks at a methodology for the use of mobile technology that challenges the tendency to simply extend traditional media onto the mobile sphere. Instead, location technology and the urban space can be viewed as an artistic canvas on which sound artists, musicians and composers can test the classical constraints of design, ruled so long by the physics of space, time, and material in order to experiment with new media content compositional strategies to create entirely new forms of art.*

the 1960's saw an emergence of multimedia work in scientific circles that embraced technology. This new experimentation in the creative arts between scientists and artists led to work that could incorporate multisensory engagement and interactivity. [27] As this collaboration continued, multimedia presentations in the 1960s and 1970s soon began to take the form of 'installations' with this word being used to describe the combined use of media such as video, music, lighting and computer technology for immersive creative experiences in a traditionally static space. [37] As information technology continued to advance, artists such as Myron Krueger began to consider the possibility of virtual experiences. In the early 1960s, Krueger coined the term 'artificial reality' (virtual reality) to describe his interactive immersive environments. The 1980's saw an investment in interactive technology where virtual spaces are navigated by developed interfaces. [33] Scott Fisher's Virtual Interface Environmental Workstation system (VIEW) included a Head Mounted Display (HMD) with two small liquid crystal display screens, a microphone for speech recognition, earphones for surround sound effects, a head-tracking device and a data-glove for the processing of the user's gestures in order to place them within the virtual environment, an idea populated by the film *The Lawnmover Man* (1992). [8] Fisher believed that engaging, immersive environments could lead to a new form of participatory, interactive electronic theatre. The majority of virtual reality applications resulted in an encumbered experience – one in which the user is bound by wearing the technology enabling the virtual interaction and which is separate from the world around them.

As artists utilized technology for media art expression, entertainment technologies such as film and gaming also applied the developing digital and information technologies in creating engaging environments. These scenarios used immersive surround sound presentations, rich visuals and interactivity. With the continued advancement of personal computer technology and gaming devices, portability of interactive entertainment experiences for the individual was made possible. [15] Portable devices can be described as handheld game consoles which are lightweight, portable, with a built-in screen, game controls and speakers. Unlike console games which are static in nature, portable devices such as Nintendo's *Gameboy* (1989) allowed the flexibility of players to engage with a game space at any time and place. [45] With the introduction of mobile technology and its subsequent increased memory and processing power, the majority of these entertainment experiences have now moved from traditional portable entertainment devices to the smartphone, signaling a merging of telecommunications and information technology industries.

Currently, not only can the media experience be undertaken in any location at any time, smartphones with integrated GPS capabilities are also able to augment real world spaces by introducing a digital narrative overlay onto a real world location. [10] In contrast to virtual reality where the user is separated from the outside world and isolated within a digitally mediated narrative, augmented reality experiences encourage the user to remain engaged with their surroundings while interacting with the digital media, hence occupying a blended, mixed reality 'third space' where the real world is changed or 'augmented' by the digital overlay, thereby giving it a different meaning. [31] Mäyrä at al points to the possibilities of augmented reality gaming as not only testing the imagination and creativity but also questioning the ideas of what constitutes reality and what it means to be present and virtual. [29] There are currently many applications that utilise GPS technology for a variety of purposes but fewer that use visual and/or audio overlays over real world locations. *Layar* [28] is a browser application that visually displays local information and reviews on the mobile phone camera view and relies on a combination of the GPS receiver, internal compass, accelerometer and mobile Internet connection. The camera captures the world as seen through its lens and displays it on the screen. The GPS information determines the exact location and the compass and accelerometer the field of view. *Foursquare* [18] is an example of a GPS mediated social networking application, where users note their location and that of their friends. An example of an augmented reality game is *SpecTrek,* [44] a ghost hunting game where the player must capture ghostly images in the camera view in order to win rewards and progress in the game. In the majority of mobile phone and portable device experiences, the location of the player is not of paramount importance to the narrative structure. However in augmented reality applications the user's physical location coordinates and movements are important elements of the narrative experience.

 ISSN 1071-4391 ISBN 978-1-906897-20-8

3. MEDIA ART AND THE URBAN SPACE

The emergence of augmented reality has not only redefined the entertainment experience but has also opened up the possibilities for artists to recontextualize media art and the urban experience by exploring the use of portable, location aware devices in which the physical space becomes the canvas. The practice of locative media art (a term coined by Karlis Kalnins) [20] utilizes location aware technology in real world locations for an emphasis upon locality and the deinstitutionalization of the traditional artistic installation, [46] hence breaking down the exclusivity barrier between artist and the general public – a concept first popularized in the 1990's by French critic Nicolas Bourriaud. [24] However locative media art has differed from the general understanding of augmented reality. Locative media art aims to enhance the social engagement with a space together with a critical understanding of oneself and culture. [24] Locative media projects such as *Can you see me now?* (2006) [1] and *Uncle Roy All Around You* (2003) [5] explore user interactions of the social and spatial relations of a narrative in a given space and their cultural understandings, allowing private narratives to become public and subject to reinterpretation. Other narrative-led location aware projects also include *Urban Tapestries* [24] which combined GPS information to enable users to explore their physical space and to map and share their knowledge and experiences of the environment. Therefore, locative media art can facilitate the understanding of the relationship between one's agency and the social and cultural structure around them.

Augmented reality is a descriptor of the technological experience rather than a social statement such as locative art [24] and refers to GPS information and smartphone technology allowing for the embedding of visual and audio information over a physical space where reality is overlaid with virtual reality. Now with the popularity and ubiquitous nature of the smartphone, artists are able to experiment with the merging of the locative media art paradigm, location technology and augmented reality. Smartphones and location technology can offer new ways of media art to engage the world and reconfigure ones understandings and experiences of space and culture. [20] This creates a sense of territory, in which there is the mapping of physical space and the production of an artistic or cultural milieu: the artist creates a new way of seeing and occupying the world. [24] By including the physical location in the virtual medium, an urban intervention is constructed to encourage encounters from outside the contained realities, hence interrupting everyday life. [48] By augmenting an urban space, places and activities that were previously viewed as mundane become reinterpreted, revealing details and experiences that were unseen, thereby providing a rich and new encounter of this new world.

4. SOUND AND SPACE

4.1 Sound Installations

With the emergence of collaborative work between the creative arts, scientists and technologists in the 1960–70's, artists strived to develop works that could appeal to the entire sensory experience. Therefore, there was a progression to incorporate or exclusively use sound to immerse the listener in a space. [27] One such example is composer La Monte Young's and Marion Zazeela's *Dream House* (1964) installations, which are an environment for sound and light installations where speakers are positioned to guide the listener through a given space. [12] This is an example where sound is spatially experienced in a given environment and extends the music from the traditional concert hall setting. [27] The sound artist Christina Kubisch, also began experimenting with sound and space by creating sound installations produced from the mutual interaction of electromagnetic fields towards the end of the 1960s. [13] The 'electrical' sound was made by loudspeakers interacting with a field of electrical wires where the sounds changed depending on the person's movement. The participant 'mixed' their own sounds as they moved through the gallery space in a timeframe of their choice. Don Ritter's *Intersection* (1993) is another sound installation where visitors interacted with sensors controlling the sound of 4 or 8 lanes of traffic rushing across a dark space. As they moved through the space, the traffic sounds changed with the result of the sound depending on the visitor's physical reaction. [26] The Canadian sound artist Janet Cardiff, also aimed to recreate real world soundscapes in static installation spaces. Her work *Forty-Part Motet* (2001) aimed to recreate the performance of Tallis's *Spem in alium* by the Salisbury Cathedral Choir by utilizing a forty channel stereophonic experience. [17] In order to receive the full effect of the installation, the listener had to stand in the centre while surrounded by the speakers. Otherwise they would not experience the surround sound effect and proper psychoacoustics (sound propagation) for the almost hyper-real sonic clarity of the recording. In these examples, sound art installations in a static space have aimed to recreate real spaces and their sonic qualities or create new interactive means of engaging and changing the audience with sound in a given space. Even though, these artists have aimed to deconstruct the elitist and exclusive nature of art installations, there is still the requirement for the audience to enter a 'space' of the artist's choice rather than experience it at their leisure. There is the additional problem that the viewer must be placed in the correct position for the sound interaction to be effective and installations recreating real events can at times appear artificial, as they may lack other sensory information associated with the experience. By positioning the work in a studio or gallery space, the work is removed from the real world and may undermine the desired immersion and engagement to a narrative. By transferring sonic art experiences from the gallery space and onto relevant real world locations, the audience is able to engage in a realistic way with the added benefit of inclusivity and accessibility for the general populace. Situated soundscapes can accurately depict real locations and their sound qualities and allow for greater interactivity and individual movement within the sound space.

4.2 Situated Soundscapes

Sound artists began to experiment with transferring their gallery installations into the real world whereby soundscapes would change depending on the movement of the participant. Max Neuhaus sought to bring sound, space and interactivity together while drawing on environmental noise, acoustical dynamics and architectural elements, thereby positioning the listener and sound inside a greater urban space. His work *Drive In Music* (1967) consisted of a series of radio transmitters located along a half-mile stretch. Each transmitter broadcast a certain frequency for that zone. As listeners drove through the given locations, the frequencies could be tuned into, overlapping and mixing as one drove from one zone to another. [47] This signaled a change for sound artists in appreciating the creativity afforded by dispersing sound across a greater real world space, effectively fixing sound to a location. Kubisch also moved her gallery work into the urban space by extending her 1980's work with electromagnetic fields to include interactions with real world locations. With magnetic headphones altered in order to perceive local electrical currents translated to acoustic sound, Kubisch developed her *Electrical Walks* (2003) site-specific sound installation. [13] As the participant moved throughout an urban space they were able to hear the audio effects of electrical currents of cell phones, elevators, light systems to name a few, hence augmenting the real world location with a unique soundscape. Therefore with situated sound art, the perception of everyday reality changes and there is a blurring of boundaries between the real and the media, the unheard becomes heard, and the urban space

 ISSN 1071-4391 ISBN 978-1-906897-20-8

is experienced in an altered way. Another example that explored the possibilities of interactive soundscapes in urban spaces is *Sonic City* (2004) which draws upon ubiquitous computing and wearable computing to create a portable music system that responds via sensors to changes in the ambient environment as the user walks through an urban environment. [22] *Sonic City* generated a personal soundscape co-produced by physical movement, local activity, and urban ambience. Using the city as an interface, *Sonic City* enabled users to create a realtime personal soundscape of electronic music by walking through and interacting with urban environments. The prototype consisted of a wearable computer that sensed the user's physical actions and mapped them to an algorithm that generated music in real-time. Sensors used included; a metal detector, an IR-sensor (infrared) measuring proximity to walls and objects, a light intensity sensor, a microphone that measured sound level, an accelerometer that sensed starts and stops and a pace sensor that set the music tempo of the session. When wearing this system, urban atmospheres, random encounters and everyday activities all participate in creating music while walking. As technology has developed, artists have sought different methods of anchoring and triggering sounds in relation to real world locations. In Mark Shepard's *Tactical Sound Garden (TSG)* (2007) [39] project, wireless (WiFi) "hot zones" were used to install a "sound garden" for public use. The participants downloaded the software and travelled to the specified location of the soundscape within an urban place. Upon entering a sound garden, participants connected to a local TSG server and downloaded a small client application along with a library of sounds to their device. As the participant moved through the sound garden, the client application periodically identified the participant's position. This positioning information was fed to the 3D audio engine running on the client, which subsequently output a realtime audio mix specific to the current location of the listener. As well as anchoring sounds to specific locations, *Tactical Sound Garden (TSG)* also utilized psychoacoustic principles such as spatialized sound to place the audio in a sound field, with the soundscape changed in relation to the user's direction. Three-dimensional audio has increasingly been utilized in creating realistic sound presentations for interactive soundscapes. Janet Cardiff's *Her Long Black Hair* (2004) audiowalk was created by using a binaural technology narrative (accurately emulating 3D human hearing) played on a Walkman together with photographs, guiding the listener through Central Park in New York City. [25]

Even though these artists have aimed to deconstruct the elitist and exclusive nature of art installations, there is still the requirement for the audience to enter a 'space' of the artist's choice rather than experience it at their leisure.

ISSN 1071-4391 ISBN 978-1-906897-20-8

With increased public access to GPS technology in the 1990's, sound artists were able to begin to explore methods of accurately anchoring sounds to specific sites that could be triggered by a dedicated GPS receiver device or a mobile phone. As the technology developed, sound installations became more sophisticated and mobile. *Sound Mapping* (1998) by Iain Mott is an example whereby participants realized a composition by wheeling four movement-sensitive suitcases within a public place, with the "aim to assert a sense of place, physicality and engagement to reaffirm the relationship between art and the every day." [24] *Sound Mapping* produces music in response to nearby architectural features, subtle movements and gestures, and by the movements of the participants. Similarly, *Aura* (2004) by Steve Symons is an example whereby a virtual sound environment is accessed by walking through a space equipped with GPS and digital compass. Individual users can "hear" the location of other participants, and work together to create sonic tapestries through their relative movements. [3]

These examples have all described unique methods of creating a new soundscape layer over a real world space. However the majority of previous site-specific sound installations have required encumbered setups. The development of GPS enabled mobile phones such as the smart phone, provided the means for artists to create increasingly unencumbered soundscape experiences in physical locations that allowed for ease of movement and an embodied control of audio to augment the local space. Additionally, with the popularity and availability of smartphones these experiences can be unique for the participant and experienced at a time of their choosing, facilitating an inclusive sound art experience. *Dimensions* (2012) developed by RJDJ, an augmented music team together with composer Hans Zimmer, is an auditory cinematic experience where the movement of the smartphone and environmental sounds create a dynamic soundscape, mediated by the surrounding urban space. [11] External sounds are recorded, filtered and added to the audio together with pre-determined music that is mixed into the overall soundscape. Another augmented reality audio experienced on the smartphone is *Soundwalk* (2009) which uses the *Layar* browser and mixes fiction and reality in a cinematic experience giving the listener the impression of actually being in a film. *Soundwalk* augments reality with additional audio content overlaid onto certain locations around Paris. [43]

The listener's perception and experience of a space can be modified depending on movement through the space and surrounding environment. Since the ground rules defining the structure of environments are changing, our idea of how we are embedded in the world is changing. Urban spaces can be experienced in an alternate way that uses sound to blur the boundary of virtual and reality, alowing the interpretion of different spaces in a new and creative way. The use of smartphone technology in artistic practice signals the development of a new art form medium that can be further extended to afford artists even greater avenues of creativity and interactivity, outside the gallery space. Pushing the limits between art, urban space and mobility, liberates us from the conventional way of relating to technology, society and physical spaces.

5. METHODS OF REDEFINING SOUND ART IN THE URBAN SPACE

In order for locative sound artists to continue to socially redefining the art space and experience, artists must expand and challenge established notions and develop new models of interaction. As technology progresses, new ideas of an interactive engagement in a real space continue to evolve, and the role of the participant is redefined. New methods of implementation must be considered in order to modify how soundscapes can evolve and respond to the environment and participant. The aim now is to look to the creation of an all-encompassing soundscape application, on several smartphone platforms, that incorporates the effect of not only the local architectural and natural environment, but also the social and economic factors that impact everyday life. In combining these factors together with the manipulation of external

 ISSN 1071-4391 ISBN 978-1-906897-20-8

sound and established music compositional idioms and guidelines, the participant is able to not only experience the locative sound artwork but also to become an integral part of its final compositional outcome.

5.1 Mobile Technology and Audio

5.1.1 Location Technology

In order to create interactive and immersive soundscapes overlaid onto an urban space, the location of the participant needs to be established. The sound design framework must be such that it is unencumbered, smooth in its transitions and automatic in the sense that the user is not consciously aware of the technology. Various methods can be used to trigger audio. In the case of locative art in an urban space, GPS technology is the most easily accessible and commonly used. However, problems with this technology continue to persist such as network unreliability and inaccuracy, which can at times consist of an eight metre delineation error. [34] This can disrupt the desired experience and immersive quality. Locations must be carefully sourced that not only support the narrative context but that also provide enough open space to enable the GPS system to register three points from three different satellites for best accuracy. Additionally, smartphones that utilise a three-axis internal compass are able to accurately determine the direction the person is facing enabling the sound artist to anchor audio to specific architectural landmarks. Research into new methods of triggering content is currently underway such as *SonicNotify* [41] which utilise inaudible frequencies from televisions and radios to trigger content on the smartphone. Additionally there has been recent work on improving the already available GPS technology with the launching of additional satellites for improved location tracking.

5.1.2 Triggering of Audio

Once the location and the direction of the device has been ascertained, and the direction, audio files can be triggered in a number of ways. The most popular smartphones platforms, the *iPhone* and *Google android* offer two distinct methods of audio playback. The first is a media player that allows for longer, linear files to be triggered and the second player is used for shorter files for 'sound effect' playback. Longer files can be used to trigger and loop pre-determined soundscapes that are relevant to the given space. Additionally, shorter files can be triggered that respond dynamically to the person's movement and direction. These can be detected by an accelerometer (ascertains speed of movement) and compass integrated within the smartphone. Gaming middleware (services beyond those available from the operating system) applications such as FMOD (for *iPhone*) [16] can act as an audio engine for the smartphone in order to trigger audio files when pre-programmed criteria are met (i.e. such as GPD data). Additionally, audio samples can be stored on the internal memory card of the smartphone and triggered by midi text files in relation to GPS data. *Sonivox Jet* [42] provides realtime mixing of a full wavetable MIDI synthesizer to create textures by customizing the wavetable. Many samples can be mixed differently according to locations with midi text files being streamed from local networks. Another method of triggering audio would be simply to stream files directly from a local server in response to a location. However, this method is unreliable and slow.

5.1.3 Manipulation of Audio

Once audio is triggered using a variety of methods, the artist can choose to either use pre-determined and recorded sound or to manipulate the audio using realtime computing on the smartphone. Examples of simple manipulations are the looping of files, playing multiple files simultaneously or changing file playback parameters such as speed of play, which would change the pitch and timbre of sound. For example, *Viking Ghost Hunt* (2010), [34] an augmented reality ghost-hunting prototype, uses the process of generative audio. This technique utilizes the playback of numerous overlapping audio files with varying pause times between them. This process depends on careful sound file creation and results in an evolving soundscape that is dynamically changing and perceived as continuous. Furthermore, middleware software such as FMOD and Pure Data [35] can again be used in filtering and manipulating audio files so that the original file is altered. This software utilizes digital signal processing technology in order to change audio parameters such as the filtering of audio frequencies to create altered sounds from the one audio file. Additionally, external audio can be recorded and digitally processed by the middleware software to created altered real world sounds that can be added to the overall soundscape mix. Again these technologies are progressing to include more functionality. For example granulation (altering the timbre by using small millisecond 'grains' of sound) of audio is now possible on the smartphone by using the *Curtis* [9] application. Even though, the processing capabilities of smartphones lack that of general computing, it is still possible to create immersive, complex soundscapes.

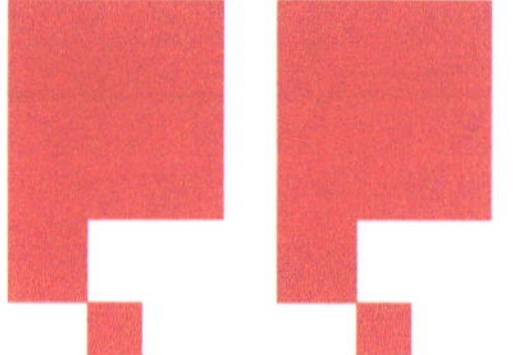

Even though the processing capabilities of smartphones lack that of general computing, it is still possible to create immersive, complex soundscapes.

5.1.4 Psychoacoustics

Psychoacoustics describes the propagation of sound in the real world, and is presented in a three-dimensional manner to enable localization, distance perception and recognition [2]. The most accurate method of spatialized audio over headphones is by the use of HRTF (Head Related Transfer Function) binaural audio filters. These filters take into account the effect of the ear structure, head and torso on the sound input before it reaches the eardrum for sound localization [21]. By utilizing software that incorporates binaural technology, spatialisationof sound can be accurately represented. Currently, it is difficult to accurately binaurally spatialize sound in real time, with middleware programs already mentioned (FMOD, Pure Data) only having the functionality to approximate (semi) binaural audio presentations. However, the artist is still able to manipulate the positioning of sound objects in any way they desire within a sound field – with the ability to spatialize multiple sounds in different spatial locations. Other programming software, such as OpenSL ES [32] for the *iPhone* also spatializes audio sound objects in a three-dimensional plane, but depends upon programming language for implementation. In the context of locative sound art, it would be creatively desirable to anchor sound objects to a real world location in such a way that they remain static in the sound field even as the participant physically changes direction in relation to it. In the previously mentioned prototype, *Viking Ghost Hunt* this was achieved by panning the sound (changing the amplitudes between two channels) in relation to head movement in the

 ISSN 1071-4391 ISBN 978-1-906897-20-8

real world. However, it was found to be unreliable and dependent on the type of smartphone that was used. [34] This is an area requiring further research that could significantly alter the creative possibilities available to artists in regards to spatial audio digital overlay on a physical location.

As well as spatialization, the use of reverberation is of importance when creating sound pieces that aspire to be immersive. Reverberation describes the propagation and interaction of sound with surfaces that create the ambience of a space. [38] Two types of reverberation can be used in sound art designs: 'artificial' and 'convolution' reverberation. Convolution reverberation is the process of simulating the reverberation of a physical (or virtual) space and is based on the mathematical process of convolution (multiplying two signals to create a third). An impulse response measurement (a recording of the reverberation) of the intended space to be simulated is recorded and then convolved with the dry audio signal to be processed. This reverberation of the processed audio signal then reacts to that of the intended physical or virtual space. [4] Real space reverberation simulation is a technique already used in film. "Worldising" – a sound concept made famous by sound designer Walter Murch, is a process where existing recordings are re-recorded in a real world acoustic space therefore taking on the characteristics of the new space. [30] Artificial reverberation is an approximation of real reverberation and involves controlling various reverberation parameters such as time delay, room size, number of early and late reflections. The use of reverberation on audio files for smartphone sound artworks can currently be accomplished to a limited extent in realtime using FMOD [16] and Pure Data. [36] Due to the current processing power possible on the smartphone platforms, it is not possible to produce convolution reverberation that is reactive to the physical space of the participant. This area would benefit from new research as the creative implications for sound art installations would be significant.

There are many technological constraints when considering the smartphone as a creative device for sound installations especially when considering psychoacoustic principles, such as reduced memory capacity and processing power. However, the avenues of creativity are endless, and the challenge that confronts the artist is to form new solutions through experimentation in order to realize the creative potential. Working with mobile technologies is simultaneously a glance into the future but also a reminder of the past; many amenities, functionalities, and power of modern computing technology on which we depend on, are increasingly becoming available on the mobile platform. Hence, the avenues of creative expression are continuously evolving and changing.

5.2 Automated Composition: The audience as performer

In order for the processes of triggering and manipulating audio to result in a sound artwork, it ultimately must be mediated by a 'performer' and a physical space. As one moves through a space, incoming data from GPS coordinates, internal compass information and accelerometer readings can trigger different audio files and digital processing in order to augment a physical space with sound. When these sounds are mixed, together they combine to create a unique soundscape for a specific location. Hence the emergent soundscape is the result of an 'embodied composition' where the smartphone acts as an automated instrument and with the movement through the space creates the 'performance'. An 'automated instrument' is a device which automatically produces sound where the formal processes are algorithmically derived and controlled. There are many early examples of automated instruments such as the Hurdy Gurdy of the fifteenth century and mechanical singing birds of the eighteenth century. Viewing music procedurally rather than purely as expression dates back to ancient times and includes early church music and the formulation of the rules of counterpoint. Wolfgang Amadeus Mozart's *Musikalisches Wurfelspiel* is an example of an algorithmically derived piece where the performer composes a piece of music based on the throw of a dice with values corresponding to precomposed measures of music [7].

Iannis Xenakis was a contemporary composer utilizing probabilities to control shapes, densities and statistical data to control changes of contour between musical parameters together with compositional processes that are outside the musical medium. Using this same concept, statistical data can be retrieved from the smartphone such as the time of day, climate and stock market values that are then 'sonified', that is, represented by sound. Therefore as the performer moves through a space, the digital soundscape can be informed by the sonification of this input data by either adding sound or by controlling various musical parameters. An urban space can be augmented with the overlaying of a given soundscape together with the sonification of social data. Creating a dynamically changing soundscape that embodies the experiences of architecture, economics, environment and technology, enabling the potential for different performers to encounter the same space differently each time. In addition to the sonification of data, external sound can be recorded, altered and added to the soundscape mix.

Compositionally, the use of external or 'found sound' objects for music making is described as musique concrète. The theoretical underpinnings of the aesthetic were developed by Pierre Schaeffer, beginning in the early 1940s, [46] where the compositional material was not restricted to the inclusion of sounds derived from musical instruments or components traditionally thought of as 'musical'. *Net_Dérive* (2008) [46] is an example of utilizing the mobile platform and GPS technology together with the concept of musique concrète, where recorded sounds of the city are processed to give the listener an abstracted soundscape experience of the urban space.

The term idiomatic writing is used to describe the process of composing music that takes into consideration the characteristics of an instrument. If we apply the principle of idiomatic writing to the smartphone and its technological frameworks, the challenge for artists is to develop formal processes of design to create soundscapes that respond in a profound way to the locative, social and interactive dynamics of an urban space. The use of interactive, participatory, and location aware technologies poses an interesting set of compositional, aesthetic and technological challenges. Firstly, the sound design framework must take into account the non-linearity of the medium and unpredictability of the interactions within an urban space. Formal compositional processes and input data that will control audio parameters must also be considered. Finally the technical constraints of realtime digital processing of audio must and its effects should be measured when developing a situated soundscape application.

6. CONCLUSION

By using many of the audio technologies on the smartphone originally developed for gaming and commercial ventures, sound artists are now able to expand on the known boundaries of locative sound art to include unique and ubiquitous experiences that can be accessed by the general public. This paper has reviewed just a few of the potential methodologies available in creating an interactive urban sound experience. Each time we experience a space, factors such as the environment, speed of ones movement, climate, time of the day and location all add to our encounter of the same space and may be experienced differently depending on our interactions. Sonification of this dynamically changing data embodies the experiences of architecture, economics, environment, technology and creativity in an audio and spatial narrative that enables society to engage differently with a location, opening up alternate explorations. Using the smartphone as an automated musical instrument for an algorithmically derived original soundscape provides a new way of relating to technology, society and the urban space. ■

ACKNOWLEDGEMENTS

We wish to acknowledge Trinity College Dublin for the continuous support and funding for our research.

 ISSN 1071-4391 ISBN 978-1-906897-20-8

REFERENCES AND NOTES

1. Rob Anastasi, Nick Tandavanity, et al., "Can you see e now? A Citywide MixedReality Gaming Experience," *ACM Transactions on Computer-Human Interaction (TOCHI)* 13, no. 1 (March 2006).
2. Daniel H Ashmead, Everett W Hill and C R Talor, "Obstacle perception by congenitally blind children," *Perception and Psychophysics* 46, no. 5 (1989): 425–433.
3. "Aura," Steve Symons, 2012, http://stevesymons.net/taxonomy/term/6
4. D. Begault, 3D *Sound for Virtual Reality and Multimedia* (San Diego, CA: Academic Press Inc, 1994).
5. Steve Benford, Martin Flintham, Adam Drozd, Rob Anastasi, Duncan Rowland, Nick Tandavanitj, Matt Adams, Ju Row-Farr, Amanda Oldroyd, and Jon Sutton, "Uncle Roy All Around You: Implicating the City in a Location-Based Performance," *ACE'04 June 3–5*, Singapore, 2004.
6. Micheal Bull, *Sounding Out the City: Personal Stereos and the Management of Everyday Life* (Oxford: Berg, 2000).
7. Karen Collins, *Game Sound: An Introduction to the History, Theory and Practice of Video Game Music and Sound Design* (Cambridge, MA: MIT Press, 2008).
8. "Comm, Tech and Culture," Comm, Tech and Culture, http://comm-tech-culture.blogspot.com/2012/02/visions-of-future-in-lawnmower-man.html (accessed April 1, 2013).
9. "Curtis," Tiny Music: Xenakis Synthesis, Curtis Roads Granulation on iPhone, http://createdigitalmusic.com/2009/06/tiny-music-xenakis-synthesis-curtis-roads-granulation-on-iphone/ (accessed April 30th , 2012).
10. Adriana De Souza e Silva, "Location Based Games: Blurring the borders between physical and virtual spaces," in *Proceedings of ISEA (12th International Symposium of Electronic Art)*, Baltic Sea, August 14–22, 2004.
11. "Dimensions," RJDJ, http://dimensions.rjdj.me/ (accessed January 10, 2012).
12. "Dream House," Mela Foundation, http://melafoundation.org/dream02.htm (accessed April 23, 2012).
13. "Electrical Walks," Christina Kubisch, http://www.christinakubisch.de/english/install_induktion.htm (accessed October 10, 2009).
14. "Epoch," Uppercut Games Pty Ltd, http://itunes.apple.com/us/app/epoch./id453164597?mt=8 (accessed April 15, 2012).
15. Pablo Fernandez, Asier Perallos, Nekane Sainz, and Roberto Carballedo, "A location-Based Transactional Download Service of Contextualized Multimedia Content for Mobile Clients," in *Distributed Computing and Artificial Intelligence 7th International Symposium* (Springer, 2010).
16. "FMOD," Firelight Technologies, http://www.fmod.org/ (accessed April 30· 2012).
17. "Forty Part Motet," Janet Cardiff, http://www.cardiffmiller.com/artworks/inst/motet.html accessed (March 20, 2012).
18. "Four Square," Four Square, https://foursquare.com/ (accessed March 20, 2012).
19. Anne Galloway, "Ubiquitous computing in the city," *Cultural Studies* 18, no. 2/3 (March/May 2004): 384–408.
20. Anne Galloway, "Locative Media As Socializing and Spatializing Practice: Learning From Archeology," in *Leonardo Electronic Almanac 14*, no. 3–4 (June-July 2006).
21. W. G. Gardner and K. D. Martin, "HRTF measurements of a KEMAR," *Journal of the Acoustical Society of America* 97, no. 6 (1995): 3907 – 3908.
22. Layla Gaye, Ramia Mazé, and Lars-Erik Holmquist, "Sonic City: The Urban Environment as a Musical Interface," in *Proceedings of NIME* 03, (2003): 109–115.
23. Drew Hemment, "The Mobile Effect," in *Convergence: The International Journal of Research into New Media Technologies* 11 (2005): 32–39.
24. Drew Hemmet, "Locative Arts," in *Leonardo* 39, no. 4 (2006): 348–355.
25. "Her Long Black Hair," Janet Cardiff, http://www.cardiffmiller.com/artworks/walks/longhair.html (accessed April 29th 2012).
26. Don Ritter, "Intersection," Aesthetic Machinery, http://aesthetic-machinery.com/intersection.html (accessed May 2010).
27. Brandon LaBelle, *Background Noise: Perspectives on Sound Art* (New York: Continuum International Publishing Group, 2006).

28. "Layar," Layar, http://www.layar.com/ (accessed December 18, 2011)
29. Frans Mäyrä, Jaako Stenros, and Markos Montola, "Pervasive games in lucid society," in *Proceedings of the 2007 Conference on Future Play*, 30–37 (New York: ACM, 2007).
30. C. Maynes, " Worldizing – take studio recordings to the field and make them sound organic," *The Editors Guild Magazine* 25, no. 2 (2004).
31. Valentina Nisi, Ian Oakley, and Mads Haahr, "Location-Aware Multimedia Stories: Bringing Together Real and Virtual Spaces," in *Proceedings of ArTech 2008* (Porto, Portugal: 2008).
32. "OpenSL ES," Khronos Group, http://www.khronos.org/opensles/ (accessed April 30, 2012).
33. Randall Packer and Ken Jordan, *Multimedia: From Wagner to virtual reality* (London: Norton and Company, 2002).
34. Natasa Paterson, Katsiaryna Naliuka, Soren Kristian Jensen, Tara Carrigy, Mads Haahr, and Fionnuala Conway, "Design, Implementation and Evaluation of Audio for a Location Based Augmented Reality Game," in *Proceedings of ACM Fun and Games 2010*, 149 – 156 (Leuven, Belgium: ACM, 15–17 September 2010).
35. "Mobile Art And Code: Pd On The IPhone," Pure Data, http://puredata.info/docs/workshops/MobileArtAndCodePdOnTheIPhone (accessed April 30, 2012).
36. Howard Rheingold, "Urban Infomatics Breakout," The Feature Archives, January 13, 2004, http://www.thefeaturearchives.com/topic/Culture/Urban_Infomatics_Breakout.html (accessed April 10, 2013).
37. Anne Rorimer, *New Art in the 60's and 70's: Redefining Reality*, (London: Thames & Hudson, 2004).
38. F. Rumsey, *Spatial Audio* (Oxford: Focal Press, 2001).
39. Mark Shepard, "Tactical Sound Garden (TSG) [TSG] Toolkit," in *International Conference on Computer Graphics and Interactive Techniques*, 219 (ACM SIGGRAPH, 2007)
40. "'Snake' Nokia," JohnJohn, http://www.johnjohn.co.uk/html/snake.html (accessed April 15, 2012).
41. "SonicNotify," SonicNotify, http://sonicnotify.com/ (accessed April 30, 2012).
42. "Sonivox Jet," Android Developers, http://developer.android.com/guide/topics/media/jet/jetcreator_manual.html (accessed April 10, 2013)
43. "SoundWalk," SoundWalk, http://www.soundwalk.com/blog/tag/reality-browser/ (accessed April 10, 2013).
44. "'Spectreck,' Google Play," https://play.google.com/store/apps/details?id=com.spectrekking.full&hl=en (accessed February 13, 2011).
45. Dan Steinbock and Johnny L.Wilson,*The Mobile Revolution* (London: Kogan Page, 2007), 150.
46. Atau Tanaka and Petra Gemeinboeck, "Net_Dérive: Conceiving and Producing a Locative Media Artwork," in *Mobile Technologies: From Telecommunications to Media*, ed Gerard Goggin and Larissa Hjorth (London: Routledge, 2008).
47. Claudia Tittel, "Sound Art as Sonification, and the Artistic Treatment of Features in our Surroundings," in *Organised Sound* 14, no. 1 (2009): 57–64.
48. Marc Tuters, "The Locative Commons: Situating Location-Based Media in Urban Public Space," *Futuresonic* (2004).
49. D. Woo, N. Mariette, N. Helyer, and C. Rizos, " Syren – A Ship Based Location Aware Experience," in *The 2004 International Symposium on GNSS/GPS*, (Sydney, 2004).

 ISSN 1071-4391 ISBN 978-1-906897-20-8

NATASA PATERSON & FIONNUALA CONWAY

interviewed by
Lanfranco Aceti & Richard Rinehart

Is there an 'outside' of the Art World from which to launch critiques and interventions? If so, what is the border that defines outside from inside? If it is not possible to define a border, then what constitutes an intervention and is it possible to be and act as an outsider of the art world? Or are there only different positions within the Art World and a series of positions to take that fulfill ideological parameters and promotional marketing and branding techniques to access the fine art world from an oppositional, and at times confrontational, standpoint?

Our work is situated at the meeting-point of disciplines – art, technology and design – and we feel that the boundaries are fluid and ever-changing. Because of that, we are constantly shifting within these spaces and find it difficult to define the territory and boundaries. Our practice lies more securely in the domain of experience design, which tends to be seen as outside the art world. However we are not interested in creating works that challenge, oppose or take a confrontational standpoint.

"In *The Truth in Painting*, Derrida describes the *parergon* (*par-*, around; *ergon*, the work), the boundaries or limits of a work of art. Philosophers from Plato to Hegel, Kant, Husserl, and Heidegger debated the limits of the intrinsic and extrinsic, the inside and outside of the art object." (Anne Friedberg, *The Virtual Window: From Alberti to Microsoft* (Cambridge, MA: MIT Press, 2009), 13.) Where then is the inside and outside of the virtual artwork? Is the artist's 'hand' still inside the artistic process in the production of virtual art or has it become an irrelevant concept abandoned outside the creative process of virtual artworks?

In our practice, the work is most certainly guided by the artists' hands. The establishment of a framework from which to allow the viewer, listener or performer to experience the work is our primary concern. We set up the rules and let them play out. Therefore, the boundaries of the extrinsic and intrinsic of our virtual work is blurred as the artist and the viewer collaborate in producing the emergent artwork.

Virtual interventions appear to be the contemporary inheritance of Fluxus' artistic practices. Artists like Peter Weibel, Yayoi Kusama and Valie Export subverted traditional concepts of space and media through artistic interventions. What are the sources of inspiration and who are the artistic predecessors that you draw from for the conceptual and aesthetic frameworks of contemporary augmented reality interventions?

The practice of locative media art utilizes location aware technology and digital overlays on real world locations with emphasis upon locality and the deinstitutionalization of the traditional artistic installation. The aim is to use art to redefine or enhance the social and physical interaction with a space in order to develop a critical understanding of oneself and culture. An early predecessor for the conceptual framework would be Richard Long with his augmenting of physical landscapes. In regards to a digital narrative real world overlay, projects such as Blast Theory's *Can you see me now* and Proboscis's *Urban Tapestries* explore one's agency and the social and cultural structure around them. As our particular emphasis is the auditory experience in a given space, works by Janet Cardiff and Christina Kubisch are of inspiration in regards to sound, space and interactivity with an urban space. Additionally, architect Christopher Alexander and his theories on urban design and the nature of space and affect are also of interest.

In the representation and presentation of your artworks as being 'outside of' and 'extrinsic to' contemporary aesthetics why is it important that your projects are identified as art?

For our work it is not important that our projects are identified as art. What is most interesting is personal interaction with a space, in the creation of an individualized soundscape, reflective of the urban space and the cultural experience. Whether this is viewed as art is inconsequential – of most importance is the emergence of a creative interaction and redefinition for the individual of their everyday space.

What has most surprised you about your recent artworks? What has occurred in your work that was outside of your intent, yet has since become an intrinsic part of the work?

It has been interesting to note that the over use of technology can take away from the artistic experience. For locative media projects, immersion where one is not distracted by the technology is desirable, hence smooth, unencumbered and easy to use setups must be implemented. The use of psychoacoustics has now become an interest in our artwork as user feedback has indicated a potential immersive/creative application. ■

 ISSN 1071-4391 ISBN 978-1-906897-20-8

NATASA PATERSON & FIONNUALA CONWAY

statement & artwork

Natasa Paterson is a Dublin based composer and performer. Dr. Fionnuala Conway is a composer and multimedia artist.

Originally from Australia, Natasa completed her M.Phil in Music and Media Technologies in Trinity College, Dublin and is currently studying for a PhD exploring sound design and composition for location aware media. Natasa is also currently the lead audio designer and composer for Haunted Planet Studios Ltd. and has worked on augmented reality projects such as Scottish Ghost Hunt, Pirates of Emerson and Bram Stoker's Vampires. Trained in piano, cello and voice, Natasa was project manager of the Irish Composers' Collective in 2010–2011 and is a member of the collective and IMRO. Natasa's compositional work include pieces for choir, piano, string quartet and the use of electroacoustic elements and she was the 2012 winner of the first Annual Ad Astra Composition Competition. Natasa is also the 2012–2013 recipient of the Fulbright-Enterprise Ireland scholarship to study Film Scoring at UCLA. Her pieces have been performed at The National Concert Hall, Samuel Beckett Theater, Cake Contemporary Centre and Centre for Creative Practices.

Dr. Fionnuala Conway has been lecturing on the M.Phil. in Music and Media Technologies course at Trinity College, Dublin, Ireland, since 2002 and was appointed Course Director in 2006. With a background in music and music technology, she has worked as composer and performer on a number of theatre productions and produced work in a wide variety of forms, from traditional materials to interactive digital media, wearable technology, installations and theatre presentation, including *Art of Decision* and *Urban Chameleon*. Her PhD thesis, *Exploring Citizenship through Art and Technology,* focuses on the creative use of technology to generate awareness of citizenship (and other social issues), with a particular focus on interactive immersive physical environments. *Art of Decision* is the practical manifestation of Fionnuala's thesis. As a multidisciplinary and multimedia artist, she is comfortable using a wide variety of media and methods to realize her work and this approach is presented in a diverse number of artworks.

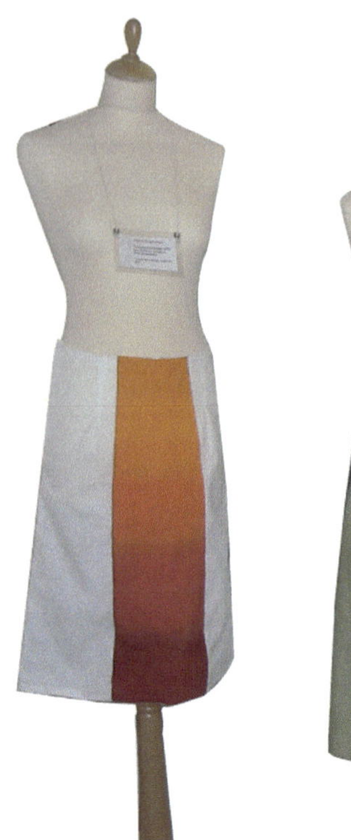
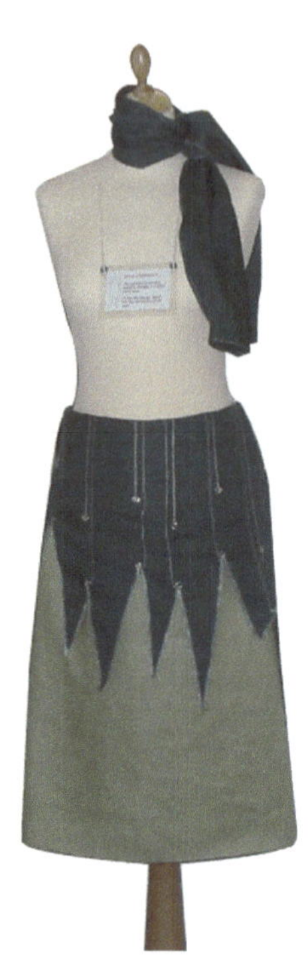
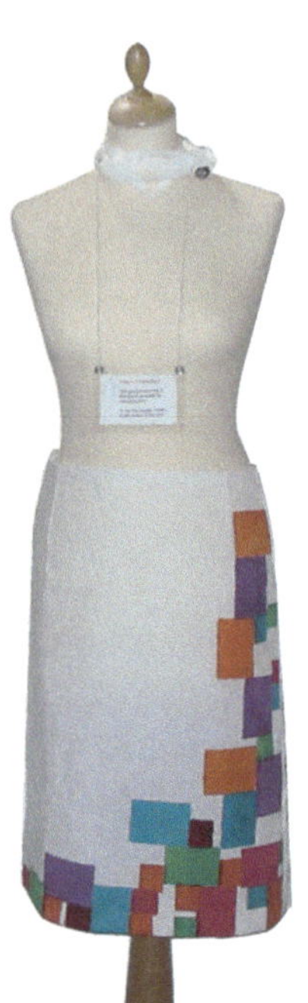

Urban Chameleon, 2003, Katherine Moriwaki and Fionnuala Conway, wearable technology. © Copyright Moriwaki and Conway, 2003.

Their collaborative interests include an exploration of compositional techniques in locative media, such as algorithmic composition and sound design, as well as, an architectural syntax that relates to urban paces, mood and design. With the advent of Global Positioning System (GPS) technology, specific locations can trigger audio backgrounds and effects, while the tracking of performer's movements using integrated smartphone orientation technology, can also contribute compositional original elements to the overall soundscape experience. Because locative media art aims to interpret the relationships between society, culture and the individual, they also have a keen interest in how the urban space can be expressed through sound. ■

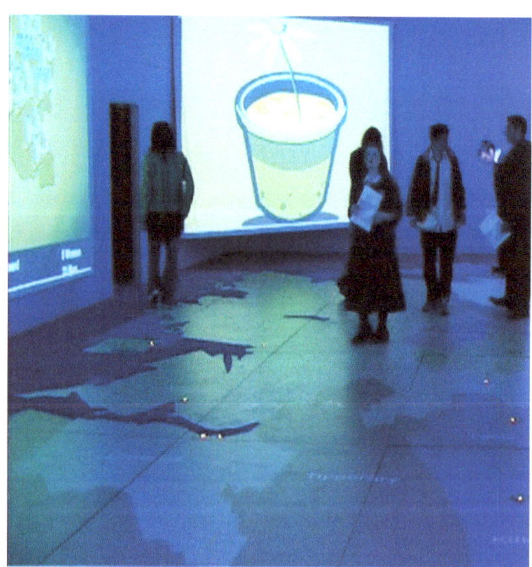

Art of Decision - DATAmap exhibit, 2005, Fionnuala Conway, interactive installation. © Copyright Fionnuala Conway, 2005.

URL'S

http://www.natasapaulberg.com
http://vimeo.com/user2288756
http://www.fionnualaconway.com
http://vimeo.com/user1135842

 ISSN 1071-4391 ISBN 978-1-906897-20-8

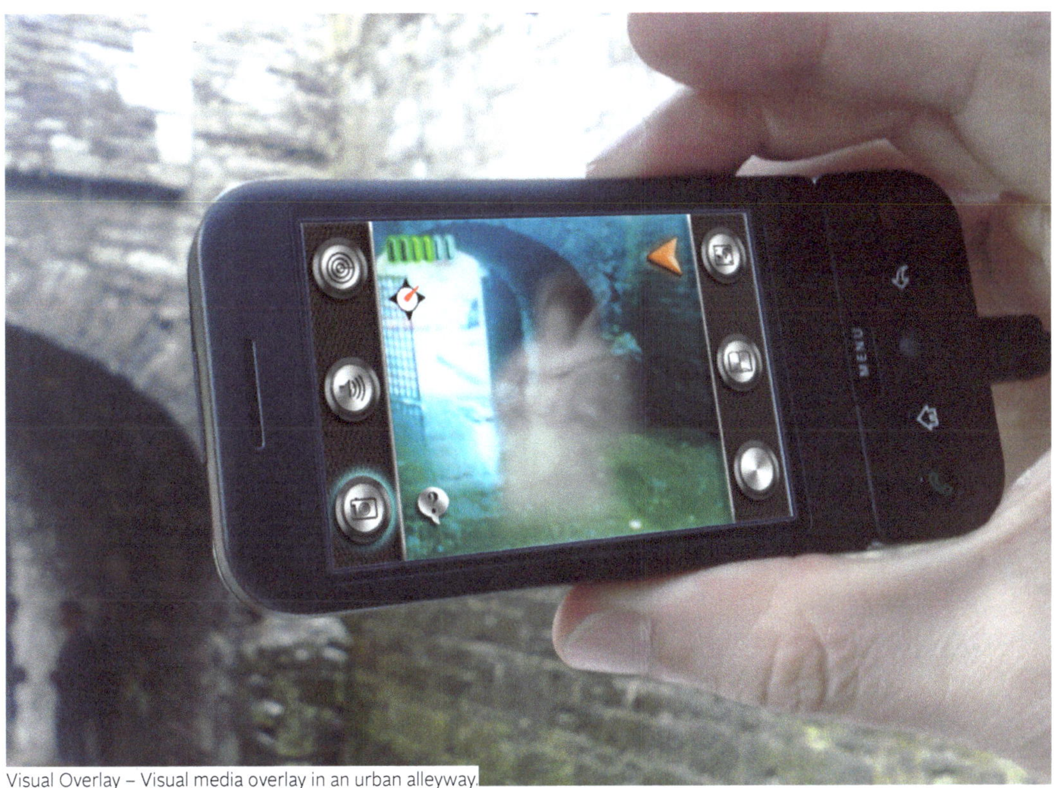

Visual Overlay – Visual media overlay in an urban alleyway.

Viking Ghost Hunt, 2009, Natasa Paterson, audio.

Courtesy of HauntedPlanet Studios Ltd.

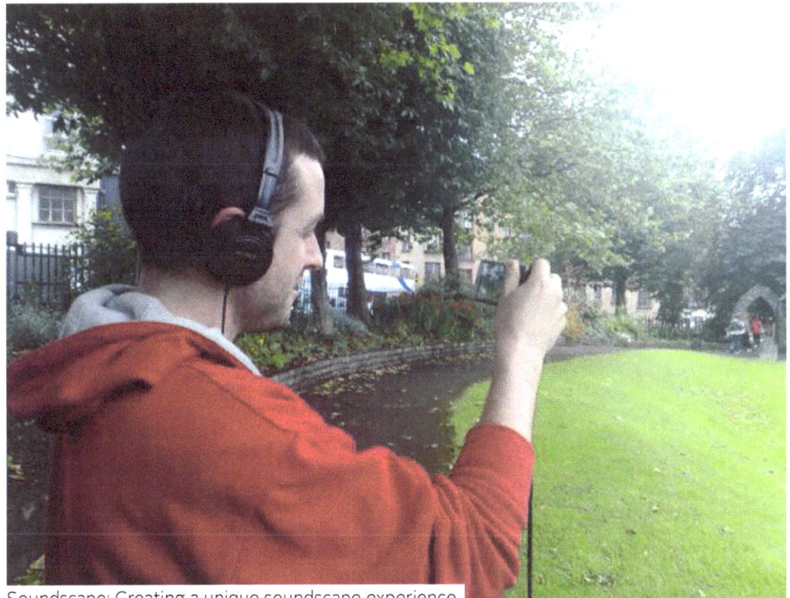

Soundscape: Creating a unique soundscape experience.

Viking Ghost Hunt, 2009, Natasa Paterson, audio.

Courtesy of Haunted Planet Studios Ltd.

A New Relic Emerges: Image as Subject to Object

REBECCA PEEL

Pacific Northwest College of Art
rpeel@pnca.edu
pnca.edu
rebeccarpeel.info
werent-or-werent.tumblr.com

The banality of objects and platitude of imagery is more insistent than ever. Nuance, in its subtlety, has the power to set something apart in the realm of infinitely reproduced/reproducible art and image-based objects that philosopher Jean Baudrillard previously classified as "only concentrated effects, miniaturized and immediately available." [1]

With the advent of the Internet, there has been a distinct state change. In its wake visual artists are able to rupture the causes and effects of contribution within any small sphere of network intervention, specifically "when the internet is less a novelty and more of a banality." [2]

When the Internet became more widely available in the 1990s, average users were led towards constrictive formats that limited their ability to interact with an interface and manipulate content that was available to other users. However, the last decade has given birth to an explosion of possibilities for information generation, storage, and retrieval. The vernacular has been shifted accordingly. Users are no longer restricted by database systems with severe edges and limits in their archiving abilities. These database systems are now in a continual state of unfolding, onto which each user is affecting his or her custom influence. By this, I am referring to the structure of content of each site that exists on the Internet which has been customized over time. With this seemingly infinite "colossally huge, searchable, public domain...now at your fingertips" as writer Bruce Sterling has described it, there is also the

 ISSN 1071-4391 ISBN 978-1-906897-20-8

consequence of overload. The Internet has itself become a new statistical model of data growth that supersedes any previous quantifiable structure in terms of breadth of information and reproduction of images. As such, Baudrillard's understanding of the simulacra becomes solidified and validated in a way that even he might not have been able to predict. If "the orders of simulacra increase as it becomes less and less possible to trace the origins of the simulations" [3] one can persuasively argue that by virtue of the internet's infinitely layered "hyperstructure" of connectivity, linking one of thousands of images to one object approaches an asymptote of impossibility.

Suppose we disregard any criticism that this daunting structure is indeed "vague, unstable, indeterminate, unidentifiable, fragmented, amorphic, and always impersonal." [4] Perhaps we will not be dampened by Baudrillard's "bleak interpretation of postmodern culture" or his "romantic concern for the loss of the real, the natural and the human" [4] and instead meditate for a moment on possibility have been stretched open as a result of this contemporary phenomenon. Upon the realization that for the most part, our ability to contribute to this structure is not stifled by law (in particular natural law). We not only have the freedom to direct our own mode of interaction but to begin directing others' experience as well. The "Internet provides the medium for disrupting models rather than confirming them." [5] The evolution of the Internet is still in its infancy, to the extent that we, as users, maintain a certain power over the direction in which it grows. "We don't have a coherent outlook or interest that can enslave us. This means we are closer to a potentially objective history than anybody has ever seen." [6]

This condition does present its own set of challenges and exciting intricacies. As Sherry Turkle pointed out in 1996, "Today's computational models of the mind often embrace a postmodern aesthetic of complexity and decentering. Mainstream computer researchers no longer aspire to program intelligence into computers but expect intelligence to emerge from the interactions of small subprograms." [7] The complexities that have surfaced from these models of the mid 1990s exemplify an incredible evolution. The Internet contains within it an entire world that is disjointed from actual reality. Generations of "digital natives" [8] communicate within varied cultures, subcultures and countercultures that are reality-based, but internet-specific. Taking this into account, however, there is an immeasurable amount of bleed between the cultures prevailing on the Internet and in the real-world interests of the active users *of* the Internet. Hosting sites and search engines are programmed to be generic and simple so that the user can apply his/her "intelligence" [7] to it, which generates overall user satisfaction. From this, there comes the often coincidental beauty of the nuance.

What becomes interesting, particularly for a visual artist, is the expansive array of opportunities embedded within a tool that is now a necessary component of everyday human existence. As Bruce Sterling suggests, "there are interesting potentials for complete digital recapturing of earlier artifacts, earlier means of production." [6] Though it may not be in anybody's basic interest to completely archive the entirety of human artifact, it has certainly become conceivable; and it has become nearly a legitimized reality since most users own devices that can remotely transmit information to the internet. We can rest assured that if there is an object, article, or occurrence of interest and a human happens upon it, the likelihood of it being captured and archived is substantial. As such, the hypothetical possibility exists for anything in the world to be found by somebody anywhere else in the world. The only requirements are, that the person who requires the information has access to an internet enabled device,

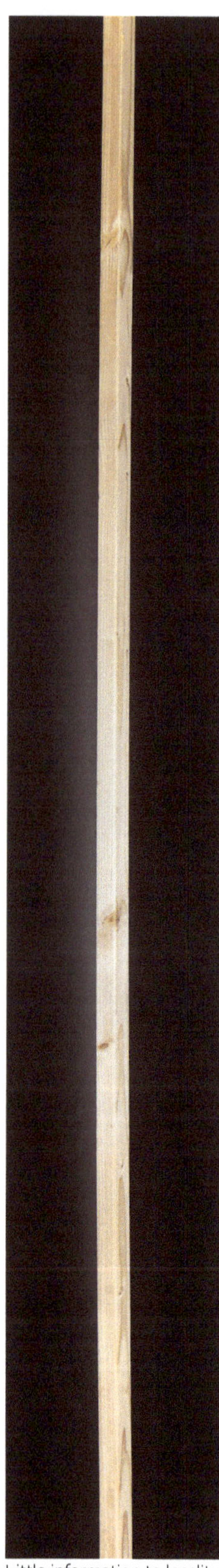

Little information to locality of the object can be inferred from the image. Image copyright of the author.

and the required data plan. It is irrelevant, at this point, whether the information is of high commercial or social value; the fact is that the objectivity of the archival database imbues potential for an object to gain a more subjective value.

The mode of this phenomenology is subsequently brought into question. How does one begin to approach the attachment of value, of any kind, to objects and images that begin with a user in physical space? How can the desired route of the Internet "explorer" lead them to gems in the "termite mounds of poorly organized and extremely potent knowledge, quantifiable, interchangeable data with newly networked relations?" [6]

Say, for instance, that you were to post a picture of a piece of wood on the Internet. For clarity's sake, we'll say that the piece of wood is an 8 foot-long 2" x 2" plank of pinewood. Say, also, that it has been photographed in front of a white wall and it is, let's say, lying in no particularly fascinating way on a concrete floor. Or, maybe we'll even say that it is photographed on an entirely black background so that all that is paid attention to is the wood. You post it onto the internet, and your photographed piece of wood will fall very quietly into the massive lumberyard of images of the same type of wood photographed against the same background.

But let's say, for instance, that you decide to put the actual piece of wood against a wall, upright, leaning. Again, you take a picture of the wood to put on the Internet. This gesture moves the object just barely out of the initial virtual iteration, which was the very generic image taken of the wood against the black background. Now, because of the special value applied to it, the wood actually exists somewhere in the world, in an actual space that has only now been represented in a virtual realm. Any person who comes across this

 ISSN 1071-4391 ISBN 978-1-906897-20-8

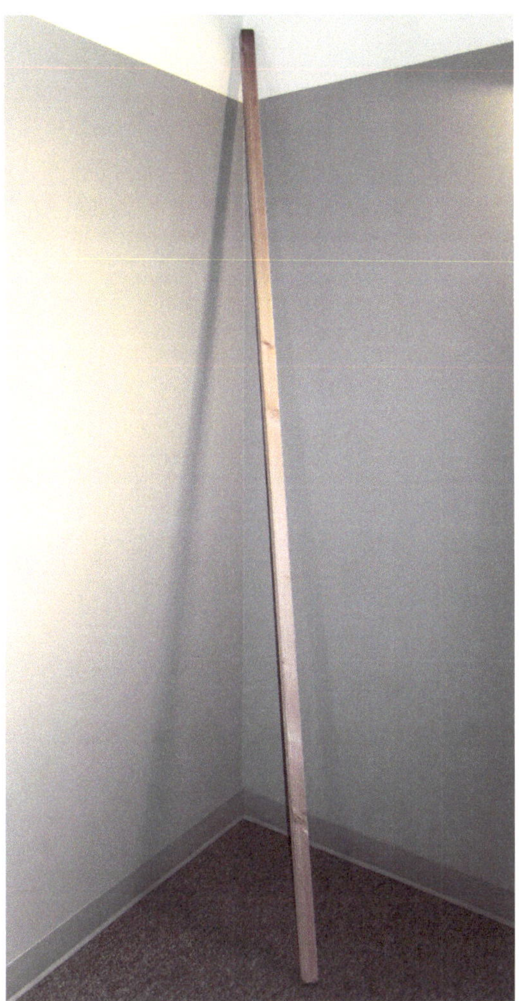

A specific site is present, not identified; the object can be understood as existing in a physical location. Image copyright of the author.

new image can see that it has been placed in a space that exists outside of the screen. However, it is still just one of a potentially infinite number of planks of wood that can lean against any number of available walls. The relative embedded interest of the original image has barely changed and it is still almost entirely reproducible.

When considering these images in relation to the expanse of distribution that they lie within, one wonders ultimately what might begin to dislocate an image on the Internet from itself when it is one of so many dislocations. It is a complex line of inquiry that yields results that are equally multifarious. However, the aforementioned overabundance of imagery may catalyze the nuanced object into making it a more effective image: "Although it sounds counterintuitive, a kind of non-reflective consciousness can be attained through an excess of self-reflexivity or self-referentiality. Even though the gesture of self-reference begins 'in' a subject, greater degrees of self-reference eventually tear it away from the subject." [9]

Now let's say you cut the wood in two places. The first of the cuts is a 23 degree angle, and the two lengths of wood are now 6' and 2'. The second cut is a 60 degree angle and the three lengths of wood are now 5' 6", 2', and 6". You now lean each piece of wood against a wall, with the end that's on the floor flush with it. The result, you will see, is an interesting arrangement of varying heights of wood, leaning against the wall at varying angles because of their new properties. You will notice that interesting negative spaces will occur, and nearly infinite compositions can be made through the lens of your camera. It is also a triptych, which alludes to and historic reference of art making. This is where the conversation within the bromidic object enters a sublime actualization that is "a kind of simulation, because it draws attention to the sheer existence of something...verifying to the point of giddiness the useless objectivity of things." [1]

Now the image of the piece of wood has departed even further from its beginning stage of relative inconsequence. The image has been altered by way of manipulation of the object itself, which, according to the image, is indivisible from the geographical site of the object. To the hypothetical Internet user who sifts through imagery in search of an interesting artifact, this would be a very peculiar nonpareil to stumble upon. It would stand out from other images, however minutely. It would have a tinge of intentionality, which flavours any triviality with artistic reference. This reference, even in its subtlety, would be uncannily palpable even if the user is a non-artist. Given the right elemental chemistry, the image would appear unusual in comparison to others. The negligible object has been removed from its ordinary iteration and ad-

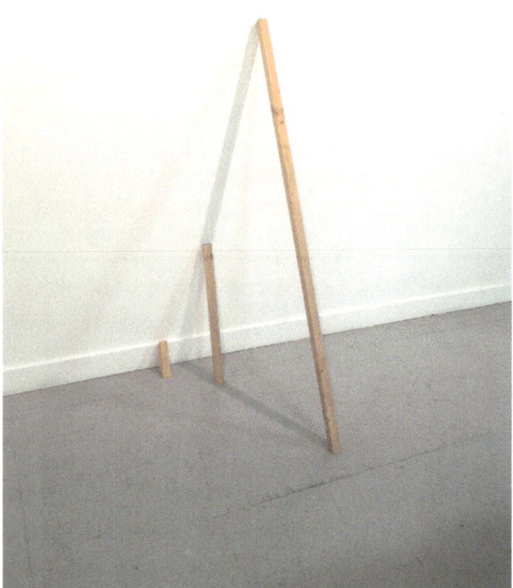

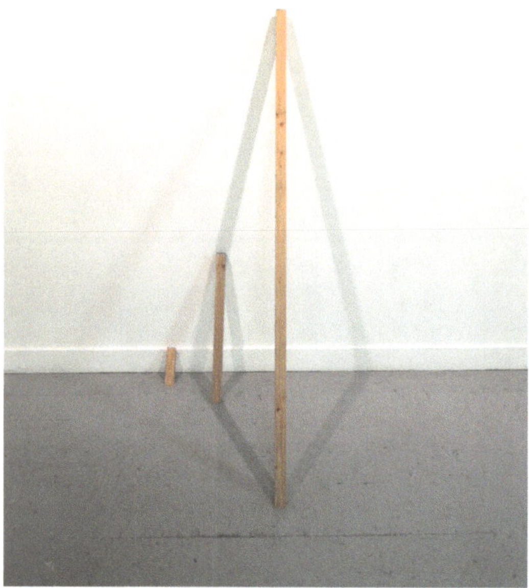

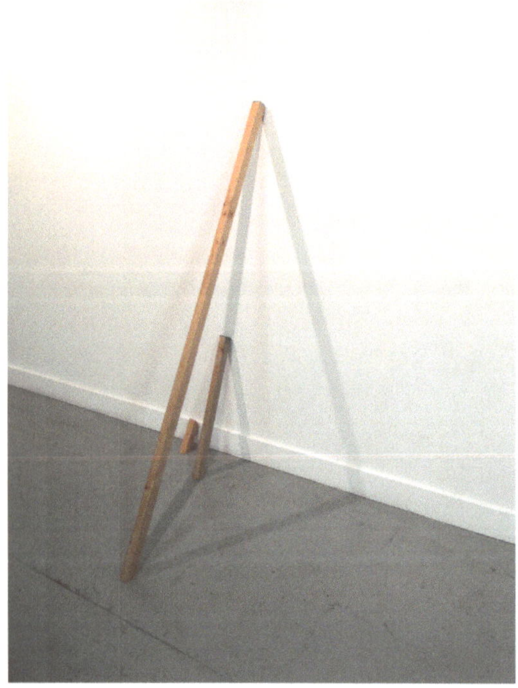

The object has been given new properties that assert the individuality of the resulting image.

vanced to a unique level of complexity. The elegance of these small gestures is the range of possibility that is infinitely implied within it. "On the Internet, one will expect to find the banal at every turn. One would also hope to find objects of seduction and artifice, objects that turn us away from our intended goals." [5] The subtle nuance is, what will become desired in an increasingly screen-based world overloaded not only with mass-produced objects but with mass-produced images. The nuance makes the infinitely reproducible once again interesting; it glorifies the timid object as a relic that does in fact belong to *somebody*, or that does exist *somewhere*. This immediately gives it value. Not monetary value, as it were, but some sort of coveted use-value.

The preceding examples surely extract reference from a Duchampian idealism. However, Marcel Duchamp enacted his interventions before the arrival of the Internet. In our contemporary locale, the rules and possibilities are constantly being re-established, never completely solidifying. With this, visual art that parallels, aligns itself with, or exists exclusively within Internet culture gains the advantage of immediacy. In

 ISSN 1071-4391 ISBN 978-1-906897-20-8

the same instant, it finds the navigation of temporality difficult. While a timestamp on an uploaded image can indicate chronology, "time" has different rules in the reality of Internet culture. A great amount of digital art that is being created for a web-only viewing experience is sweeping along as quickly and as frequently as plastic toys are being pumped out of factories. These images, as important as they are to help future historians locate a movement, are once again amassing. The ingenuity of each individual image is becoming lost amidst increasingly similar and analogous elements. There is a flashy, colorful silkiness to many of these images. Ironic reference to classical forms and Greek Canon sculptures is rampant. Photoshopped waves, lines, wavy lines, watery textures, desert-like textures, gradient overlays, obscure non-sequitur one-liners are, upon first glance, pleasing and sometimes ingenious. However, these products are in danger of cycling and recycling themselves. As crafty as they may have been to begin with, they are so rampant and redundant that they quickly expire their novelty. Browsing through imagery has, for many, supplanted leisurely activities such as reading newspapers. In the same vein, what's been seen once, often becomes old news. The differences, though, are vastly notable. For one, anybody can participate. Secondly, there are options such as "share" and "reblog." This allows the chance for a curious image to resurface over and over, depending upon its success with an audience. What results, then, is the need for an image to be instantly captivating.

Images like these are made using a specific set of computer-based tools that are globally accessible, and they are inherently recognizable as such. What is, at times, most highly considerable about these images is the range of subtle appearances of the human hand. The "artifact" of a digitally manipulated image is what fundamentally distinguishes it from others of its genus. This is an opportunity to put into effect the simple, subtle, and honest interventions to alter the impact of virtual images on a viewer. It involves creating, re-creating, or re-contextualizing physical objects in a way that emphasizes the presence of the object. Providing a foundation for a virtual interaction with an actual, physical object is fertile investigative territory since what people are often looking for, from images and objects, is a certain familiarity: "...when people consider what if anything might ultimately differentiate computers from humans, they dwell long and lovingly on those aspects of people that are tied to the sensuality and physical embodiment of life." [7] But it doesn't stop there. "...the virtual body sets us astray from our assumptions about what it means to have a 'real' body...." [7] If this assumption is accurate, it seems apposite to be reminded of our proximity to the physical, sensual world; to the objects that share space with our bodies.

Let's return for a moment to the cut piece of pinewood. Whatever image you might create within the photoframe can be further engaged upon with induction of new elements. You could begin to make small assemblages that more closely hinge the image to its global site; objects that hint towards physical dimension and spatial occupation. The same principle applies, but an expansion occurs by adding new objects. For example, suppose you add a ball in front of your leaning pieces of wood. Suddenly those pieces of wood will be influenced differently than before. Next, hang a rag on one of your pieces of wood and your image changes drastically again. Depending on what color, pattern, fabric, or texture the rag is, whether the ball is a soccer ball or a popcorn ball, and so on, the potential interpretation will shift.

This ball, rag, and wood assemblage now has latent points of interest to be discovered. Anybody who sees it will understand that these are ordinary objects, but that they have been arranged and formatted in a way that makes them slightly "extra-ordinary." The connections between objects must be investigated since contextual information about the creation of a specific assemblage is not typically or readily available. These objects will have a certain mystique, but the interventions that have been taken upon them and the setting they have been placed in is disjunctive with the Internet. There is a separable quality about the image regarding the space where the image itself is held.

This is where the highly accessible computer tools come into use. The viewer now has the option and the power to relocate these objects *back* into the virtual. For example, suppose that the user who finds the image interesting is compelled to remove the background from behind the assemblage. In the vernacular of Photoshop, this user might magnetic lasso, magic-wand, eraser tool the original context of physical space to manipulate the amount of influence it has over the image of the objects. What is left is a digital image of the original assemblages that is removed from direct correlation with the time and space it originally existed in.

Now, the image has been sincerely situated in virtual space. The photoshopped image can be made into a graphic interchange file (.gif), the pixel quality of which is visually distinct. It can be made into a .png file as well, which preserves some pixelation of the image but keeps the transparency of the background, allowing the image-object to be mobile and free-floating. In theory, then, these virtual objects can be placed in the context with other images that attend to their physical locality. This creates a potent theoretical paradox.

Apart from creating the novelty of an Internet object, it may seem extravagant; but the importance lies in directing the course, through which, one learns how to consume content from the Internet. It is an undeni-

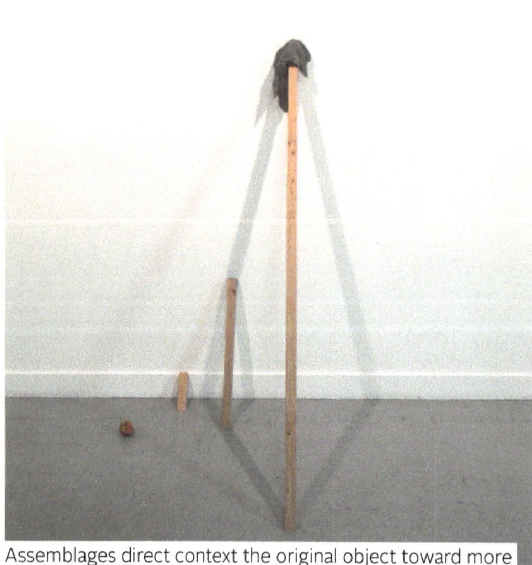

Assemblages direct context the original object toward more subjective interpretations. Images copyright of the author.

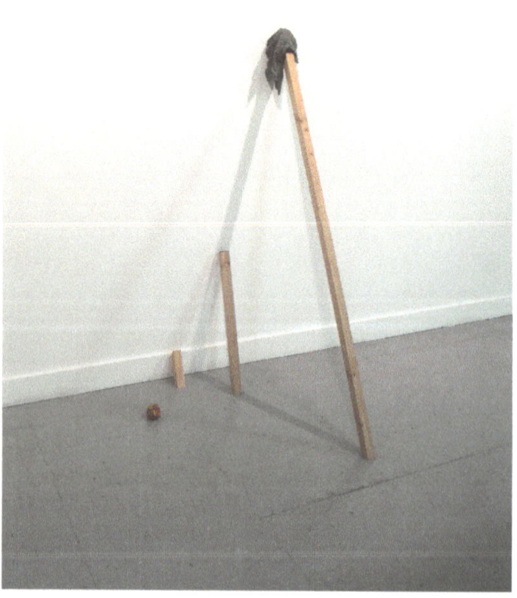

 ISSN 1071-4391 ISBN 978-1-906897-20-8

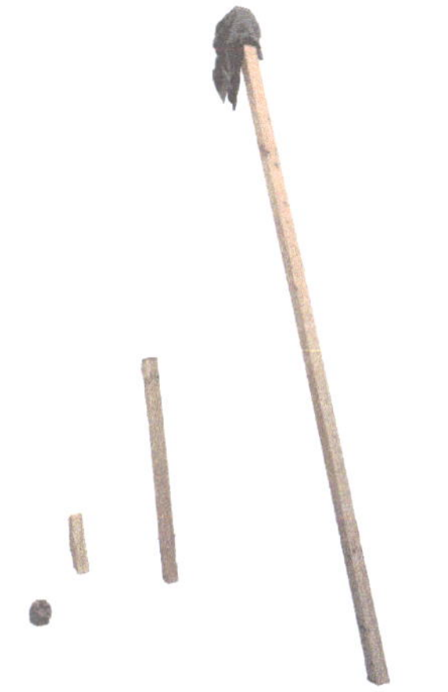

Pixelation that is unique to graphic interchange files denies the illusion that the image exists outside of virtual space any longer. Image copyright of the author.

able necessity for all current and future Internet users to be presented with certain intellectual challenges if, as theorist Paul Virilio asserts, "no information exists without dis-information. And now a new type of dis-information is raising its head, and it is totally different than voluntary censorship. It has to do with some kind of choking of the senses, a loss of control over reason of sorts." [11]

Baudrillard seemed to think that by removing direct interaction with physical space, that we are in turn rendering our bodies into obscurity. "This body, our body, often appears simply superfluous, basically useless in its extention...since today everything is concentrated in the brain and in genetic codes, which alone sum up the operational definition of being." [10] Baudrillard is concerned perhaps that we are interacting with spaces that detract from the romance of our solidarity in time and space; I think it is our opportunity now to reform our iterations in this ultra-sensory environment that do not detract from our physical presence, but rather enhance our interpretation of it. ■

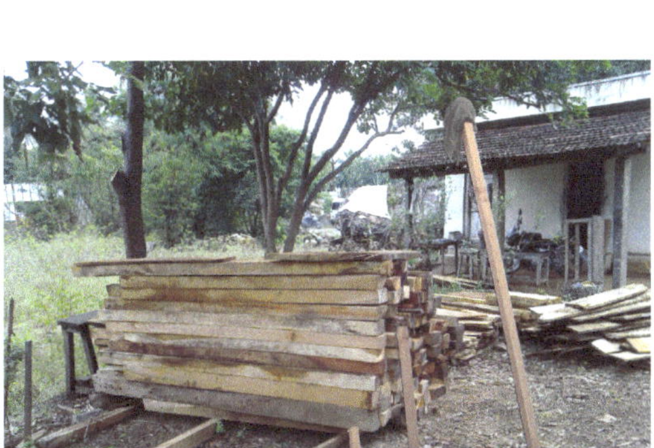

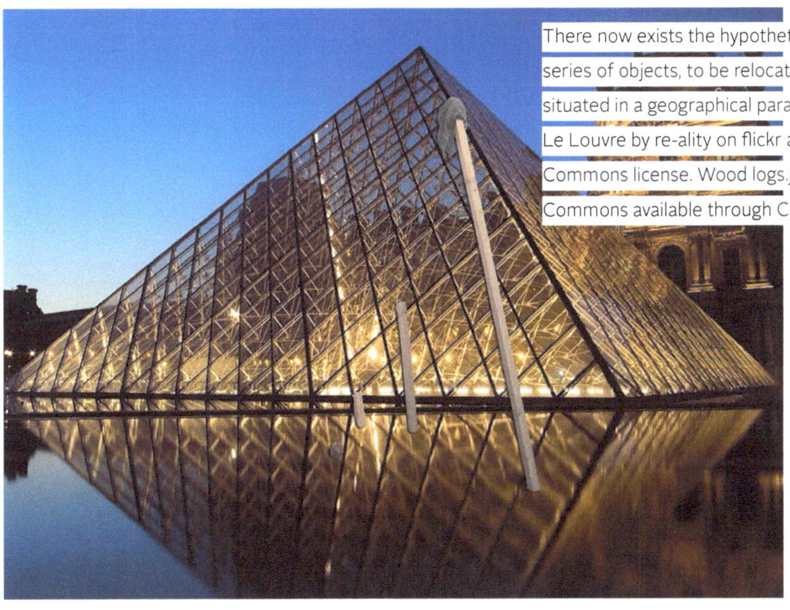

There now exists the hypothetical potential for this object, or series of objects, to be relocated to a new image context and situated in a geographical paradox.
Le Louvre by re-ality on flickr available through Creative Commons license. Wood logs.jpg by Parvathisri on Wikimedia Commons available through Creative commons license.

REFERENCES AND NOTES

1. Jean Baudrillard, *The Ecstasy of Communication*, trans. Bernard and Caroline Schutze, (New York: Semiotext, 1988), 18–29.
2. Gene McHugh, *Post Internet* (Brescia, Italy: LINK Editions, 2011).
3. Joanna Topor, "Simulation, Simulacrum (2)." IThe Chicago School of Media Theory, 2002, http://csmt.uchicago.edu/glossary2004/simulationsimulacrum2.htm (accessed November 21, 2011).
4. Temenuga Trifonova, "Is There a Subject in Hyperreality?" in *Postmodern Culture* 13, no. 3 (May 2003), http://pmc.iath.virginia.edu/issue.503/13.3trifonova.html (accessed November 21, 2011).
5. Mark Nunes, "Jean Baudrillard in Cyberspace: Internet, Virtuality, and Postmodernity," in *Style* 29, no. 2 (Summer 1995): 314–327.
6. Bruce Sterling, "Atemporality for the Creative Artist," *Wired*, February 25, 2010, http://www.wired.com/beyond_the_beyond/2010/02/atemporality-for-the-creative-artist/ (accessed December 4, 2011).
7. Sherry Turkle, "4.01: Who Am We?" *Wired*, January 1, 1996, http://www.wired.com/wired/archive/4.01/turkle_pr.html (accessed December 4, 2011).
8. Marc Prensky, *Digital Natives, Digital Immigrants*, (Bradford: MCB University Press, 2001), http://www.marcprensky.com/writing/Prensky – Digital Natives, Digital Immigrants – Part1.pdf (accessed November 21, 2011).
9. Brad Troemel, "Peer Pressure: Essays on the Internet by an Artist on the Internet," (lulu, 2011), http://www.lulu.com/items/volume_72/11774000/11774401/1/print/Brad_Troemel_Peer_Pressure_2011.pdf (accessed October 25, 2011).
10. Jean Baudrillard, *The Ecstasy of Communication* in *The Anti-Aesthetic: Essays on Postmodern Culture*, ed. Hal Foster, 129, (Port Townsend: Bay Press. 1983).
11. Paul Virilio, "Speed and Information: Cyberspace Alarm!" *CTheory.net*., eds. Arthur and Marilouise Kroker, August 27, 1995, http://www.ctheory.net/articles.aspx?id=72 (accessed December 4, 2011).

 ISSN 1071-4391 ISBN 978-1-906897-20-8

REBECCA PEEL

interviewed by
Lanfranco Aceti & Richard Rinehart

Is there an 'outside' of the Art World from which to launch critiques and interventions? If so, what is the border that defines outside from inside? If it is not possible to define a border, then what constitutes an intervention and is it possible to be and act as an outsider of the art world? Or are there only different positions within the Art World and a series of positions to take that fulfill ideological parameters and promotional marketing and branding techniques to access the fine art world from an oppositional, and at times confrontational, standpoint?

I believe the border is much less concrete than it is often perceived. It behaves like many natural divisions in substances or in biological tissues or in climates, for instance...that is, there are often palpable *qualities* of both "inside" and "outside" that make them recognizable, respectively, but there is a large area that allows for interpretation and interaction between the two states.

What is amorphous about this intermediate area is the rules for which we now define "art." Anymore, an intervention that might appear prosaic in an "outside" context, for example, a sandblasted wall, will gain something when moved "inside" the artistic context. It invariably must be looked at differently because, after all, the *intention* was different. The knowledge and information informing the action inside was not, by default, the same knowledge and information that would inform the action in the context that speaks to the more recognized *purpose* of the action. What happens, then, when an action such as the one described is done with artistic intent outside of an institutional setting? Does it *require* a document? Of course it doesn't, it can still exist, but it begs the tree-in-the-forest question. In order for extrinsic art to apply to an artistic discussion, it demands evidence. Otherwise, it will be looked over as the same action as the prescribed purpose of the action, the one with an unaltered intention. In this way, "outside" and "inside" is still a binary situation, but they are quite symbiotic. In many contemporary circumstances, including the aforementioned, the two are actually indivisible.

"In *The Truth in Painting*, Derrida describes the *parergon* (*par-*, around; *ergon*, the work), the boundaries or limits of a work of art. Philosophers from Plato to Hegel, Kant, Husserl, and Heidegger debated the limits of the intrinsic and extrinsic, the inside and outside of the art object." (Anne Friedberg, *The Virtual Window: From Alberti to Microsoft* (Cambridge, MA: MIT Press, 2009), 13.) Where then is the inside and outside of the virtual artwork? Is the artist's 'hand' still inside the artistic process in the production of virtual art or has it become an irrelevant concept abandoned outside the creative process of virtual artworks?

Such as it has always been, the artist has immediate control over how transparent his/her "hand" will appear in a piece of art, despite if it is virtual or not. It is difficult, if not impossible, to state that it is irrelevant. To some, it might be irrelevant because the *virtual*, being in many ways its own medium and its own artist, is used to state the conditions of its own world, and therefore must be allowed to speak for itself. For example, Alexei Shulgin's *Form Art* project implicates specificities of the internet as sterile and objective tools to create fascinating displays of humour and composition. It pokes fun at internet and gaming history while maintaining an elegant formalism that bluntly articulates that the internet and its capabilities are able to diversify the vernacular of sculpture.

However, the desire by some to retain individuality is ever-pervasive and this desire can transcend media. Laura Brothers is exemplary in her ability to make digital compositions maintain an expressionist quality that successfully allows her work to morph between a digital/virtual conversation and that of abstract drawing and painting. The mode of interpretation of virtual phenomena by human beings remains quite similar to an interpretation of the actual; virtual information and physical information alike are processed inside of the brain. The output, then, will be an individual expression that has been filtered through the body, through sensory processing. The output, by default, will be touched with life.

In relation to the *parergon,* though, virtuality certainly becomes a fertile space to find areas of rupture between a traditional practice and an exploratory vision that, perhaps, has less to do with "making art" and more to do with traversing uncharted territory.

Virtual interventions appear to be the contemporary inheritance of Fluxus' artistic practices. Artists like Peter Weibel, Yayoi Kusama and Valie Export subverted traditional concepts of space and media through artistic interventions. What are the sources of inspiration and who are the artistic predecessors that you draw from for the conceptual and aesthetic frameworks of contemporary augmented reality interventions?

The tie to the Fluxus movement is quite appropriate. Gestures that expand and abbreviate time and space in an accessible, "do-it-yourself" manner are a crux of virtual artistic interventions. Yoko Ono's participatory poems were revolutionary and prophetic in regards to how space and time dissolve in a virtual environment. Just as Ray Johnson engaged in acts that travelled geographically with his mail art, artists can interact with mediums such as email, Craigslist and eBay (Ben Schumacher). I recently started Exposition Article, a tumblr site aimed directly towards the collection of fluxus-style gestures that assume the sensibility of the digital age. The immediacy that we can attain with our image making, collaborating, and communicating without regard to geographical location poses a vast expanse of recognizant opportunity. I can appreciate global instantaneous travel of ideas and expression, but I can also appreciate this dislocation in the small scale. In an upcoming show, I will breach site-specificity via digital intervention. A series of photographs will be taken from the perspective of the architecture, printed, and then either reflected back towards or placed slightly near its original location. This does little but to elucidate the power of digital technology not only to provide quick access to location, but also to deceive us.

In the representation and presentation of your artworks as being 'outside of' and 'extrinsic to' contemporary aesthetics why is it important that your projects are identified as art?

If my work was not identified as art, it might not be identified. I tend to want to give value to banal occurrences, if only for the sake of revealing art's authority over any type of object, image, or scenario. However, I wouldn't necessarily be able to say that my work is entirely extrinsic to contemporary aesthetics; I see quite a lot of artists delving into similar inquiries. After all, the idea is not particularly new; Marcel Duchamp did a great job of bringing this authority to light in the start of the twentieth century. The difference is, in fact, the existence of the internet. I have the advantage and the liberty of using not only found objects, but found *tools.* I can create a computer-mediated scenario that pulls out areas of interest from within a global connection zone and allow the extremities of the internet's capabilities exemplify themselves.

 ISSN 1071-4391 ISBN 978-1-906897-20-8

Rafael Rozendaal loves the internet because "Coca Cola is using the same internet as me; the Guggenheim is using the same internet as me." The idea that the internet is a level playing field in which all users have equal opportunity as participants gives the visual artist a great array of possibilities for interaction and intervention. One can simply post one's work on his or her social networking site and blog, or one can use the internet as a way to sidle up next to other virtual entities and create a discourse in comparison.

This is not to mention that digital personae can be modified as the user behind the screen sees fit and/or is capable of. In cases of criminal activity, this notion can be dangerous; for artists, it can be instrumental and important. If nothing else, it would be a constructive gesture to make performance-driven work that reiterates that possibility of danger, or perhaps that underlines the thrill of constructing oneself in virtual reality.

What has most surprised you about your recent artworks? What has occurred in your work that was outside of your intent, yet has since become an intrinsic part of the work?

I have been learning that a mechanically impartial approach to process-based work has, in my case, given a typical viewer the impression that they are being challenged or mocked; handed a dry joke without a punch line. The first instance of this happened in *Ersatz*. The basis of the process began in a certain space of raw futility: futility of a material (wood) to be another material (aluminum); futility of one of the pieces of wood to use a joint to raise itself off the ground and the other to have a joint that does anything at all; the futility of images gleaned from Google's *Similar Image Search* to successfully mimic a photographed image of the wood. This futility ultimately translated as wry humour. I was puzzled and fascinated by this. I began to realize that because of the ambiguity and banality of the images and objects presented, it became apposite for the viewer to either anthropomorphize them to a certain degree, or to enter a vulnerable space of exploration to find relationships between the components. Futility, articulated through a series of controlled and digitally-mediated interventions, resurfaced in a peculiar way. The viewer was directly responsible for his or her own understanding of the relationships, despite how painfully equitable they were in theory. I was, in turn, held accountable for this intriguing fortune, and dubbed a "prankster."

Since this lynchpin, I have directed a certain amount of focus towards these phenomena. I have adopted the idea in much of my work that I should only be a hand where a hand is needed, and limit my artistic liberties as much as possible. What surprises me most about this method of approach is that it does exactly the opposite. The objects, the interventions, the context are so completely transparent in function that they are also transparent when I stand behind them; the responsibility is focused and directed straight towards me, the artist. This creates the supposition that I am playing a game, inviting the viewer to dare enter. To say that none of the humour is intentional would be untruthful, however, where the work requires decision, I indeed appreciate taking advantage of inherent quirks in material, structure, and format. ■

REBECCA PEEL

statement & artwork

Rebecca Peel is a Portland-based artist interested in the intermediacy of site-specificity.

She believes that one of the best ways to evaluate provocative phenomena is not necessarily to point at its perfection, but rather to strip it of embellishment, using temerarious banality to chronicle the intricacies of a world in motion.

Her media and approach is mixed. Formal gesture and traditional media are often intervened upon via digital process to create a sense of anachronism. Painting, ceramic sculpting, wood and metal work are all in her vernacular, but she is particularly intrigued by the fluidity and motility of tools like tumblr and Google's Similar Image search.

Rebecca likes the idea of skydiving. ■

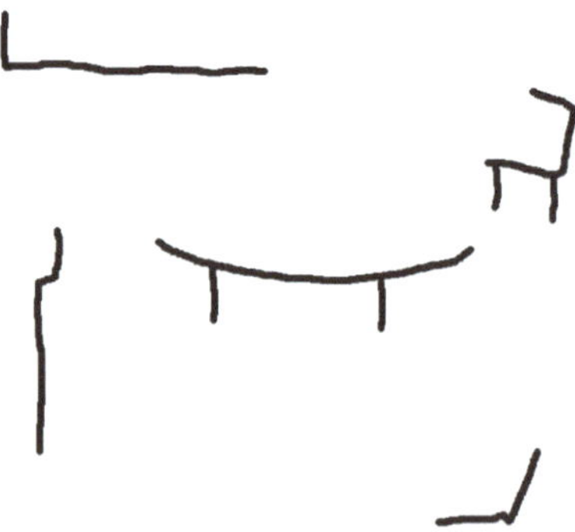

CTLWLI, 2011, Rebecca Peel, Microsoft Paint.

 ISSN 1071-4391 ISBN 978-1-906897-20-8

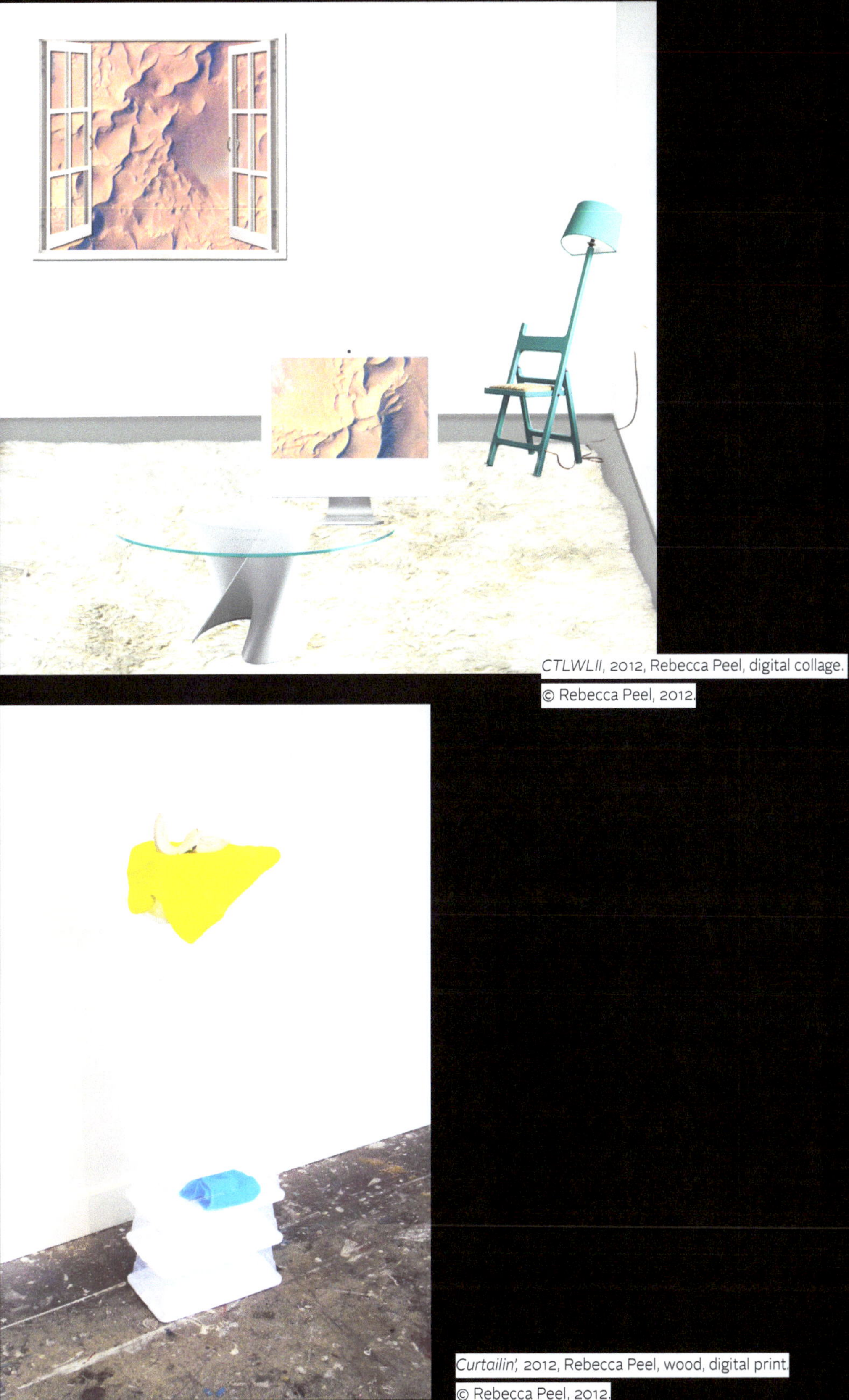

CTLWLII, 2012, Rebecca Peel, digital collage.

Curtailin', 2012, Rebecca Peel, wood, digital print.

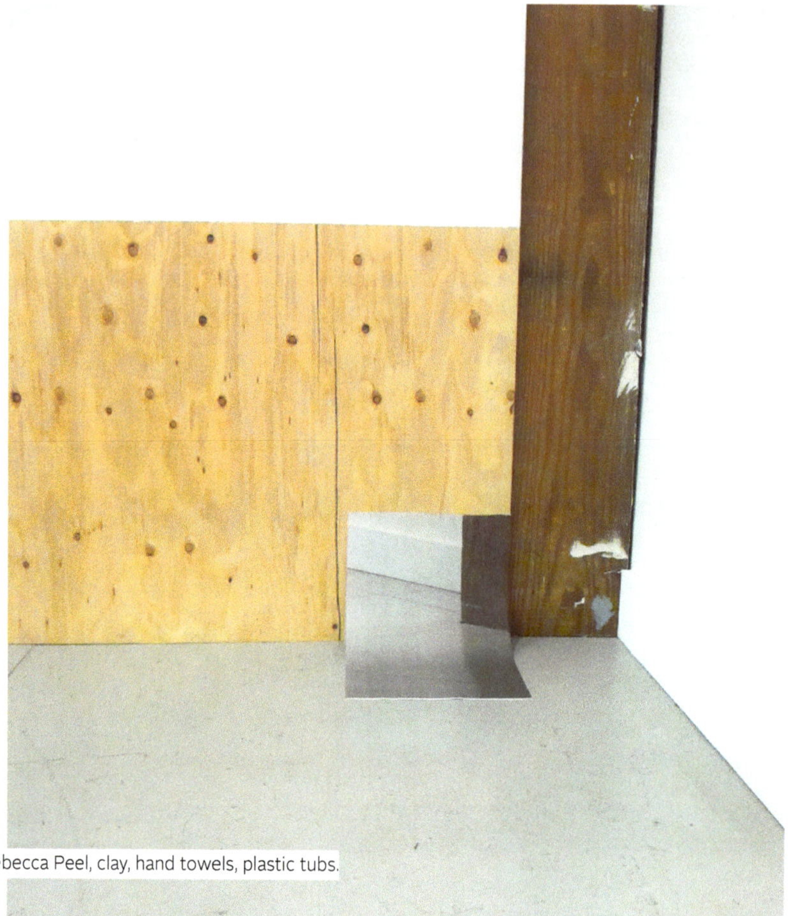

Celebration of Middles, 2012, Rebecca Peel, clay, hand towels, plastic tubs.

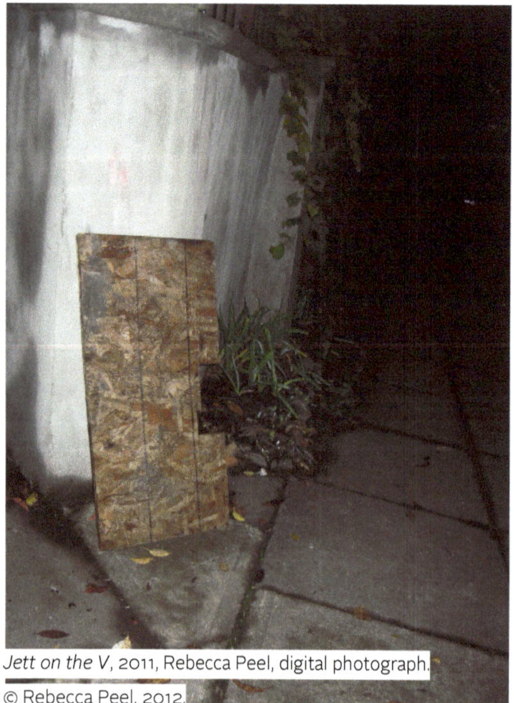

Jett on the V, 2011, Rebecca Peel, digital photograph.

 ISSN 1071-4391 ISBN 978-1-906897-20-8

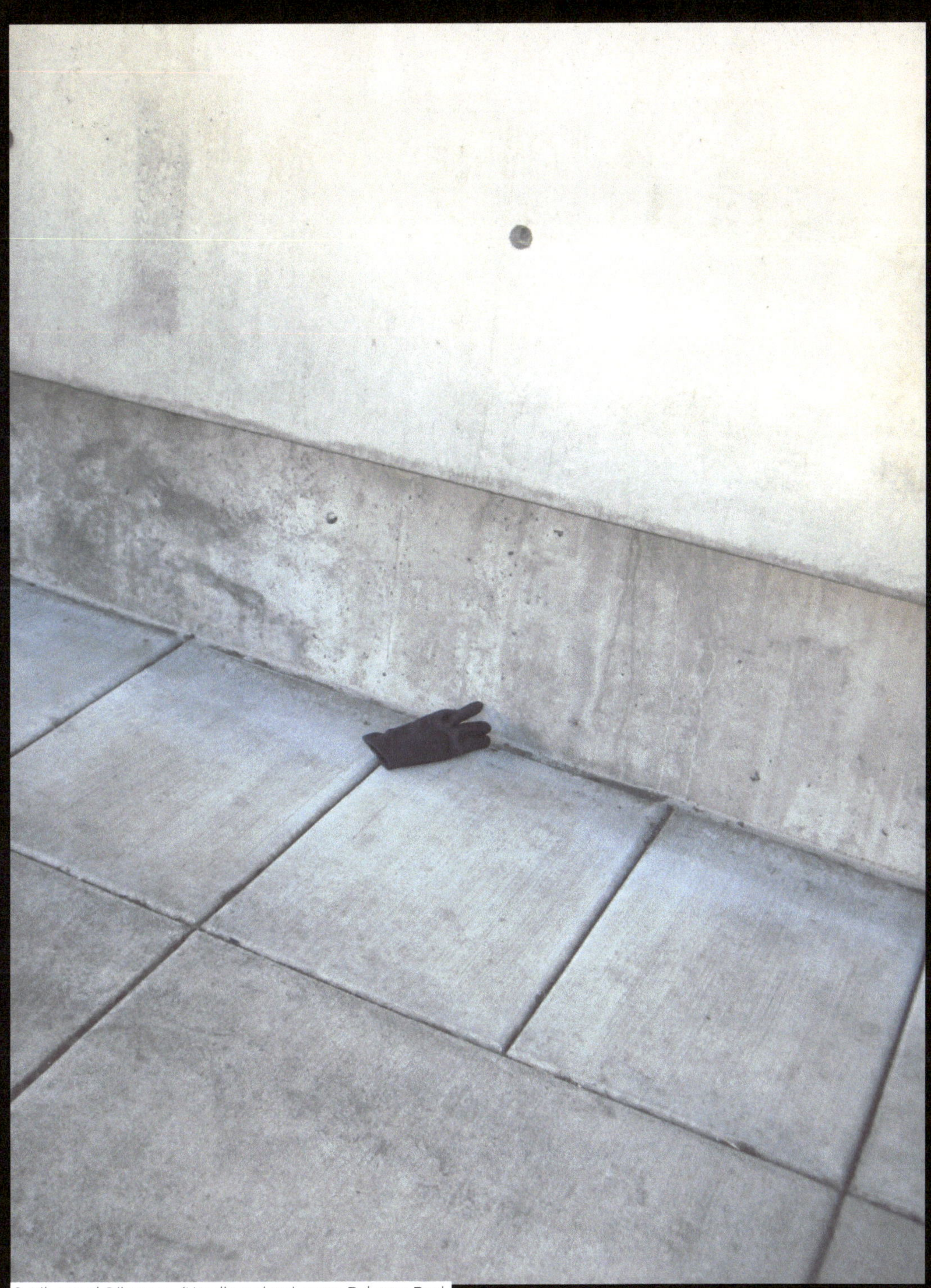

O-Liberated-Dilemma- (Handless glove), 2012, Rebecca Peel, digital photograph. © Rebecca Peel, 2012.

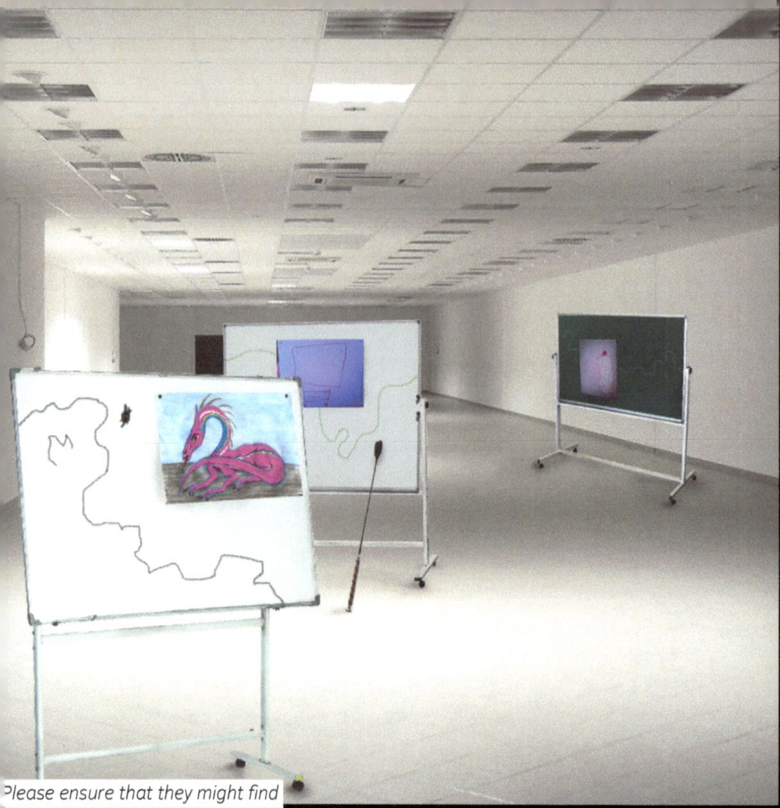

Please ensure that they might find their way out easily, 2011, Rebecca Peel, digital installation. © Rebecca Peel, 2011.

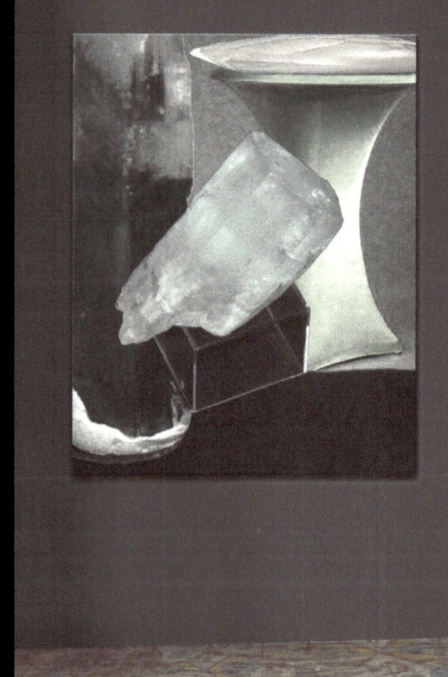

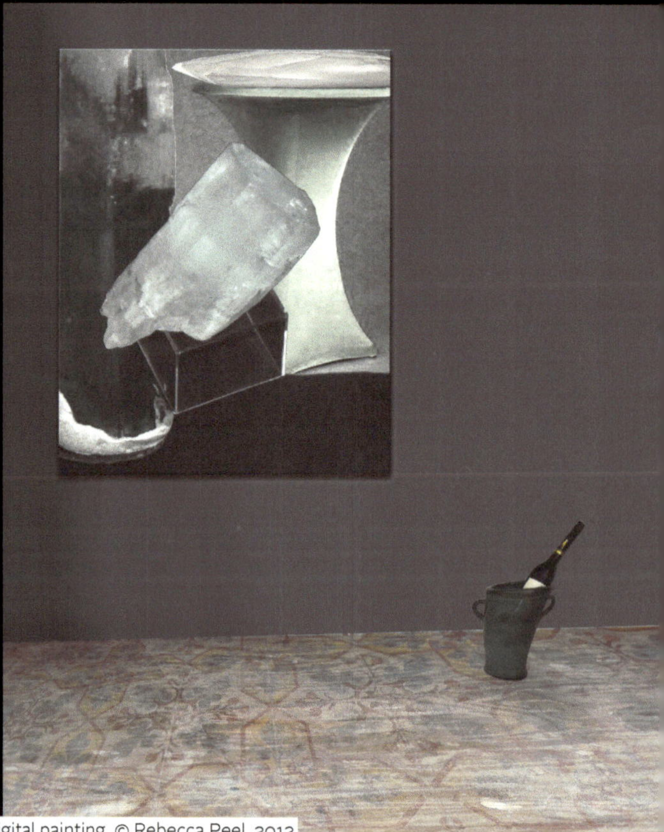

Syllabic Painting (slurry), 2012, Rebecca Peel, digital painting. © Rebecca Peel, 2012.

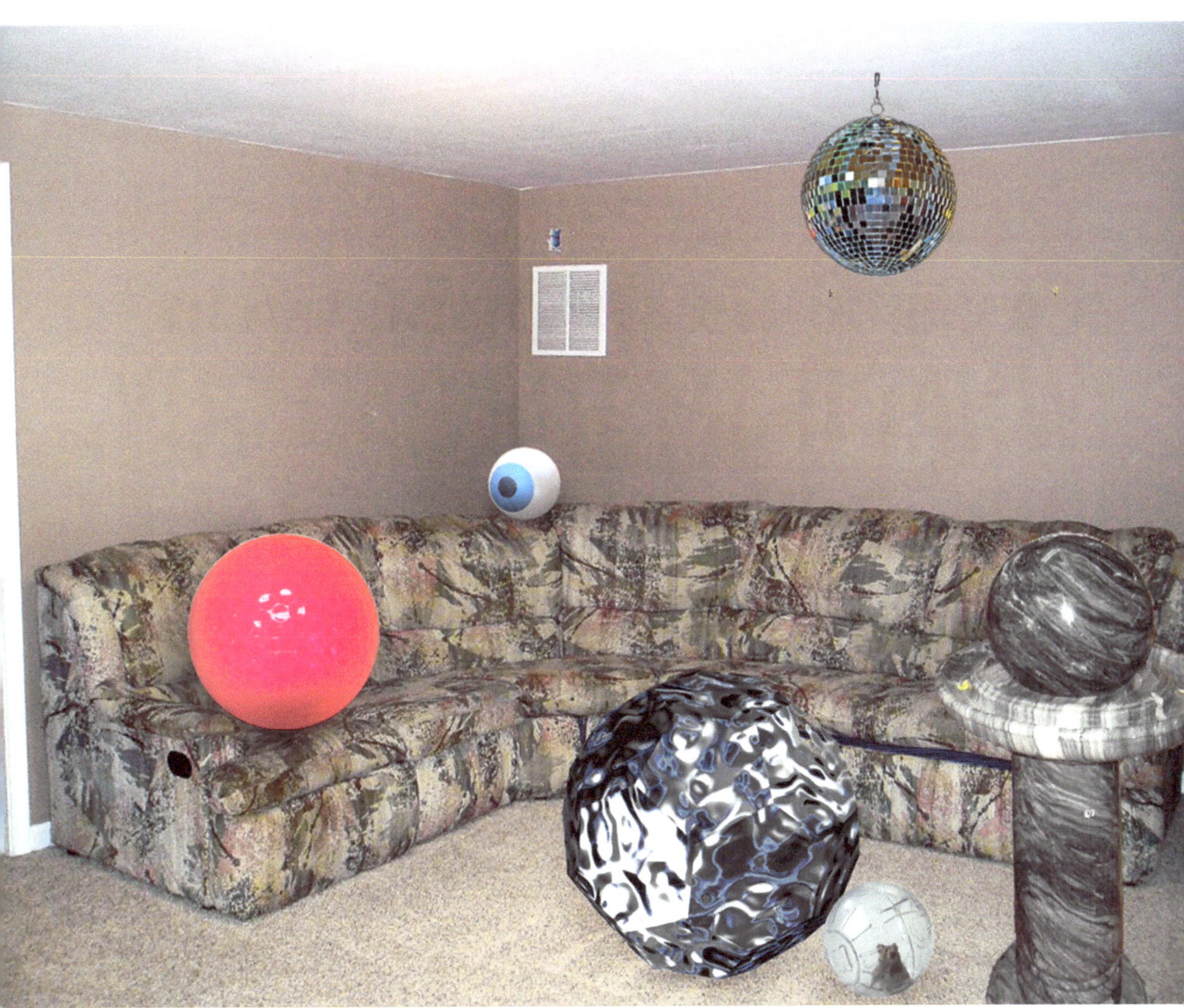

Tally, 2012, Rebecca Peel, digital installation. © Rebecca Peel, 2012.

Re-visualizing Afghanistan in WHAT IF IM THE BAD GUY: Using Palimpsest to Create an AR Documentary

AARON A. REED & PHOENIX TOEWS

Aaron A. Reed
UC Santa Cruz
PhD Student, Computer Science
aareed@gmail.com
http://www.soe.ucsc.edu/people/aareed
http://www.aaronareed.net/

Phoenix Toews
Independent
phyrworks@gmail.com
http://www.augmentedmountain.com

Sharp-edged fragments of faces loom above the grassy expanse behind a concrete building, in pieces thirty or forty feet high: a giant eye, a pixilated nose. At first these fractured portraits seem hopelessly jumbled. However, as one moves through the space and becomes more familiar with the experience of seeing these virtual objects overlaid over the environment, it starts to seem that perhaps there are places from which these fragments would line up, would appear to form a single, unbroken image. Coming to this realization is one entry point into *what if im the bad guy*, an experimental augmented reality (AR) documentary created in a new framework for AR narratives called *Palimpsest*.

Based on the stories of three US soldiers in Afghanistan and three unarmed civilians they shot and killed in early 2010, the piece embeds narrative fragments into an explorable, outdoor 'playing field.' Some of the fragments can be regarded from a perspective that causes them to re-align, triggering point-of-view re-stagings of the killings from the perspectives of various accused soldiers; other fragments represent moments in their stories, and can be repositioned

 ISSN 1071-4391 ISBN 978-1-906897-20-8

***what if im the bad guy** is an augmented reality documentary based on the stories of three US soldiers in Afghanistan accused of war crimes.* *Narrative fragments are embedded into an explorable, outdoor "playing field" where the participant is invited to find a point of view from which the story makes sense, and to explore the often-hidden motivations, contexts, and realities behind the surface of an at-first unapproachable news event. The piece is built on a new open-source framework for AR narrative called Palimpsest, which combines a powerful scripting language with a sophisticated low-level 3D engine capable of producing highly reactive and configurable narrative environments in real spaces.*

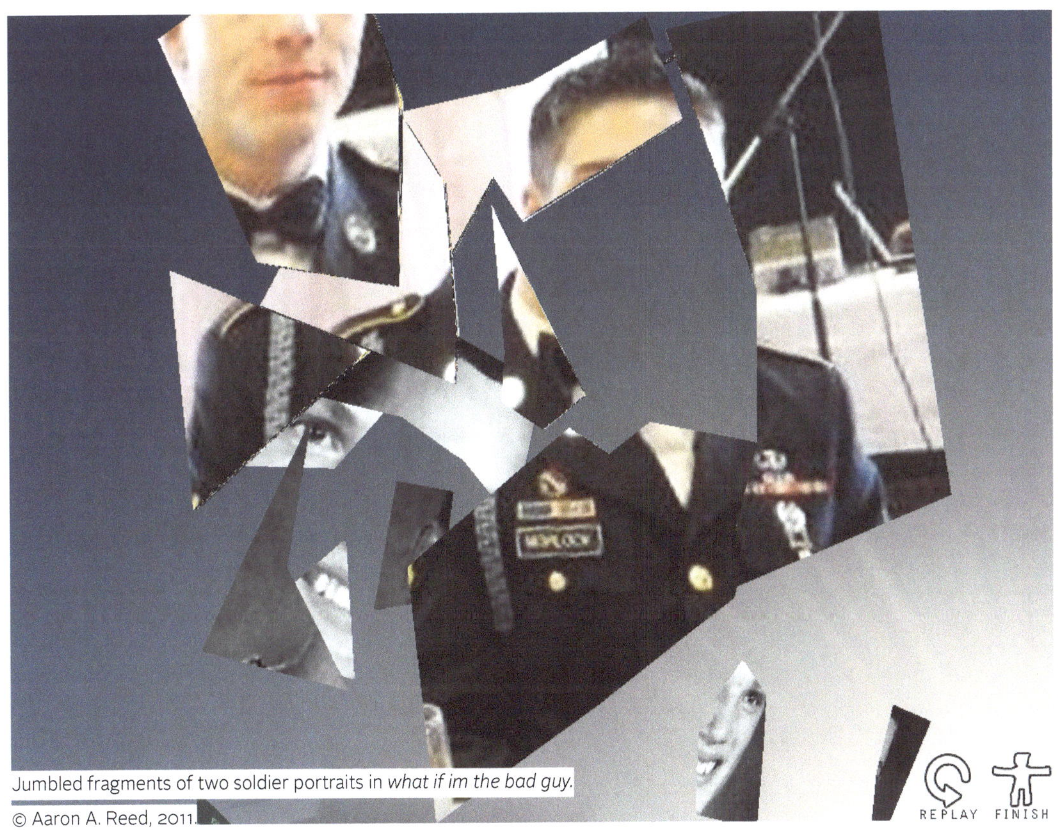

Jumbled fragments of two soldier portraits in *what if im the bad guy*.

by the viewer into configurations that offer different windows into the narrative: chronological, thematic connections, serendipitous juxtapositions. In various ways the participant is invited to find a point of view from which the story makes sense, and to explore the often-hidden motivations, context, and realities behind the surface of an at-first unapproachable news event. The field becomes a space for re-enactment, reflection, mourning and investigation.

The piece was created as part of a collaboration between an artist/coder and a writer/game designer, both MFA students on the UC Santa Cruz Digital Arts & New Media program at the time the piece was completed. (Though born from intensive theoretical discussions between both authors, the final piece was largely the work of Aaron A. Reed, while the technological innovation behind it largely driven by Phoenix Toews.) We share a strong belief in the promise of Augmented Reality (AR) to provide not just amusing diversions, but new ways of seeing truths that the corporate and governmental entities increasingly colonizing our digital lives might prefer remain obscured. As we enter the age of Google AR glasses and the internet of things, it becomes increasingly possible to alter, censor, or invent the experiential reality of technology users, providing access to altered realities for (especially) non-privileged and overlooked viewpoints. *bad guy* is an overlooked news story made re-visible for its viewers, and Palimpsest is a new software platform for enabling such re-visualizations: in the remainder of this article we'll describe both in a little more detail.

***

The *bad guy* project was born from a visceral reaction to a disturbing news story and incredulity over the next few weeks at how few people had heard about it and how little the press followed up. The story outlined, in brief, the shocking tale of a platoon of US soldiers in Afghanistan that had been systematically murdering unarmed civilians for sport, then planting weapons on the bodies to make it appear the victims were insurgents. [1] The killings, which took place throughout the spring and summer of 2010, were not stopped until an unrelated incident accidentally brought them to the attention of Army investigators. (During the investigation of this initial incident, photographs documenting a soldier's beating at the hands of his platoon-mates appeared online; one of these shows a tattoo reading "what if im not the hero // what if im the bad guy," a quote from the film *Twilight*.)

At the time we first encountered this story in the final months of 2010, media coverage was sparse, and details were still coming out in bits and pieces. However, despite the shocking picture emerging, it was not a page one story: among our peers, few were even aware of it. We began to see this as symptomatic of the weariness and disgust felt by most Americans with the war in Afghanistan, then approaching the end of its first decade with no end in sight. Journalist Gary Younge was writing at the time:

> *The American people, it seems, are bored with war. Like a reality show that's gone on too long, it ceases to shock, shame or even interest....The conversation has moved on; the trouble is, the troops haven't.* [2]

We came to feel the story was going untold, not because it was not worth telling but because most people refused to hear any more stories from Afghanistan. We began to wonder whether we could use new technology to tell these stories in a way people had not heard before, a way they had not already trained themselves to tune out. *Palimpsest* was already well into development, and we began discussing how AR's

 ISSN 1071-4391 ISBN 978-1-906897-20-8

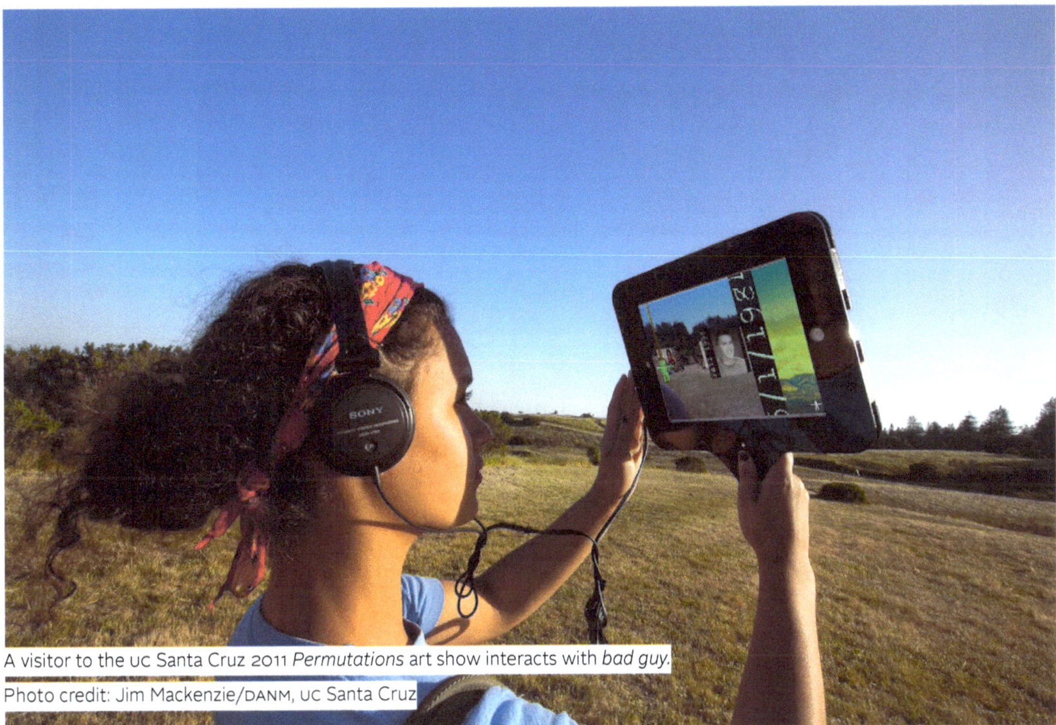

A visitor to the UC Santa Cruz 2011 *Permutations* art show interacts with *bad guy*.
Photo credit: Jim Mackenzie/DANM, UC Santa Cruz

ability to physically instantiate virtual objects could make it a tool for bridging the divide between a war half a world away and the unreality of news reports about it.

An early conceptual framework we developed was the notion of perspective. Humans use visual and spatial metaphors constantly to talk about how we process ideas and understand each other: I can see your point of view, get where you're coming from, or where you're going with that; I can talk past you, appreciate your perspective, or meet you halfway. The concept of "finding the point of view from which the story makes sense" became a key phrase in our early thinking about the work. We also explored metaphors of map and mapping, but realized early on, that navigation through the space was less important than getting participants to enter the space at all (a notion echoed in Wendy Chun's assertion that "in an info-rich society, a map is not a solution but a further problem.") [3] There was also the question of site-specificity: would we ask participants to travel to rural Afghanistan locations where the killings took place, and if not, what value could positioning pieces of that story in other places in the world have? We decided that our project was explicitly to bring those inaccessible places into uncomfortable proximity with an American audience: to place the events in a familiar setting and force participants to take a perspectival relationship to them. Conversations with D. Fox Harrell also helped us focus on the way AR's proprioceptive qualities could establish a connection between participants and the people in our story: the feeling of being *this* close to someone, or *that* far from safety.

Born from these discussions, and a great deal of research, was an experimental documentary told through AR and based on the stories of three of the accused American soldiers, as well as three of their Afghan victims. [4] Participants held an iPad 2 like a mirror in front of them in a custom case to view the embedded virtual objects, and wore headphones to hear positional audio, instructions, and narration. The installation code was written in Lua, which Palimpsest uses as a scripting language to tap into a powerful low-level 3D engine. With this technical framework we could embed participants in a complex, GPS-positioned and motion-tracked space capable of containing dozens of animated, interactive 3D objects and sounds, with a high enough frame rate and tracking accuracy to create a convincing augmented environment.

bad guy consists of four major thematic elements, presented as an at-first disorienting maelstrom of ob-

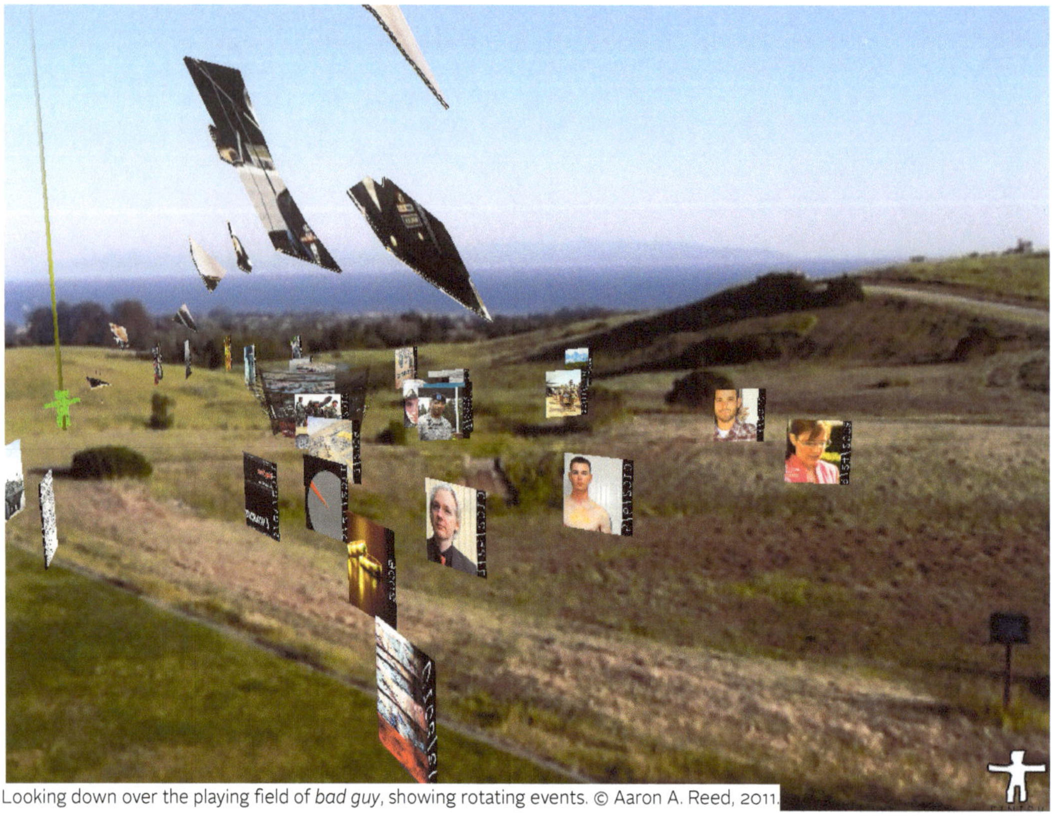

Looking down over the playing field of *bad guy*, showing rotating events. © Aaron A. Reed, 2011.

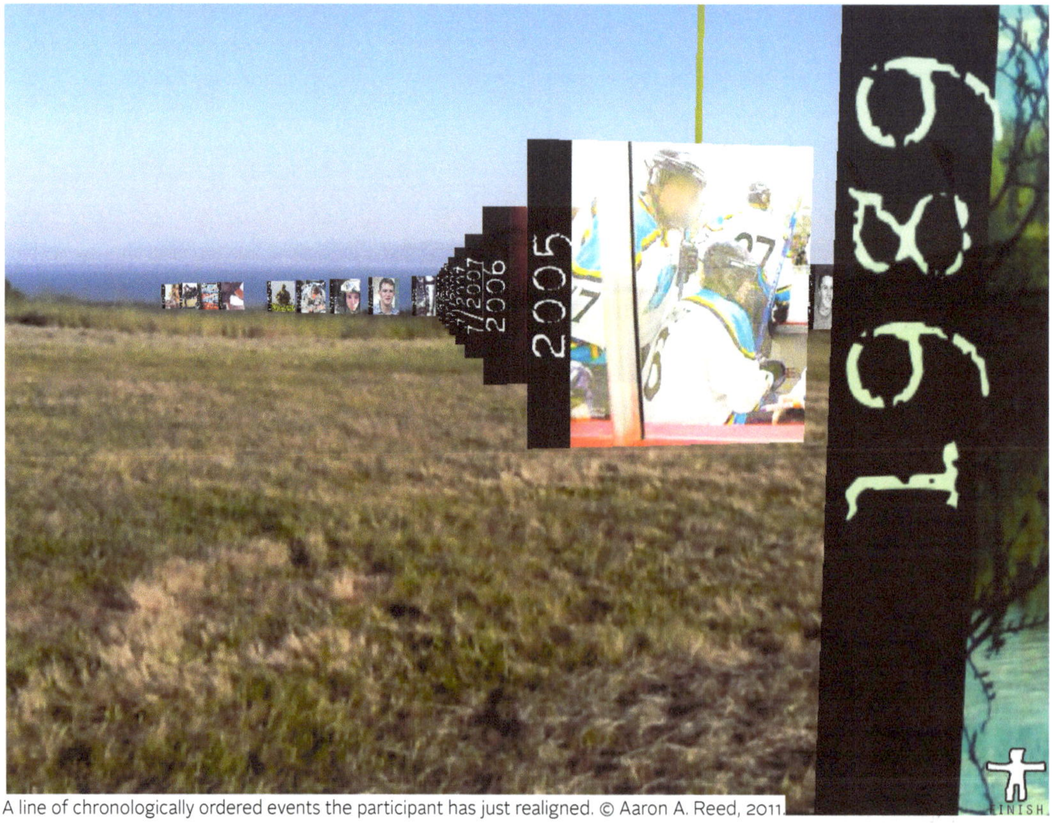

A line of chronologically ordered events the participant has just realigned. © Aaron A. Reed, 2011.

 ISSN 1071-4391 ISBN 978-1-906897-20-8

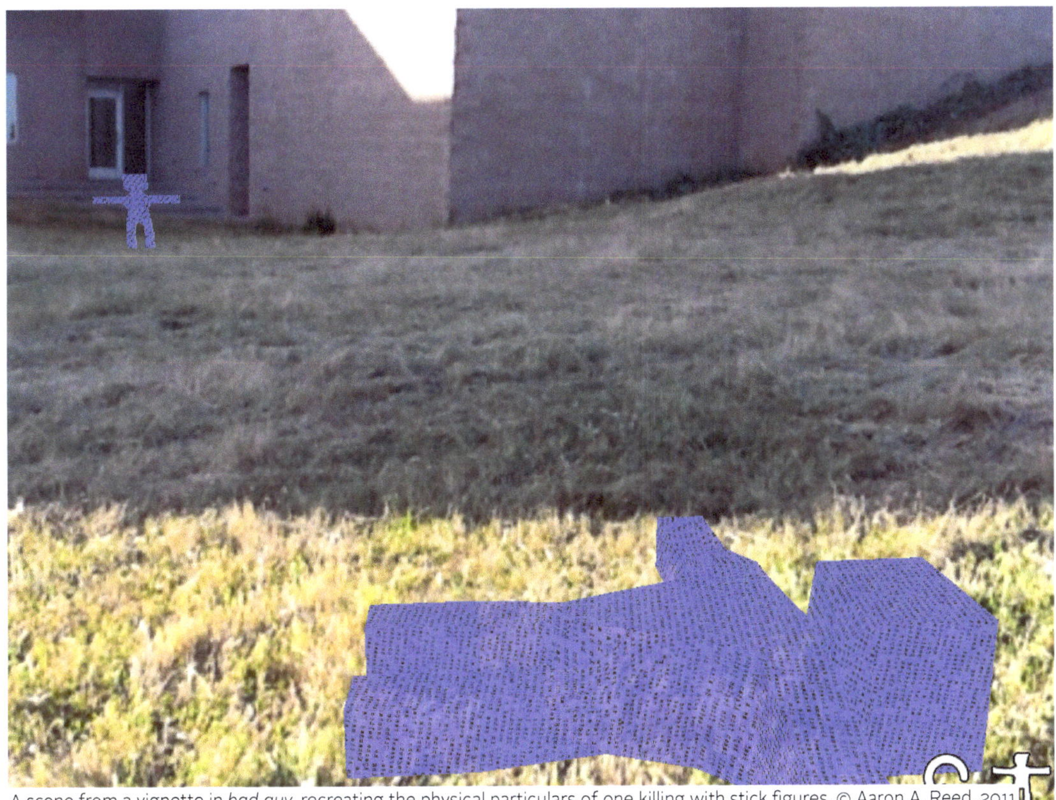

A scene from a vignette in *bad guy*, recreating the physical particulars of one killing with stick figures. © Aaron A. Reed, 2011.

jects and sounds spread out over a "playing field" approximately 100 meters across. [5] The most significant element is a collection of "events," each corresponding to a nugget of information unearthed by the press about the soldiers and the killings. When first encountered, the events (each embodied as a square image two meters to a side) are all revolving slowly around the center of the playing field, which is suffused with a sound of grinding machinery, suggesting a medieval orrery (another era's attempt at using technology to understand a complex world). When approached and touched, the events expand to reveal a text description, a date, and a series of keywords representing location, participants, and thematic labels such as *Promises*, *Strategy*, or *Deception*. Touching a keyword causes all the events associated with that keyword to rearrange (with a groaning mechanical sound suggesting tortured machinery) into a chronologically-ordered column along the direction the participant is currently facing. The participant can then walk forward to explore the events that happened after the one selected, or turn around and walk the other direction to explore what happened before. Any new event encountered can be touched to bring up new information and keywords. The participant thus creates an ever-changing configuration of events determined by his or her movement through and interaction with the space. Much like a journalist cutting and pinning newspaper articles to a wall to discover patterns and connections, we hoped the playing field of *bad guy* could be a dynamic space where participants could rearrange and reorder the pieces of this story in an attempt to make personal sense of them.

The second major element of the piece is three fractured portraits of the three accused soldiers, looming as giant fragments suspended in the air above the playing field. From most perspectives, the three fractured photos interpose or obscure each other, seeming hopelessly jumbled; but as the participant moves through the space, they begin to notice that each set of fragments will line up from a certain location to reassemble one portrait. (We suggest here traditions such as anamorphic art, where parts of the image are hidden in plain sight or only revealed from the right perspective.)

When participants stand at a spot where a portrait aligns, they trigger one of three events that retell a killing from the point of view of the aligned soldier. Blocky stick figures textured with words from news reports of the killings are positioned in a tableau recreating the spatial relationships between the soldier (standing at the player's position) and other nearby actors in the scene. A narrator describes how the killing took place, during which the stick figures change position: when a victim is shot, his figure changes from being upright to face down on the ground. These events recreate, in as much detail as possible, from available reports, the exact physical positioning of the actors involved in each killing: if a victim was "about 50 feet away," the stick figure representing him is placed that distance from the player's location; if the soldier whose eyes you're looking through was short, the stick figures of the other soldiers are increased in size so they seem taller than you as you look around at them. While we could not bring participants to the site of the killings, we could try to make them feel the spatial realities of being surrounded by others, the shortest one in a group, or just a few paces from a man being shot.

The three victims are also represented in the piece. At the spot where each victim is first seen in a vignette is an angry series of overlapping, slowly spinning funnel shapes suggestive of a frozen explosion. The shapes are formed from distorted images of the accused soldiers and text fragments of dry details about the killings. An audio montage of warfare, war protesters, mourners, and news coverage of the killings originates from each memorial; this can be heard across the playing field but becomes louder as one steps closer. If one approaches each shape and then steps inside, all sound stops and other imagery vanishes, replaced by a wraparound panorama of a beautiful, tranquil landscape, and floating text marking the name, occupation, and date of death of the victim (often the only information known to Western media). The player can remain in this memorial space as long as they like before stepping outside back into the external chaos.

The final element of the piece is its conclusion. After initial introductory narration, the participant is given very little direction and few explicit goals, but rather invited to explore the piece for as long as is desired. A button on the viewing device can be pressed to end a session with the piece. When this happens, a new stick figure is created at the precise location and orientation of the player; it literally appears around them and they must step outside of it. When they do, they see that the playing field is now filled with other silent stick figures, marking the spots where each prior participant chose to end the piece. The participant then walks back to return the equipment through a field of these figures, leaving their own marker behind to join them.

***

In the conceptualization and implementation of this piece, we drew on inspiration from many sources, both cultural, artistic, and technological, while also consciously aiming to push the boundaries beyond the work we were familiar with. AR has already developed traditions both as an interventionist device and a sculptural surrogate. Craig Freeman's *Border Memorial: Frontera de los Muertos*, for instance, places a virtual skeleton effigy at each location where human remains have been recovered near the US/Mexico border, "allow[ing] people to visualize the scope of the loss of life." [6] Making the dry GPS coordinates of an obscure database into an instantiated, located memorial re-visualizes the human cost of the public and political policies around immigration issues. While works like this may have strong user emotive engagement, the tools for creating them (in this case, the

 ISSN 1071-4391 ISBN 978-1-906897-20-8

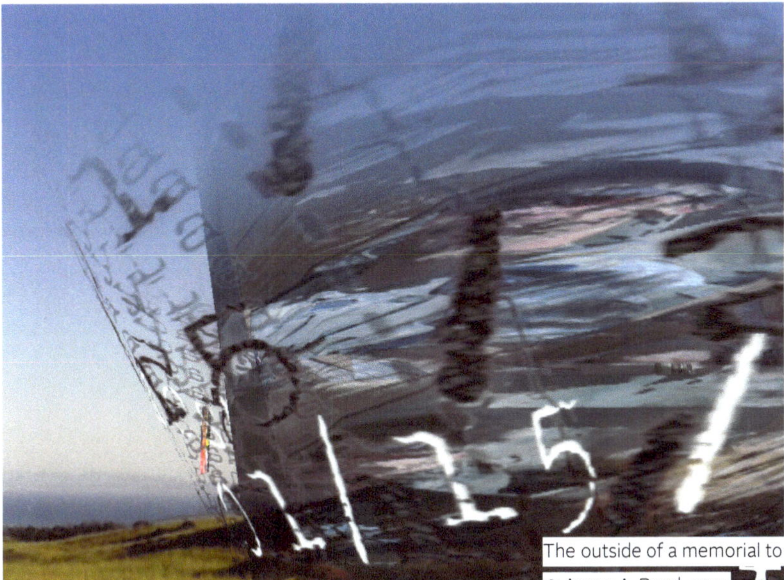

The outside of a memorial to one of the victims in *bad guy*.
© Aaron A. Reed, 2011.

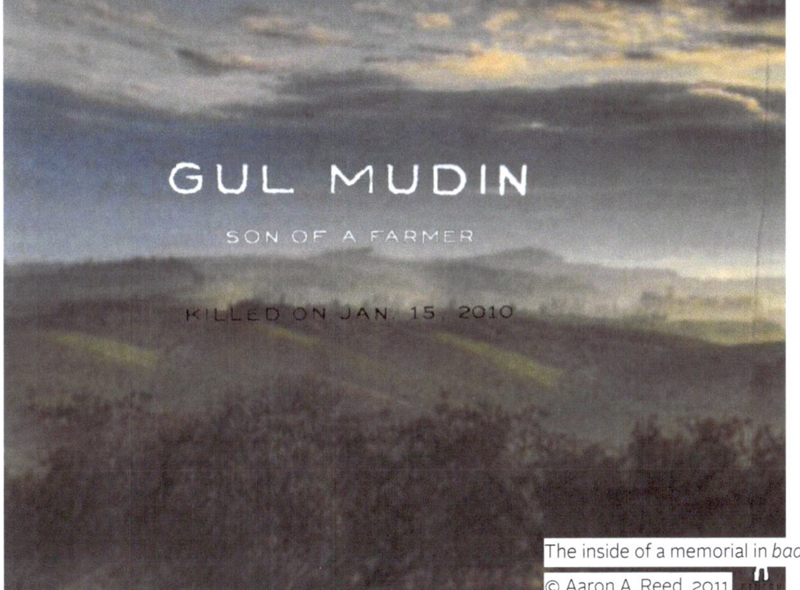

The inside of a memorial in *bad guy*.
© Aaron A. Reed, 2011.

Layar platform) remain either technologically limited or financially difficult to access. The use of AR to create virtual sculpture (even on scales not feasible in reality, as with *Border Memorial*) is one way the medium can innovate, but tools for creating more reactive or procedurally involved work are still rare.

One goal of the Palimpsest Augmented Reality Toolkit is to provide such a tool-- one both powerful and freely available-- to wider audiences. [7] Palimpsest has been created with the specific intent of supporting the construction of nonlinear AR narratives and documentaries using a framework capable of both hardware-pushing graphics and algorithmic power. Palimpsest authors write code in a simple but powerful scripting language built on top of a low-level AR browser for the iPhone and iPad. The system provides hooks to respond to movement, rotational, and touch actions from the user, and to script positional 3D objects, animations, and sounds. Changes in heading, proximity to particular locations, and other behaviors are all scriptable. While singular GPS coordinates are useful for creating symbolic representations of spaces, they do not represent the way that people interact

We spent significant amounts of time engaging with particular locations we knew (or grew to know) quite well, with the intent of incorporating our cultural knowledge of place with the technology we were building.

with their local environment: with Palimpsest, places are conceptualized as collections of objects and possible interactions, an area of potential rather than a singular point in space. This gives us the ability to re-visualize a physical place as a reactive space with rich narrative potential.

The creation of Palimpsest was the direct result of numerous discussions, walks, and whiteboard drawings between the authors. We spent significant amounts of time engaging with particular locations we knew (or grew to know) quite well, with the intent of incorporating our cultural knowledge of place with the technology we were building. Our envisioning of the breadth of spatial narrative possibilities within the places we encountered, profoundly impacted the design of Palimpsest. Inherent in the design process was a desire to create technologies that foster community involvement within one's own locality, a reversal of the trend towards globalizing technologies that tend to shift power away from the local. AR has a particularly powerful potential for re-engaging the local by creating a dialog between the virtual/global/networked environment and the personal/physical/local environment. We hope that Palimpsest will push the dialog towards a more engaging and complex discussion than what has formerly been possible.

Without a long tradition of AR narratives to build upon, we mostly drew inspiration from other media in assembling *bad guy*. Framing a story as a series of fragments to be reassembled into a coherent whole has been explored in film (Michael Haneke's *71 Fragments of a Chronology of Chance*, [8] to name one example) and in computer-based media such as *Bleeding Through: Layers of Los Angeles, 1920–1986*, [9] a multimedia project presenting fragments of narrative about a fictional character embedded in a real historical context. A more embodied approach was taken by Jessica Faith Hayden and Christopher Molla's installa-

 ISSN 1071-4391 ISBN 978-1-906897-20-8

tion *Seemingly External Things*, [10] which furnishes a Silver Streak trailer with period objects that conspire with hidden technology to share fragments of story through video, audio, and motion when touched. In the VR project *Three Angry Men*, [11] the participant can move between chairs arranged around a table to witness a fictional drama from the perspective of any of its three characters. All of these pieces explore the dual meaning of perspective as referring to both what is visible and what is believed: as we uncover new fragments, we continually change our relationship to the characters in the story, positioning ourselves relative to them and their actions in the narrative space.

Using virtual spaces to explore real-world events also has precedent. Tamiko Thiel's *Beyond Manzanar* recreates a Japanese internment camp in virtual reality (VR), with similar experiential goals as we had with our own project: "As you explore the camp your kinesthetic sense is engaged to underscore the emotional impact of confinement." [12] The game art installation *Waco Resurrection* asks participant to wear VR helmets that put them in the head of cult leader David Koresh, pumping disturbing voices from God into the headphones while they play a first-person shooter game defending the compound and empowering followers. [13] Outside of AR/VR, other software-based projects have engaged with real-world tragedies in journalistic or critical ways, including *Super Columbine Massacre RPG!*, *JFK: Reloaded*, and *Six Days in Fallujah*; what's disturbing is that many of these pieces were threatened, pulled, or shut down in the face of real or imagined public outrage. [14] [15] Virtual spaces are not yet universally seen as acceptable places to engage in serious dialogue about real-world issues: in *dead-in-iraq*, a piece where the names of US soldiers killed in Iraq were typed into the chat box of in-progress games of "America's Army," [16] the artist frequently received threats and vitriol both from players and non-players of the military-funded recruiting game.

We remain, however, strongly committed to the potential of virtual spaces for re-visualizing the forgotten or invisible. *Oyster City* is a new Palimpsest-based project being produced as a collaboration between Meredith Drum, Rachel Stevens, and author Phoenix Toews. An eco-psychogeographic walking tour that takes place in an area of lower Manhattan, the piece tells the story of the rise and fall of the oyster trade in New York City, and invites participants to draw connections between the oyster trade, ecological and environmental sustainability issues, and social, political, and cultural histories. *Oyster City* will be part game and part historical narrative. A participant will be able to "collect" various virtual objects by visiting a series of sites that are intimately connected with the history of oysters in the city. Physical traversal from site to site will be required to piece together the various parts of the narrative, and the collection and movement of objects will open new narrative trajectories for the participant. *Oyster City* is expected to debut in fall 2012. Other projects are also underway: a collaboration with the Silicon Valley Toxics Coalition to create augmented reality tours of superfund sites in the Bay Area is under construction, as well as several collaborations with both national and international artists. Palimpsest itself is currently being prepared for release as an open-source, freely available system.

In early rounds of the discussions that led to *what if im the bad guy*, we considered the disturbing possibility of subscribing to "channels" of reality, imagining AR apps that would only let you see what the entities behind each channel wanted you to see. With each passing month this seems less like science fiction. Big interests will continue exploiting the steep technological barrier to creating sophisticated AR, providing access to only the content (and eventually, realities) that serve their purposes. Palimpsest is named after the practice in an earlier era of reusing the same precious paper to inscribe new writing, even though traces of the old would inevitably remain. While digital technology offers the temptation to completely eradicate the past (or undesirable presents), we hope putting access to AR into the hands of a broader audience will help keep more stories, viewpoints, and realities visible. ■

ACKNOWLEDGEMENTS

We would like to thank our thesis committee members, Elliot Anderson, Jennifer Gonzalez, D. Fox Harrell, Michael Mateas, and Noah Wardrip-Fruin for conceptual, technical, and moral support on our projects. *what if im the bad guy* and Palimpsest were supported by grants from the Florence French Financial Aid Fund for Art.

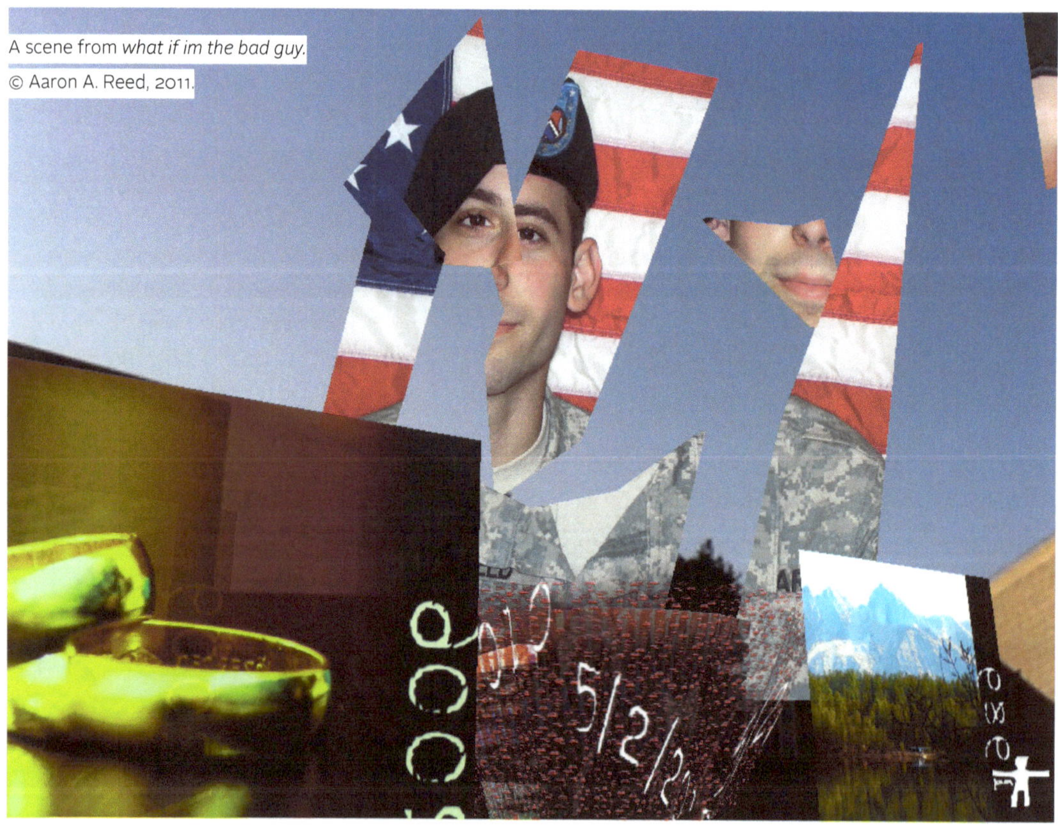

A scene from *what if im the bad guy.*

 ISSN 1071-4391 ISBN 978-1-906897-20-8

REFERENCES AND NOTES

1. Andrew Purcell, "Porn, hashish and killing for kicks ... what fuelled a GI death squad in Afghanistan," *Herald* (Glasgow), October 3, 2010.
2. Gary Younge, "Forgetting Afghanistan," *The Nation*, November 8, 2010, http://www.thenation.com/article/155501/forgetting-afghanistan (accessed April 29, 2012).
3. Wendy Chun, "Codes, Crises and Critical Pleasure" (keynote address, Critical Code Studies @ USC, Los Angeles, CA, July 23, 2010).
4. The American soldiers chosen were Calvin Gibbs, Jeremy Morlock, and Adam Winfield; the victims were Gul Mudin, Marach Agha, and Mullah Alahdad of Qala Gai.
5. Aaron A. Reed, "A Sequence of Possibilities: Constructive fictions, quantum authoring, and the search for an ideal story system," (MFA thesis, UC Santa Cruz, 2011).
6. Border Memorial: Frontera de los Muertos, "Project Description," http://bordermemorial.wordpress.com/border-memorial-frontera-de-los-muertos/ (accessed April 29, 2012).
7. Phoenix Toews, "Place is a Palimpsest: Augmented Reality and Experience of Place" (MFA thesis, UC Santa Cruz, 2011).
8. 71 Fragmente einer Chronologie des Zufalls, dir. Michael Haneke (1994).
9. Rosemary Comella, Andreas Kratky and Norman Klein, "Bleeding Through: Layers of Los Angeles, 1920–1986," The Labyrinth Project/Zentrum für Kunst und Medientechnologie, 2001 (Microsoft Windows DVD-ROM).
10. Jessica Faith Hayden, "Seemingly External Things: Evocative Objects and Imagined Landscapes in the Installation Practice" (MFA thesis, UC Santa Cruz, 2010).
11. Blair MacIntyre, Jay David Bolter, Jeannie Vaughan et al., "Three Angry Men: Dramatizing Point-of-View using Augmented Reality," *ACM SIGGRAPH 2002*, (2002): 268.
12. Beyond Manzanar, "History and project origins," http://www.mission-base.com/manzanar/history/origins.html (accessed May 27, 2011).
13. *Waco Resurrection*, 2004, Eddo Stern et al., computer Game/installation/hardware/mixed media.
14. Stephen Totilo, "Columbine Game Yanked From Slamdance Festival Amid Controversy, Protest," *MTV News*, January 9, 2007.
15. Associated Press, "Company pulls plug on Fallujah war video game," April 30, 2009.
16. *dead-in-iraq*, 2006-ongoing, Joseph DeLappe, performance; http://www.unr.edu/art/delappe/gaming/dead_in_iraq/dead_in_iraq%20jpegs.html (accessed April 23 2012).

AARON A. REED

interviewed by
Lanfranco Aceti & Richard Rinehart

Is there an 'outside' of the Art World from which to launch critiques and interventions? If so, what is the border that defines outside from inside? If it is not possible to define a border, then what constitutes an intervention and is it possible to be and act as an outsider of the art world? Or are there only different positions within the Art World and a series of positions to take that fulfill ideological parameters and promotional marketing and branding techniques to access the fine art world from an oppositional, and at times confrontational, standpoint?

There's clearly an outside to the art world, although for artists working out there I'm not sure whether (or what!) they might be interested in launching back into it. I think especially within new media art there's a lot of people creating work informed more by contexts and paradigms outside art and art historical traditions: frameworks from hacking to storytelling to game-making to DIY building. Speaking only for myself, I find that I spend most of my time when making work not thinking consciously from an "art world" perspective; it tends to be only in moments of reflection and self-critique between projects that I step back into that headspace to think about how my work intersects with those traditions and frames.

"In *The Truth in Painting*, Derrida describes the *parergon* (*par-*, around; *ergon*, the work), the boundaries or limits of a work of art. Philosophers from Plato to Hegel, Kant, Husserl, and Heidegger debated the limits of the intrinsic and extrinsic, the inside and outside of the art object." (Anne Friedberg, *The Virtual Window: From Alberti to Microsoft* (Cambridge, MA: MIT Press, 2009), 13.) Where then is the inside and outside of the virtual artwork? Is the artist's 'hand' still inside the artistic process in the production of virtual art or has it become an irrelevant concept abandoned outside the creative process of virtual artworks?

VR/AR certainly blurs the lines between reality as seen by the viewer and reality as seen by the artist. Alternate reality games have explored this terrain for years, even before they were called that (the 2001 video game Majestic was centered around the notion of the story invading your reality through all of your available devices). Now that we live in a world where control of reality is no longer science fiction but a matter of who makes it to market first, this question of the boundaries of work (whether art, commerce, or interface) is no longer theoretical but vitally important. Artists will most likely be on the forefront of questioning what the new role of boundaries is in augmented spaces: whether the augmenter has a moral obligation to keep their hand visible, and how much blurring of boundaries augmentees will find practically and comfortably acceptable.

Virtual interventions appear to be the contemporary inheritance of Fluxus' artistic practices. Artists like Peter Weibel, Yayoi Kusama and Valie Export subverted traditional concepts of space and media through artistic interventions. What are the sources of inspiration and who are the artistic predecessors that you draw from for the conceptual and

 ISSN 1071-4391 ISBN 978-1-906897-20-8

aesthetic frameworks of contemporary augmented reality interventions?

My work in AR has been informed largely by artists and practitioners interested in making the formerly invisible visible. Wafaa Bilal's "Domestic Tension" was a huge influence on me, for its attempt to make something that was an abstraction for most Americans (civilian death in Iraq) into a visible reality both in its gallery exhibition and online, explicitly implicating participants in both contexts. From another angle, I've admired work that's used technology to make visible the implicit ideologies and assumptions of its audience, such as Michael Mateas's Terminal Time, a piece where audiences responses to an interactive documentary causes the narration to increasingly pander to the ideologies of the current viewers. I've also been inspired by work done by my colleagues in the Digital Arts and New Media program at UC Santa Cruz, including Phoenix Toews' use of AR to visualize underground contaminants in suburban neighborhoods, and Meredith Drum's "Louisiana Re-storied," an interactive documentary exploring the largely silenced consequences of the petroleum industry in southern Louisiana.

In the representation and presentation of your artworks as being 'outside of' and 'extrinsic to' contemporary aesthetics why is it important that your projects are identified as art?

I wouldn't say this is particularly important to me: in fact, maybe something I like about the label "story" for much of my work is that this can seem a less loaded term with which to introduce a new experience to a lay audience. With my AR piece "what if im the bad guy," despite its presence in the context of my MFA exhibition, I definitely shied away from overtly labeling it as art, preferring to call it a "documentary" or an "experience" that participants could explore on their own terms. I suppose if an individual finds something useful about conceptualizing my work as "art" then they're free to, but I'm much more interested that they encounter it at all than that they label it a particular way.

What has most surprised you about your recent artworks? What has occurred in your work that was outside of your intent, yet has since become an intrinsic part of the work?

Creating computational fictions continues to change the way I write and think about writing. While I initially conceived of this kind of writing as collaboration with a capricious, sometimes unreliable co-author-- the algorithms responsible for all or part of my interactive stories-- I've recently come to a realization that I'm really collaborating with myself. Part of this has come from increasing my skills as a programmer to the point where I no longer feel uneasy giving myself that label, and the ability to turn more and more advanced techniques towards proceduralizing various aspects of my ideas, styles, and philosophies. This reification of parts of my artistic process into executable code has forced a precision of thought which I did not put into my fiction, but now that it is there I can not imagine writing without it. ■

AARON A. REED

statement & artwork

My work explores the largely unmapped territory at the intersection of computation and traditional literary practice.

While swaths of this terrain have been labeled as "hypertext fiction," "interactive fiction," "e-poetry" etc., my projects increasingly involve sorties outside these semi-established zones into new ways that interactive stories can be informed by sophisticated algorithmic processes.

While mostly working with text-based narratives, I've also worked on graphical games and augmented reality installations. As the number of devices in our lives that can present us with computationally-driven story is increasing, augmented reality provides a preview into a future where the devices fade away into the background, giving artists (and other entities) the ability to directly inscribe stories onto our lived reality. This can't help but profoundly change the way we think about and tell stories, both fiction and non-fiction, and experimentation in this space continues to be fruitful. ■

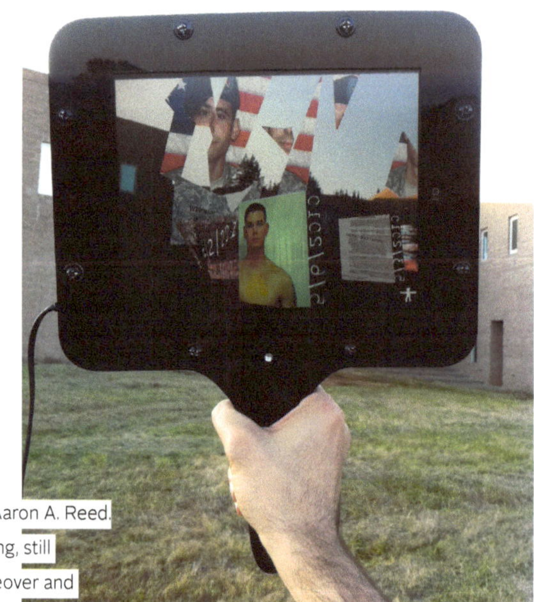

what if im the bad guy, 2011, Aaron A. Reed. iPad 2, Palimpsest, Lua scripting, still photography, 3D objects, voiceover and ambient audio, text. © Aaron A. Reed, 2011.

 ISSN 1071-4391 ISBN 978-1-906897-20-8

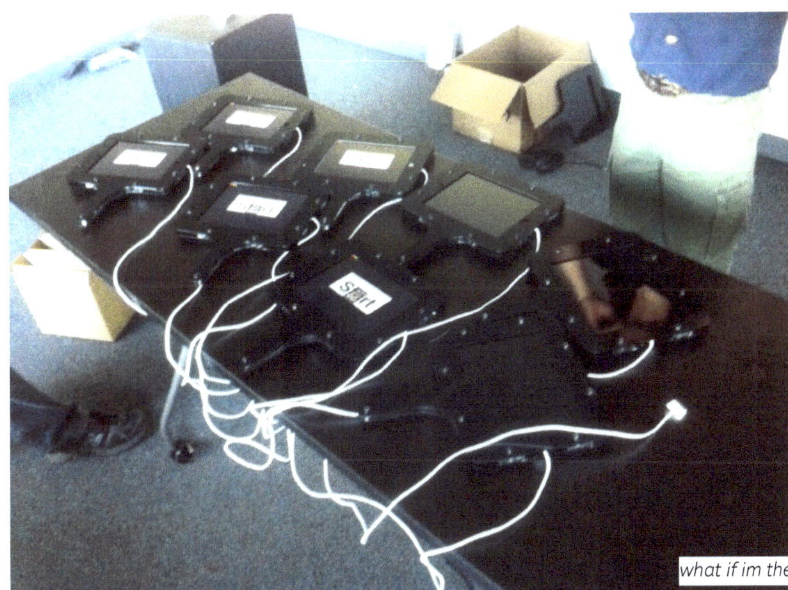

what if im the bad guy, 2011, Aaron A. Reed. iPad 2, Palimpsest, Lua scripting, still photography, 3D objects, voiceover and ambient audio, text. © Aaron A. Reed, 2011.

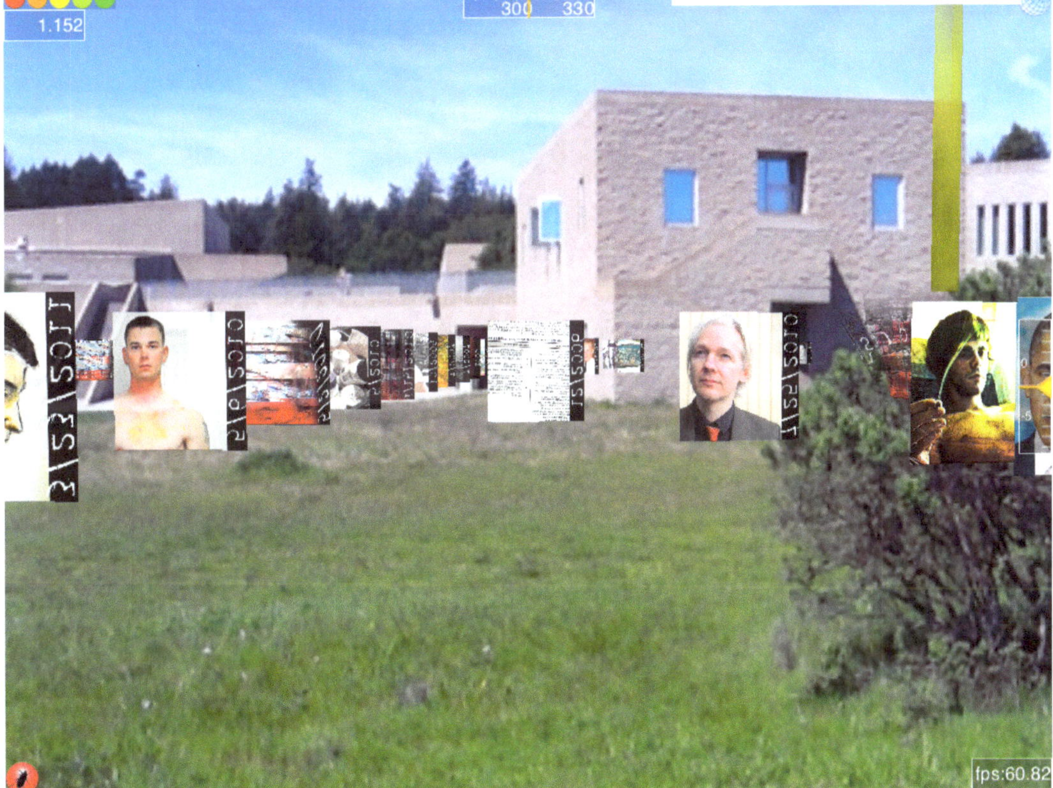

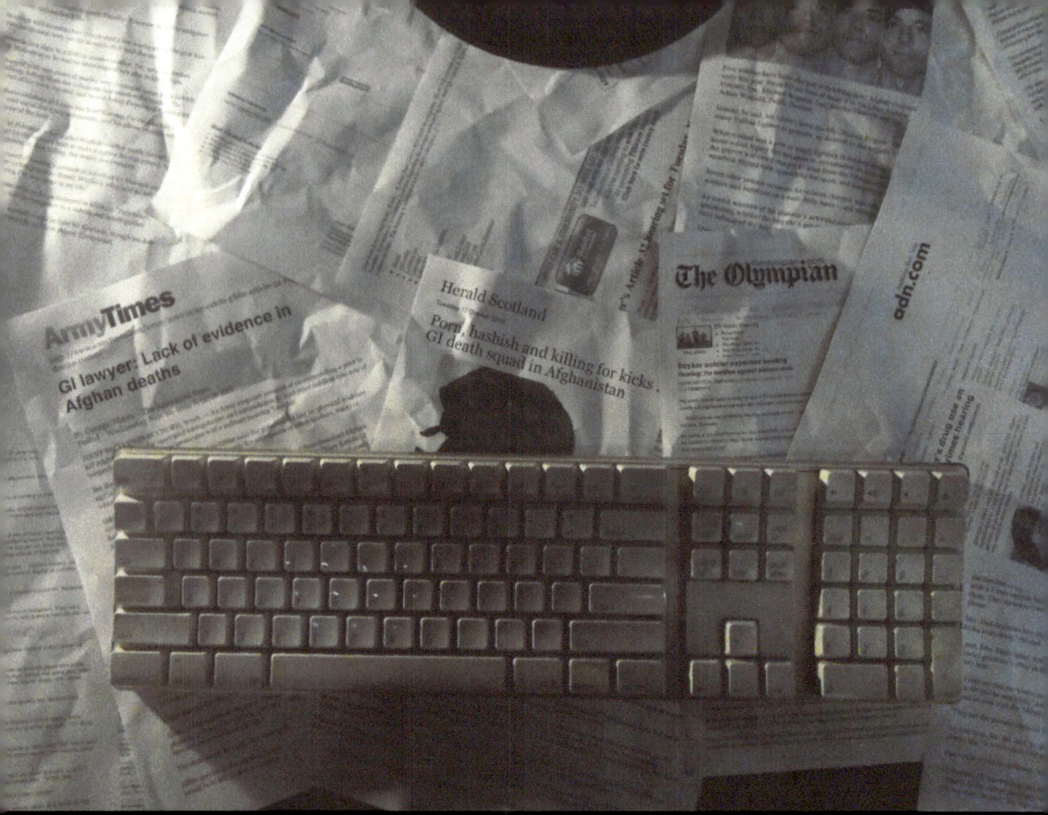

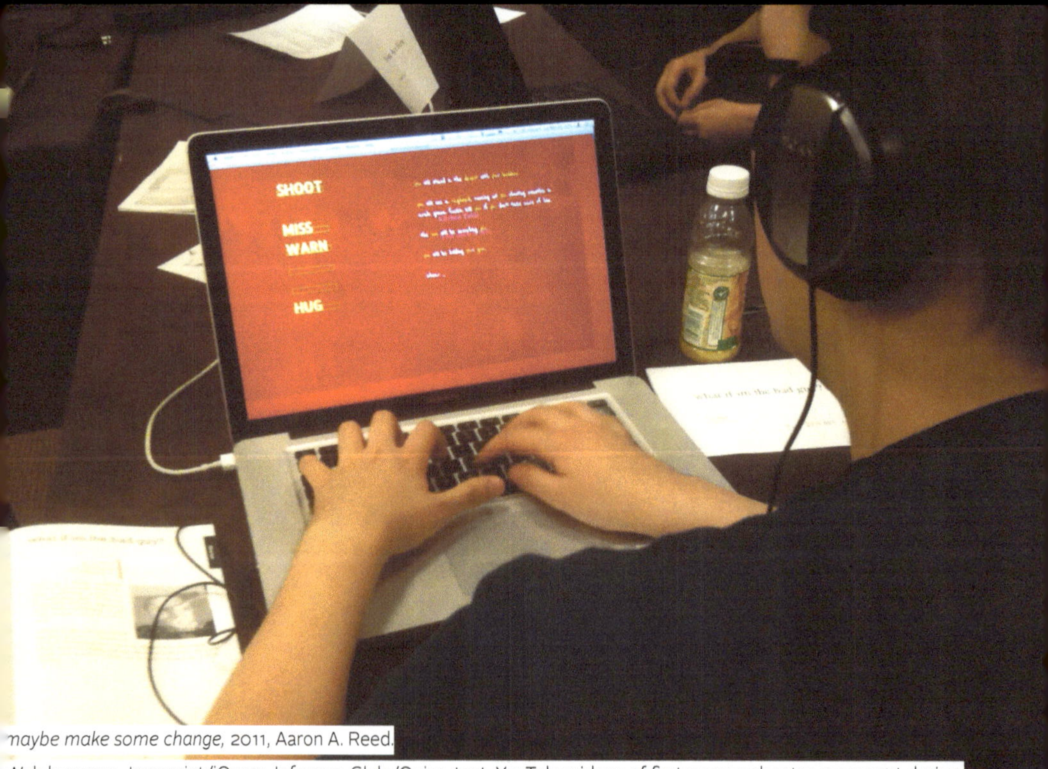

maybe make some change, 2011, Aaron A. Reed.

Web browser, Javascript/jQuery, Inform 7, Glulx/Quixe, text, YouTube videos of first-person shooter games set during contemporary wars, audio of soldier/civilian interactions in Afghanistan, still images. © Aaron A. Reed, 2011.

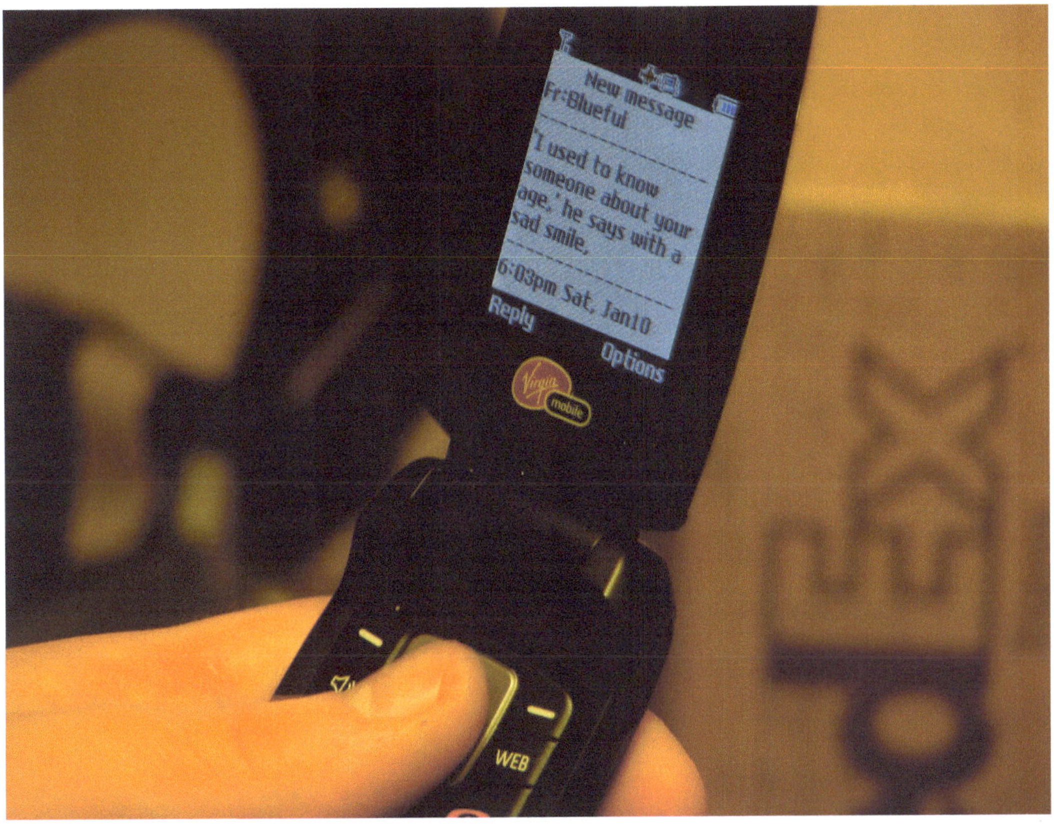

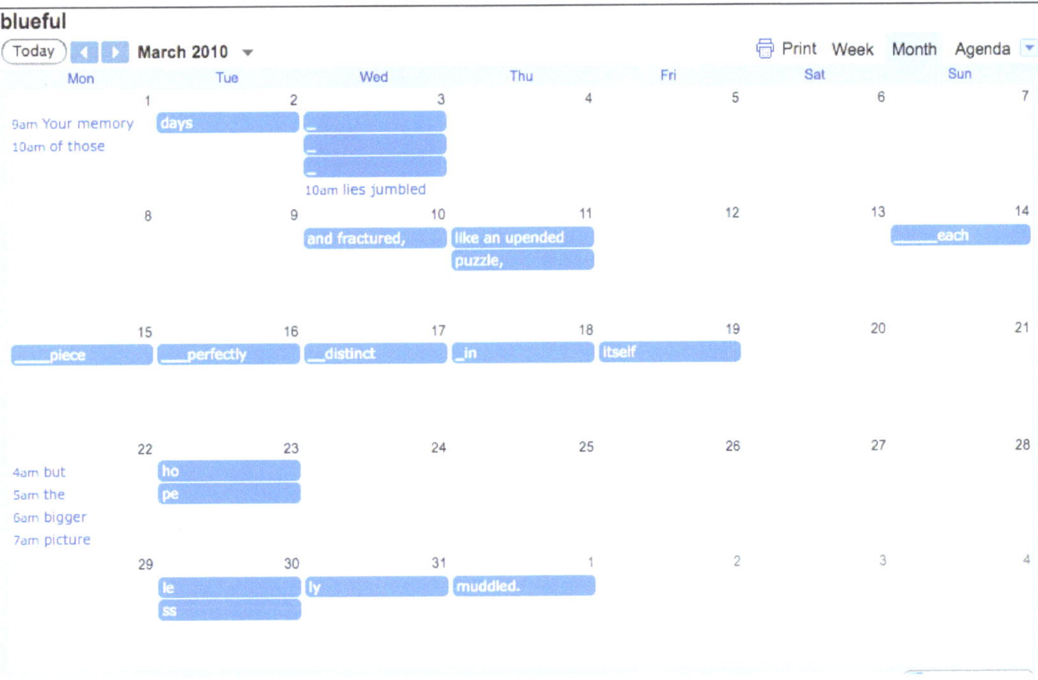

blueful, 2009, Aaron A. Reed.

Text nodes on Amazon.com, Craigslist, CafePress, and forty other websites.

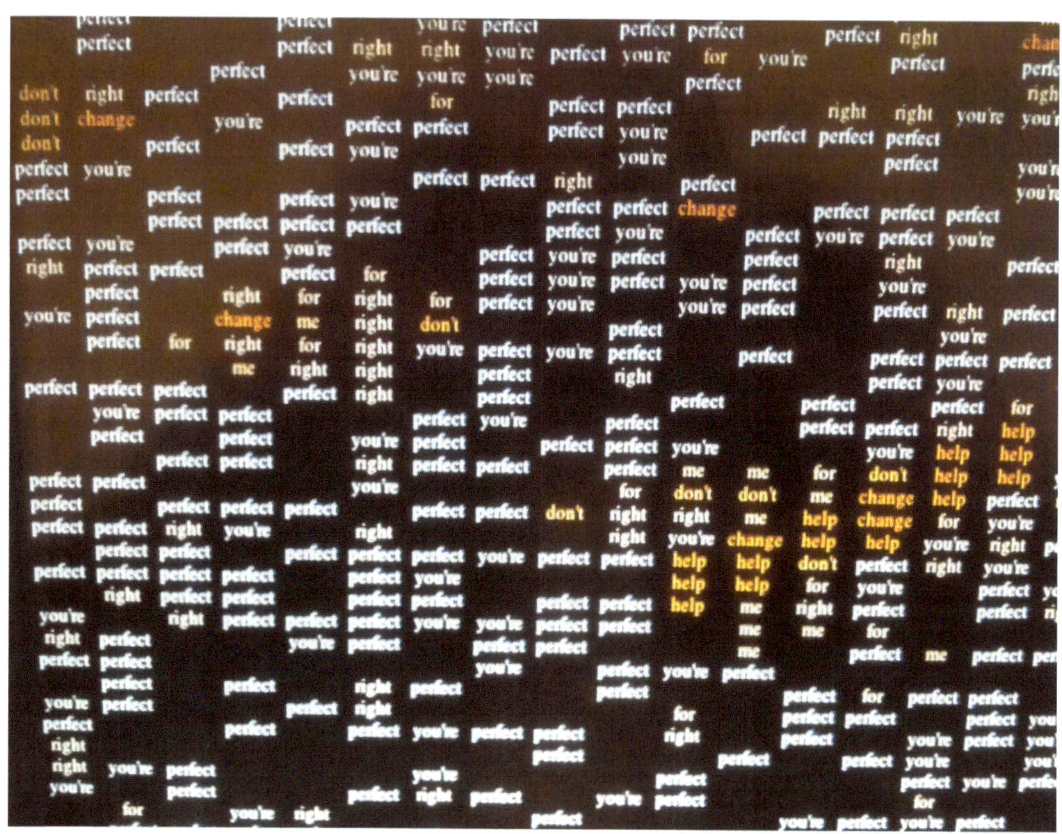

Minimalist Story Generator #2, 2010, Aaron A. Reed.

Javascript/jQuery, touch screen. © Aaron A. Reed, 2010.

 ISSN 1071-4391 ISBN 978-1-906897-20-8

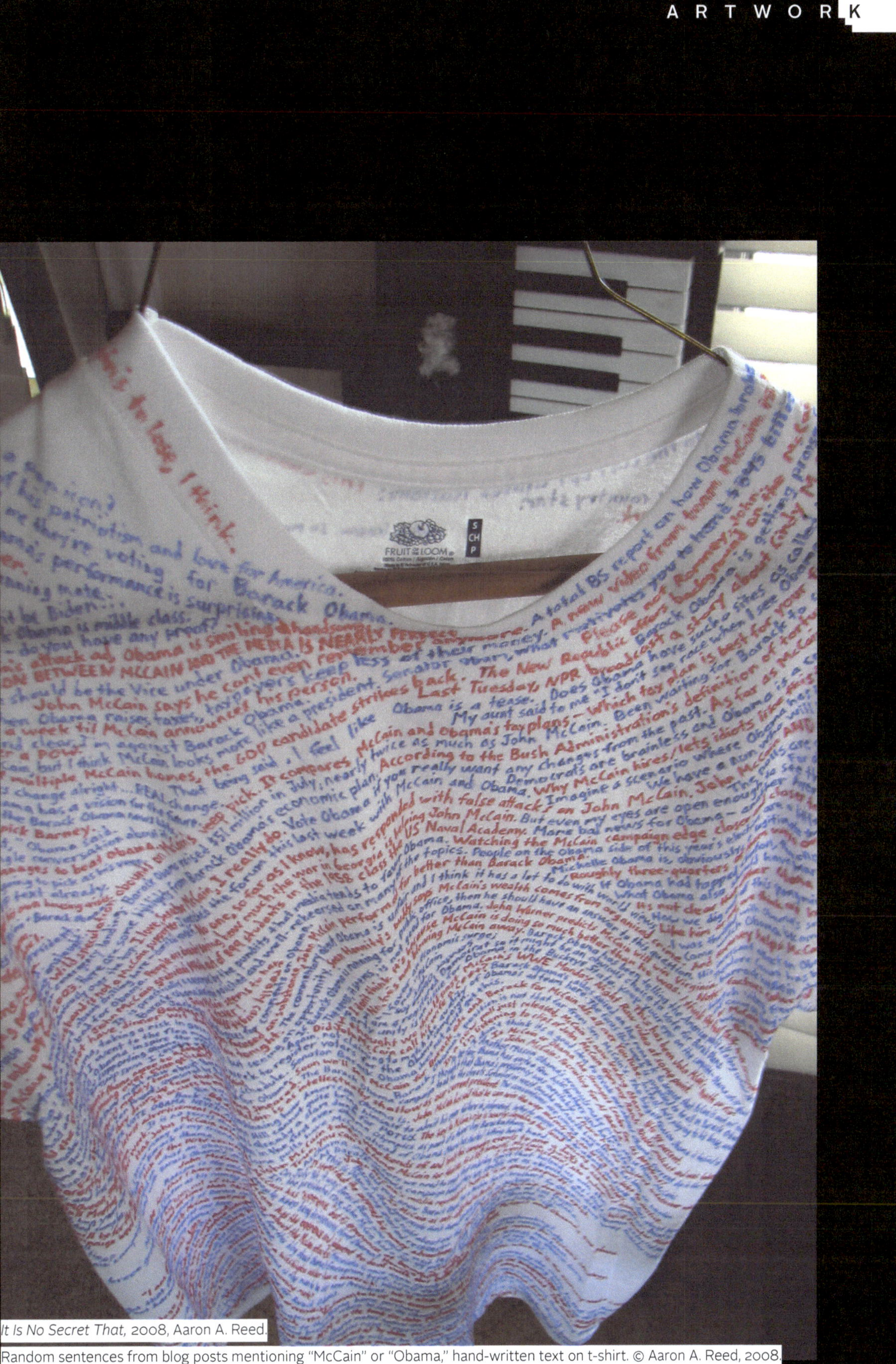

It Is No Secret That, 2008, Aaron A. Reed.

Random sentences from blog posts mentioning "McCain" or "Obama," hand-written text on t-shirt. © Aaron A. Reed, 2008.

www.ingramcontent.com/pod-product-compliance
Lightning Source LLC
LaVergne TN
LVHW070121110826
845147LV00002B/163
9781906897208